Understanding Crime
Concepts, Issues, Decisions

Joseph F. Sheley

Tulane University

Wadsworth Publishing Company, Inc., Belmont, California

Sociology Editor: Stephen D. Rutter
Production Editor, Copy Editor: Brian K. Williams
Cover Designer: Detta Penna
Illustrator: Barbara Hack

© 1979 by Wadsworth Publishing Company, Inc., Belmont,
California 94002. All rights reserved. No part of this book
may be reproduced, stored in a retrieval system, or
transcribed, in any form or by any means,
electronic, mechanical, photocopying, recording, or otherwise, without
the prior written permission of the publisher.

Printed in the United States of America
   2 3 4 5 6 7 8 9 10—83 82 81 80

Library of Congress Cataloging in Publication Data

Sheley, Joseph F
  Understanding crime.

  Bibliography: p.
  Includes index.
  1. Crime and criminals. 2. Social problems.
I. Title.
HV6025.S457   364   78-27441
ISBN 0-534-00695-7

For Roslyn and my parents

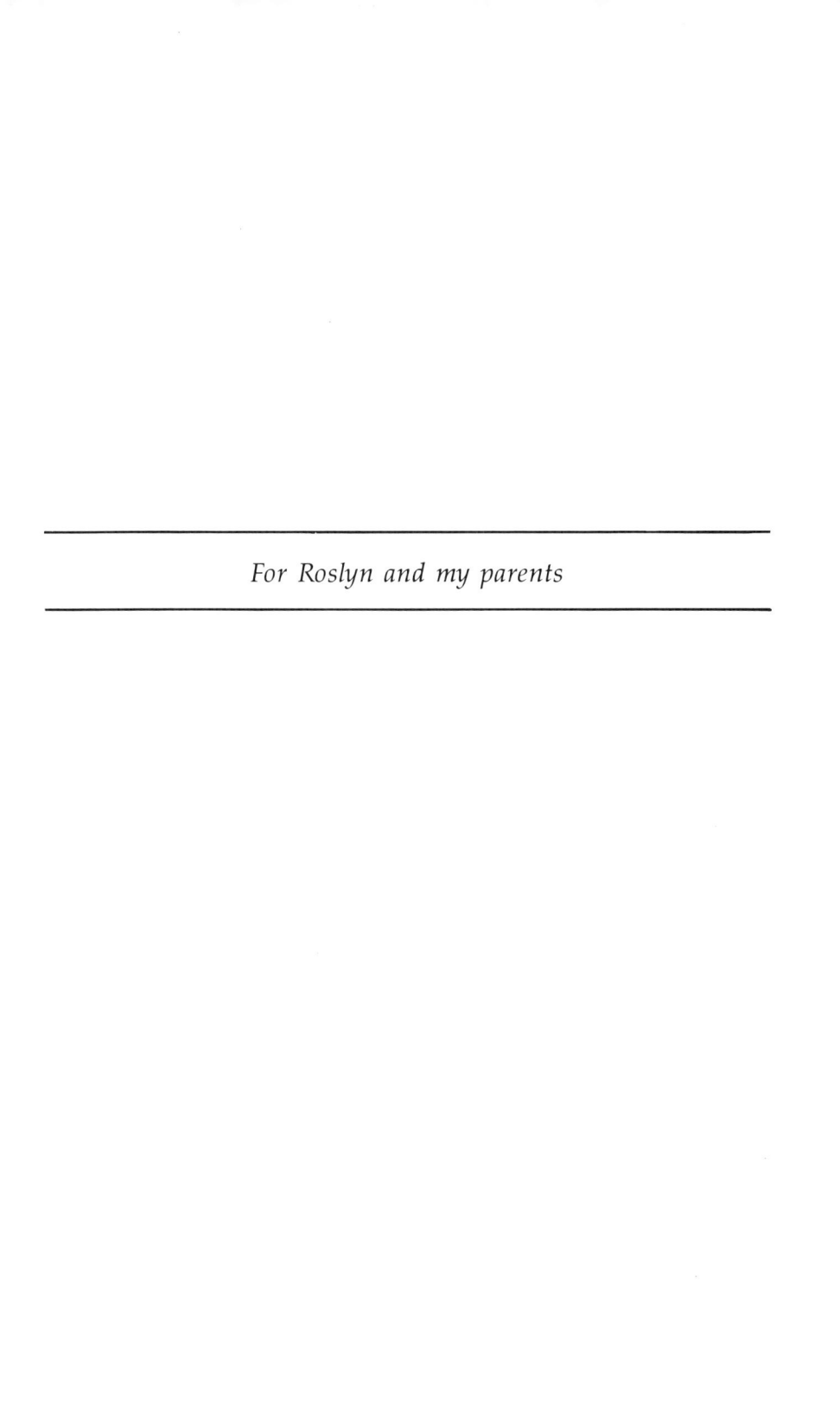

Contents

Preface vii

Introduction 1

Part One — *Crime: Facts and Myths* 7

Chapter 1 — *The "Crime Problem"* 9

Defining Social Problems 9

Crime as a Social Problem 10

How the Public Views Crime and Criminals 10

Three Sources of Public Concern 11

Inconsistencies in Crime Fears 15

The Cost of Crime Fears 15

Responses to Crime: Pressures on Legislatures and Criminal Justice Systems 17

Limiting Civil Liberties 17

Narrowing Procedural Rights 18

Summary 23

Chapter 2 — *Crime Facts and Figures* 27

Uniform Crime Reports Problems 28

Two Alternative Ways of Estimating Crime Rates 31

How Much Crime?   34

Trends in Index Crimes   35

White-Collar, Corporate, and Political Crime   37

White-Collar Crime Wave?   41

Organized Crime   41

Crime Statistics: Taking a Critical Approach   43

Summary   48

Part Two   *Criminals and Victims*   53

Chapter 3   *Patterns of Criminal Behavior*   55

Overview of Criminality Patterns   56

Gender and Criminality   59

Age and Criminality   64

Socioeconomic Status and Criminality   67

Race and Criminality   69

Two Examples of Epidemiological Analysis: Robbery and Embezzlement   71

Implications for Causal and Policy Analysis   76

Summary   77

Chapter 4   *Theories About the Causes of Crime*   81

Popular Guesses About the Causes of Crime   81

More Formal Theories About the Causes of Crime   86

Directions of Causal Analysis   92

Biological Explanations   93

Psychological Explanations   95

Sociological Explanations   98

Sociological Crime Theories Appraised   108

Causal Analysis and Anticrime Policy   109

Problems with Attempted Structural Change: The MFY Program   111

Summary   113

Chapter 5   Victims   117

Patterns of Victimization   117

Victim-Offender Relationships   124

Theoretical and Policy Implications   129

An Example: Victims of Commercial and Corporate Crime   132

Summary   133

Part Three   Creating Crime and Criminals   135

Chapter 6   Criminal Labels   137

The Interest-Group Conflict Perspective   138

The Labeling Perspective   146

Summary   156

Chapter 7   The Criminal Justice System and Its Products   161

Criminal Justice Agencies   161

Peripheral Agencies   164

The Criminal Justice Filter   166

Process Versus Production   167

The Police   170

viii   Contents

        The Courts   177

        An Example: Bail Decisions and the Production of Official Criminals   184

        Summary   186

Chapter 8   *Corrections System*   *191*

        What Is "Correction"?   191

        Changing Corrections Orientations   192

        Jails   194

        Prisons   195

        Community-Based Corrections   209

        The Future of Corrections   214

        Summary   215

Conclusion   *219*

Chapter 9   *Summary and Observations on Crime Control*   *221*

        Summary   221

        Responses to Crime   223

        Limited Procedural Rights   224

        Increased Penalties for Crimes   225

        Locking Up Career Offenders   226

        Gun Control   228

        Conclusion   230

        Author Index   *233*

        Subject Index   *236*

Preface

Criminology courses are generally best sellers in most colleges, and criminology professors are faced with making their courses meaningful for students from a variety of majors. A number of "encyclopedic" texts are available to aid the instructor. Most try to summarize the field of criminology in the same way that natural science texts represent their fields—by surveying research findings. Combined with the skills of the instructor, these books (some more than others) can make the criminology course interesting for the student. However, they cannot make criminology meaningful.

In constructing the meaningful criminology text, I am not suggesting that we rehash that tired debate about "relevance" of courses for students. I do not feel that criminology professors must make students see crime through the eyes of offenders, victims, and police officers. Yet, crime is considered a social problem, and the criminology course should therefore have more meaning for students than many other of their courses do.

In *Understanding Crime*, I have tried to make criminology meaningful by addressing the manner in which crime touches the average student. Most college students are neither perpetrators nor victims of serious crime, nor do they know personally many victims of serious crime. However, like most members of our society, they exhibit a great deal of fear of "street crimes," both attitudinally and behaviorally. Most make personal decisions that are potentially costly—as an extreme example, keeping guns in the home for protection, which can often lead to accidental shootings. More importantly, fear of crime leads to demands for "law and order," encouragement of legislation and criminal justice system efforts to curb crime through restraints on individual rights, and approval of tax spending for anticrime research and programs.

Since tax dollars spent on crime represent dollars not spent on other pressing problems and since individual rights, once forfeited, are not easily regained, we owe it to ourselves to formulate as accurate a picture of the "crime problem" as possible before supporting various anticrime policies. If criminologists can impress these notions upon their students and instill in them a critical approach to all they hear and read about crime ("How can I be misled by these statistics?" "What negative effects may follow policy based on this theory?"), then criminology becomes meaningful for students.

Understanding Crime is able to employ this critical framework while still permitting coverage of most traditional and recent criminological concerns. All bear, in one way or another, on public attitudes toward crime and its prevention.

In Part One of the book, public perceptions of the "crime problem" are set against what is actually known about crime. Chapter 1 reviews the recent history of public concern with crime and the sources of that concern. In line with the book's emphasis on the costs of responding to crime fears, the impact of these fears on personal habits, social solidarity, the economy, and procedural rights is explored. In Chapter 2, the many problems encountered in trying to gain an accurate picture of crime are examined. With these problems in mind, recent trends in violent and property offenses and in white-collar, political, corporate, and organized crime are discussed.

Part Two is devoted to descriptions of criminals and their victims and of the various theories that attempt to account for their involvement in crime. Again, we stress the fact that common stereotypes of who victimizes whom and for what reasons are often inaccurate. Chapter 5 presents an analysis of aspects of victim characteristics which is absent from most criminology textbooks. Not only is victimization often a nonrandom occurrence, but it is also not always simply a matter of the active criminal preying upon the passive victim. Various patterns of victim-offender interactions are examined for anticrime policy implications.

In Part Three, we examine yet another dimension of the "crime problem"—namely, the extent to which it is created by political and criminal justice system interests within our society. Chapter 6 explores the labeling and conflict perspectives and encourages the student to ask not only what can be done about crime but also why we are concerned with crime (especially "street crime") in the first place. Who shapes our views of legal behavior and to what end? In Chapter 7, this theme is more specifically applied to the police and courts. These segments of the criminal justice system are not simply processors of criminal suspects. Rather, they are producers of such products as official crime rates and official criminals. Chapter 8 examines the corrections system and its negative role in the crime situation.

Understanding Crime concludes with a reemphasis of the need for a critical approach to crime statistics and theories in an attempt to avoid costly "knee-jerk" anticrime policies. The positive and the negative potential of a number of possible policy responses to the crime situation—limiting procedural rights, increasing penalties for crimes, incarcerating career offenders and instituting gun-control laws—are examined in light of what we know and, more importantly, what we do not know, about crime in this society.

A number of people helped me with this book. Stephen Rutter of Wadsworth initiated and shepherded the project, and Brian Williams provided expert copy editing. Judson Landis of California State University at Sacramento offered constructive counsel and criticism at several points, as did Thomas Carroll at the University of Missouri, Sherry Corbett at Miami University, Arthur Ferrari at Connecticut College, Paul Friday at Western Michigan University, and Gene Kassebaum at the University of Hawaii at Manoa. My colleagues at Tulane University were extremely supportive of my work. Evelyn Seidule, Peggy Keeran, and Harolyn Landow assisted in typing and library research. Roslyn Sheley provided help with the tables and figures. My special thanks to all of them.

Introduction

An unusual double suicide occurred in New York in the fall of 1976. As reported in the New York Times (1976), the victims, Hans Kable, seventy-eight, and his wife Emma, seventy-six, were much like many older couples living in the Bronx. Things had changed considerably during the years they had occupied their neat little apartment. Crime had become a persistent problem for them. Everyone feared it. The Kables had been victims of crime in their neighborhood, most recently of assault and robbery in their own apartment. They were afraid to remain there, yet they could not bear the thought of uprooting and trying to begin life anew somewhere else. One day, the Kables laid out their best clothes on their bed, wrote a note explaining their dual fear of crime and of relocation, and hanged themselves in their bedroom.

The Kables' double suicide received extensive news media coverage and dramatized American society's perception that crime is intruding into the lives of average citizens as never before. As we shall see in the coming chapter, the American public fears crime immensely, and its demands for solutions to the "crime problem" become more vocal every day.

Among the targets of demands for solutions are sociologists. Traditionally, the sociological subfield of *criminology* has addressed crime-related issues. Criminology is the scientific study of crime as a *social* phenomenon (as opposed, for example, to a legal, historical, psychological, economic, or forensic phenomenon). That is, crime is a matter of sociological interest because it violates social rules and draws a social response, because a criminal act is a social act occurring in a social setting, and because crime is implicated in society's cultural and structural framework.

To be more specific, criminologists study the following issues:

1. *The Creation and Use of Laws.* Criminology is in part concerned with the development of laws, the functions of law in a society, law as an instrument of social change, and the functions of legislation and law enforcement for interest groups within a society.

2 Introduction

2. *Criminal Justice Administration.*   Criminologists are interested in the police and the legal profession as occupational categories; the criminal justice system and its bureaucratic and organizational processes; and, importantly, the criminal justice system as a primary producer of a community's criminal population and crime rates.

3. *The Patterns of Crime.*   Some criminologists study the pattern of crime for a community at a given point in time and over various time periods. This area of criminology, also referred to as the *epidemiology* of crime, involves not only the study of trends, patterns, and the impact of crime but, incidentally, the analysis of definitions of crime and criminals and the reasons why some behaviors are considered criminal and others are not.

4. *Causes of Crime and Criminality.*   Criminology also studies the conditions affecting societal crime rates and the causes of individual and group involvement in criminal behavior. This study of causes, known as *causal analysis,* also attempts to identify distinctive types of criminal careers and their development. Traditionally, the major goal of causal analysis has been the formulation of strategies for crime prevention.

5. *The Societal Reaction to Crime.*   Criminological theory and research focus on the forces influencing a society's definitions of criminal behavior, the ways in which a society reacts to individuals and their acts, the process by which individuals come to be called criminals, and individuals' reactions to society's definition of them.

6. *Custody, Punishment, and Rehabilitation of Criminals.*   A final branch of criminology is the study of society's methods of dealing with criminals. Most research in this area is designed to evaluate the success and deterrent effects of correctional programs, from the point of view of both the public and the individual offender. Much of this research concerning prisons and other correctional agencies is also used in developing sociological theories of bureaucracy.

Criminology has always tried to be responsive to the crime concerns of its day. However, it has traditionally directed its responses less at immediate than at long-range solutions to crime. As a subfield of sociology, criminology has channeled its efforts primarily toward building a general body of knowledge about societal norms (rules, laws), deviance (rule violation), and social control (restraining individual pursuit of self-interests thought to be detrimental to society). Thus, crime is studied as a form of deviance and methods of combating crime as forms of social control. The ultimate goal of such an approach is the development of a sophisticated set of sociological principles to allow broad-based solutions to problems like crime, rather than reliance on ad hoc, patchworklike remedies.

As public concern about crime has grown, public patience with searches for long-range solutions to the crime problem has worn thin. Shifting with public sentiment in recent years and spurred by the availability of government and private foundation grants, criminologists are now more willing to address more specific crime questions, with an eye to more immediate crime-control strategies. For example, much research has recently been conducted to provide criminal justice planners with knowledge about community-based rehabilitation programs for juvenile offenders. Empey and Erickson's *The Provo Experiment* (1972) serves as a landmark for such research. The authors used sociological theory and methodology to investigate the claim that probation and supervised treatment in the community are superior to incarceration in discouraging future delinquencies. They found no basic differences in the success of these types of corrections. Results aside, the study provided a research model by which future correctional innovations could be evaluated.

Research like this is called *social policy research*. It attempts to identify or better conceptualize social problems, map strategies to combat the problems, and conduct research to evaluate the costs and the effects of the strategies. Presently enjoying a great deal of popularity among criminologists, policy research assumes that criminology can, and should, make immediate, significant contributions to the solution of major social problems. Most policy studies are large-scale, governmentally funded projects. Many have involved experimentation with various correctional programs. However, the list of topics for study seems to be growing. Recent studies of the effectiveness of police patrols on lowering crime rates serve as examples (see, for instance, Kelling et al., 1974). The question of reducing robbery and burglary rates through decriminalization of narcotics also represents a policy-research problem.

Through policy research, criminologists seem able to successfully claim that they are at least partially addressing public demands for solutions to the crime problem. Yet, criminology's impact on the average citizen's concern with crime is questionable. Crime touches most people through the fear it instills; people are anxious about their safety and that of their possessions. Most citizens are unaware of the governmental policy research in which sociologists participate. From the citizens' point of view, criminological theory and research that do not directly and visibly address their fears are interesting but not particularly relevant.

Criminology need not change radically to become more responsive to public concerns. Basically, it must accurately assess public perceptions of crime and the content and quality of crime fears. People base decisions on these perceptions and fears. Some decisions involve organizing one's personal life to minimize the chances of being a crime victim: buying a gun, barring windows, or, as in the extreme case of Hans and Emma Kable, taking one's life. Other decisions concern the citizen's involvement in legal and political responses to crime. Even in as power-differentiated a society as ours, few governmental decisions can forego at least tacit public approval. Directly or indirectly, the public approves or disapproves the spending of the tax dollar on crime-control programs. More importantly, the public explicitly or implicitly condones or condemns crime control measures that limit individual rights.

Whether at the personal or governmental level, decisions about potential crime solutions like those just described carry important consequences. They must therefore be based on the most accurate knowledge available. Three important questions should be addressed in any personal or governmental policy decision:

1. What is the nature and scope of the problem at hand (that is, how accurate are the assumptions and figures relating to the problem)?
2. Will the proposed remedy actually aid in solving the problem?
3. What incidental side effects may accompany implementation of the proposed remedy?

Criminology can be made relevant for the average citizen by providing information that can aid in both asking and answering these three questions. The goal of this book is to summarize current criminological thought on crime in this society in such a fashion that its readers can make better sense of the crime situation as it affects them, better formulate personal decisions concerning the crime situation, and better evaluate general governmental anticrime policies. Surveys indicate, for instance, that the public increasingly favors capital punishment for certain crimes (Hindelang et al., 1977:325-27), that it supports at least some form of gun control (Hindelang et al., 1977:345-51), and that approximately one-third support unrestricted governmental computerized file-keeping on citizens, searches without warrants, and electronic surveillance of suspected criminals (Hindelang et al., 1977:324). These attitudes are apparently based on perceptions of crime as being highly troublesome for society. Yet we can be certain that most citizens have not systematically assessed the crime situation they see as threatening, the potential effectiveness of the preventive measures mentioned above, or their potential negative side effects.

This book will disappoint readers who are looking for ready solutions to the crime problem. It has none to offer. Instead, it tries to provide a framework for asking questions about crime and solutions for it. Those who read the book, it is hoped, will become very skeptical of all they hear about crime and will begin to ask questions first and act later. To this end, we will devote the coming chapters to assessments of the accuracy of public views on crime and theories to explain them, the role of the victim in various offenses, sources of definitions of people and acts as criminal, and the role of the criminal justice system in producing and controlling crime.

References

Empey, L. T., and M. L. Erickson
    1972   The Provo Experiment: Evaluating Community Control of Delinquency. Lexington, Mass.: D. C. Heath.

Hindelang, M. J., M. R. Gottfredson, C. S. Dunn, and N. Parisi
    1977   Sourcebook of Criminal Justice Statistics—1976. Washington, D.C.: U.S. Government Printing Office.

Kelling, G., T. Pate, D. Dieckman, and C. E. Brown
    1974   The Kansas City Preventive Patrol Experiment—A Summary Report. Washington, D.C.: The Police Foundation.

The New York Times
    1976   "Couple, recently robbed, take their own lives, citing fear." October 7, sec. 1:5.

Part One Crime: Facts and Myths

Both individually and collectively, people address social problems according to what they *think* they know about them. But, as we shall see, there are great dangers in many of today's "gut reactions" toward crime. ☐ Chapters 1 and 2 describe public perceptions of the "crime problem" and compare them with available information about crime.

1

The "Crime Problem"

Americans have nearly always felt threatened by immorality, deviance, and crime; however, never so much as today. This chapter analyzes concern about crime as a "social problem" and explores the shape, source, accuracy, and costs of the public's fear of crime and its influence on criminal justice policy.

Defining Social Problems

What are "social problems"? They are social phenomena that, at base, people perceive as threats to society. That is, social conditions become "problems" for society when significant numbers of people define them as such.

The definition of a situation as a social problem—whether crime, drug abuse, or whatever—generally does not occur overnight. It begins with the alarm sounded by a few, is then given coverage by the mass media, and finally creates widespread public concern and elicits governmental attention. Whether or not the perception of the problem moves beyond the alarm sounded by the initial few depends greatly on the social identity and legitimacy of those few. Doomsday prophets, for example, do not gain the public's attention as easily as do scientists, legislators, religious leaders, or government administrators (Turner, 1969).

If we understand that social problems are socially constructed, then we can also see that perceptions of situations as threatening or harmless may not be accurate. For instance, with hindsight we can see that some very real dangers, such as early deaths of chemical-plant workers owing to chemically induced cancer, were not recognized as social problems when they first occurred. By contrast, other situations once considered threatening, such as the "witches" of colonial Salem or the 1950s "red scare," can now be viewed as having been relatively harmless threats. In any case, whether correctly or incorrectly diagnosed, a situation defined as a social problem precipitates alarm, fear, and demands for solutions.

Crime as a Social Problem

Crime is currently defined as a particularly threatening problem by the majority of people in American society. Although there is little consensus among experts about *objective* measures of social threat from crime—that is, agreement as to how many crimes really constitute a danger for society—there is a great deal of public consensus that life in America is hampered by fear of crime. During the past decade, numerous surveys have found crime consistently rated as a major concern in most communities (Hindelang et al., 1977:4). A 1973 survey of New York City residents, for instance, reported that crime was considered *the* most threatening of nineteen social problems (New York Times, 1974). A more recent U.S. Census Bureau survey found crime ranked second only to noise as the most undesirable neighborhood problem in the United States (New Orleans Times-Picayune, 1976b).

Government legislators and administrators seem to agree with citizens that crime is a serious problem. Public expenditures for law enforcement and criminal justice exceed $17 billion yearly (U.S. Department of Justice, 1977). The Law Enforcement Assistance Administration, founded in 1968 in response to the first major public fears about crime, today spends over $800 million a year. Obviously, public fear of crime is very strong and has expensive consequences.

How the Public Views Crime and Criminals

Surveys indicate that the crimes people fear most are "street crimes," threats to personal safety while one is out in public. Indeed, for most people, the word "crime" appears to symbolize a violent attack with a weapon while one is out at night. In fact, a 1972 poll (Hindelang, 1974:113) reports that nearly half of the nation's citizens fear walking alone at night in areas within a mile of their home. In 1967, a special President's Commission on Law Enforcement and Administration of Justice suggested that the fear of crime might, at base, be a fear of strangers (President's Commission, 1967a:50).

In general, crimes that appear to concern the public the most are those seven the yearly *Uniform Crime Reports* by the Federal Bureau of Investigation label the "index crimes":

1. Homicide.
2. Aggravated assault.
3. Forcible rape.
4. Robbery.
5. Burglary.
6. Larceny.
7. Automobile theft.

The fact that the FBI reports detailed information for these offenses only—and we have prominently displayed them above because we will return to this list in coming chapters—helps foster this concern. More importantly, however, fear of such crimes, as Nettler (1974:3) writes, reflects a natural human desire to be safe from attack on one's self or property.

The public tends to view criminals as being a special class of people who live outside of law-abiding communities and neighborhoods and enter them to commit crimes. Most major crime today is attributable, the public believes, to a relatively small number of hardened criminals—villainous public enemies who necessitate a "war on crime." Interestingly, they are also seen as products of environmental and developmental deficiencies, such as bad companions and poor family supervision, but this aspect of criminality is generally downplayed in the public mind. Whatever its causes, once criminality is achieved, the public considers it a permanent individual condition. As we shall see shortly, this view greatly colors responses to the "crime problem."

Three Sources of Public Concern

The way people think and act stems partly from their own experiences and partly from others' accounts, as transmitted, for example, during political campaigns and through the mass media. Let us examine these sources.

Personal Experience

Available evidence suggests, interestingly, that personal experience plays only a small part in public attitudes toward crime. According to one survey, people's personally witnessing a crime, being the victim of a crime, or having an acquaintance who was victimized is not related to fear of crime.[1] Similar results are reported by a second survey, though it notes that personal victimization and fear are more highly related for serious crimes alone. Both reports also suggest that most people, even those living in high-crime areas, tend to see their own neighborhoods as being safe. It seems, then, that even objectively measurable danger does not influence attitudes toward crime.

Most people soon forget minor victimizations. One study found that people asked to recount crimes committed against them during the previous year tended to report only those that occurred during the few

---

[1] This and other findings cited in this section are taken from summaries of research reported in the President's Commission, 1976b:86–87.

months immediately preceding the survey. When asked to recall the worst crime they had ever experienced, 79 percent of the respondents said it had occurred during the past five years; 60 percent within the past two years; and 50 percent within the previous eighteen months. However, statistical probabilities indicate the chances are slim that this is when they really happened, which suggests that even serious crimes committed against us do not shape our attitudes for a long time. Perhaps political campaigns and the mass media are more important than personal experience in generating public concern about crime.

Political Campaigns

The presidential election year 1968 fostered many slogans about "law and order," "war on crime," and "safe streets," and public concern about crime consequently became particularly noticeable. It is misleading to suggest that a political campaign manufactured our "crime problem." However, American political campaigns search out issues that reflect public concern, specify and crystallize them, bring them to public and media attention, and otherwise legitimize them. Such appears to have been the case in 1968. If crime was not a true social problem before the campaigns, it certainly was one during and after them.

The 1968 anticrime platforms continue to inspire political campaigns. As Conklin (1975:25) points out, promises to reestablish law and order and to make streets safe are especially effective in mobilizing political support for a candidate, for crime arouses deep-seated fears for personal safety and for the preservation of the social order. Part of Jimmy Carter's 1976 presidential nomination acceptance speech illustrates the point:

> It is time for the law to be enforced. We cannot educate our children, create harmony among our people, or preserve basic human freedom unless we have an orderly society. Crime and lack of justice are especially cruel to those who are least able to protect themselves. Swift arrest and trial, and fair and uniform punishment should be expected by those who break our laws.

The Media

Like political campaigns, the media respond to and stimulate fears of crime, and are therefore probably the greatest influence on public attitudes about the topic. Basically, control of information to the public represents, in many ways, control of the public, since people structure much of their views of the world around media information. Because the American press is relatively free and can pursue and report most aspects of crime, a crime wave may be perpetuated or eliminated according to how the media choose to cover the subject.

The media tend to influence public perceptions of crime in three important ways: (1) by making it a national problem, (2) by selectively reporting crime news to the public, and (3) by perpetuating criminal stereotypes in the entertainment media. Let us discuss each of these.

1. Crime as a National Problem. Once primarily a community problem, crime has only recently become a matter of national concern—that is, defined by the public as a nationwide problem. The shift in concern from community to society has meant that rural, as well as urban, areas have been included among those communities with "crime problems." Mass-communications networks are especially implicated in this shift. News once was slow traveling; word of Abraham Lincoln's death, for example, did not reach the western states for weeks. John F. Kennedy's assassination, however, was news within minutes. Robert Kennedy's was broadcast practically as it occurred. Crimes of all kinds now gain national interest by being televised to nearly all members of society simultaneously. The Watergate coverup crimes and the exploits of Patty Hearst and the Symbionese Liberation Army were daily news. Everyone receives much the same details of a crime. Everyone is afforded the same chill when a mass murder occurs. As mass communications increasingly "shrink the globe," those in relatively crime-free areas become involved in and identify with the drama of crime as never before. On-the-spot TV coverage has shown, for example, that participants in a crime situation, especially victims and witnesses, are usually ordinary people rather than a strange breed of city dweller. All this has transformed what may once have been community problems (for example, routine vandalism) into one major problem—a national trend toward lawlessness. That is, what were once small, isolated problems are now perceived as being interrelated symptoms of a larger crime problem.

2. Selective Crime News Coverage. The news media are often accused of distorting the picture of crime in America. Critics contend that the media select crime news items primarily on the basis of their sensationalistic features. Actually, one study (Roshier, 1973:34–35), reports that the factors influencing crime news selection are the seriousness of the offense, whimsical or unusual circumstances connected with it, sentimental or dramatic elements of it, and the involvement of famous or high-status persons in any aspect of it. Some argue that the more trivial the motive for a crime, the more likely its inclusion in the news. Sutherland and Cressey (1974:246) contend that "crime waves" are generally fabricated by the press. A sensationalistic crime occurs, receives coverage in one community, and, before long, editors in other communities begin giving attention to hitherto unnoticed similar crimes.

Although the news media do not ignore the question of their obligations to the public, neither do they grant these obligations the same importance as "selling news." As business enterprises, the media cannot devote their energies to discerning and communicating a *representative* picture of crime to the public. Representative crime—that is, property and white-collar offenses—is not the "news" the public desires. Nor does the government consciously attempt to persuade or employ the news media to present a full picture of crime in America. Instead, the government generally restricts itself to presenting data on a few selected offenses, primarily violent crimes and a few property crimes.

Research conducted by F. James Davis (1952), though now somewhat dated, suggests that the public needs more accurate crime news. Studying the relationship of official crime rates to crime news and crime news to public opinions about crime, Davis concluded that crime rates and crime news coverage are unrelated and that the public's conception of crime more accurately reflects the picture of crime presented in the newspapers.[2]

3. Media Stereotypes of Crime and Criminals. While there is much debate about the extent to which the entertainment media, especially television, encourage and promote indifference to crime by stressing violent activity, little is known about how these media shape public attitudes about the amounts and types of crime in this society.

If the public *is* influenced by the entertainment media, it is clearly in the wrong direction. Recent research (Dominick, 1973) has found that the least committed offenses (violent crimes such as murder and assault) appear most often in television dramas, but that property offenses (burglary and larceny) receive little coverage, though they constitute the bulk of real-life crime. In addition, violent crimes as portrayed on television are generally shown to be the result of greed or attempts to avoid detection for other offenses, whereas in actuality most violent crimes are crimes of passion committed during arguments. The racial and occupational characteristics of criminals and victims are also distorted—victimization of poor blacks, for example (a common occurrence in real life), is rarely seen in television dramas. Finally, television shows exaggerate the necessary use of violence in police work and seemingly sanction the use of illegal police tactics (Arons and Kalsh, 1977).

We must emphasize, however, that there is no evidence that persons who watch television crime dramas believe they reflect real-life

---

[2] Davis is somewhat cautious about the quality of evidence on which he bases his second conclusion. Further, a more recent study of newspaper crime reporting in England suggests the media do not influence public views of crime (see Roshier, 1973).

situations. Still, it is likely that some segments of the population—for instance, the aged, the very young, recent immigrants—would be more apt than others to be influenced by such television portrayals. Clearly, more research in this area is necessary.

Inconsistencies in Crime Fears

Whether or not, as the above discussion suggests, the mass media are indeed shaping public opinion about crime, the President's Commission on Law Enforcement and Administration of Justice (1967b: 88–89) reports what it considers inconsistencies in public fears about crime. It notes, for example, that the public stereotype of crime emphasizes violence, though property offenses are actually more common. In addition, it finds, the public is apparently far more tolerant of property crime than of violent crime. On the one hand, this seems reasonable, since people usually place personal safety above safety of their property. But, on the other hand, the average citizen's risk of being a victim of a violent crime is relatively negligible—one chance in 550. Hospitalization is required only once in every 3,000 cases of violent attack (President's Commission, 1967b:14–16). Property crimes result in much higher victimization rates. The commission notes (Pp. 88–89) too that the public's fear of strangers may be exaggerated, for violent crimes are far more likely to occur between acquaintances. Finally, the public stereotype of crime is distorted by the emphasis on standard FBI-index offenses such as murder and robbery. Yet, as we shall see in Chapter 2, crimes against businesses and public institutions touch *everyone* through higher costs and taxes, though the public gives such offenses little attention.

The Cost of Crime Fears

Whatever their causes, public fears about crime have three detrimental consequences: personal, social, and economic.

Personal Consequences: Withdrawal and Retreat

Whether based on fact or fiction, fear of crime colors the thoughts and actions of many Americans, and most responses to this fear involve some form of social withdrawal. Surveys report that as much as 43 percent of urban populations and 16 percent of the nation as a whole remain off the streets at night for fear of criminal attacks. Those who venture forth generally use cars and taxis, avoiding public transportation when possible. Most people lock their doors at night; 25 percent do so during the day, even when other household members are present. One study summarized (with other studies) in the President's Commission (1967b:87–88) reports that fear of crime prompted 28 percent of urban dwellers to purchase new locks for their doors and 10 percent to install locks and bars on windows.

Individuals are arming themselves against criminals as well: 9 percent of urban residents (19 percent in high-crime areas) report carrying weapons (usually knives) for protection when going out at night. More than a quarter of one national sample kept watchdogs in their homes for protection.

The ultimate response is actual retreat: Fear of crime influenced between 20 and 30 percent of the respondents in one study to contemplate moves to new, "safer" locations.

Social Consequences: Erosion of Solidarity

As mentioned earlier, fear of crime is primarily a fear of strangers, which results in suspicion, withdrawal, and a weakening of societal unity and of the informal mechanisms of social control (Conklin 1975:131). But, paradoxically, retreat from strangers to avoid victimization may create *more* crime, for a breakdown in interaction between people also means a breakdown in citizens' informal surveillance and correction of potential offenders. When people desert the streets and become aloof and indifferent to the plights of others as they try to seal themselves off from crime, they actually may make the streets *safer* for criminals, who are then relatively free to attack the people who do venture out. Thus, we observe a possible self-fulfilling prophecy: fear of crime that, as suggested above, may not be wholly realistic may produce the very situation that makes it realistic.

Economic Consequences: Billions of Dollars

Beyond the costs to each of us individually in increased personal security measures, various government agencies spend over $17 billion a year on criminal justice services. An additional $1.35 billion a year is spent on private security guards for homes and businesses (which pass the cost on to the consumer). Burglar alarms and other security systems cost over $200 million annually. Crime insurance amounts to another $300 million or more each year (President's Commission, 1967a:53–59). While it is difficult to ascertain how many guns people buy annually for self-protection, they no doubt cost further millions of dollars. It is equally difficult to estimate how much communities with a so-called "crime problem" lose when new industries decide to avoid them, but here again millions, perhaps billions, of dollars are involved.

Responses to Crime: Pressures on Legislatures and Criminal Justice Systems

The public response to crime fears is focused on criminals, not on the causes of crime. This response reflects peoples' frustration with alleged "liberal coddling" of criminals and the seeming inability of scholars and scientists to find "cures" for the crime problem. As a result, the public has developed a "lock 'em up" philosophy, feeling crime can best be combatted by isolating for extended lengths of time those "few hardened criminals who commit most of the serious crimes in this society."

State legislatures respond to this discontent by passing bills designed to make control of criminals easier: lengthening prison sentences, eliminating parole for some offenses, and developing "multiple billing" procedures so that sentences of repeat offenders may be doubled or tripled. Despite the harshness of these solutions, most people feel such remedies are relatively ineffective, and as public fears about crime continue so does the search for new solutions.

At present, a minority of social critics are concerned that America is overreacting to the crime problem. They argue that before truly drastic measures are considered, there must be much research into the nature of the crime problem and the potential effectiveness of crime-prevention measures. As in television westerns in which the new sheriff rids the town of hoodlums and then himself becomes a dictator, solutions to problems sometimes cause more damage than did the problems themselves. Often the damage is irreparable; once a solution is implemented, it may be impossible to offset its undesirable effects. An inaccurate picture of crime or a poorly researched "remedy" cannot only waste tax dollars but also vastly alter individual rights.

Limiting Civil Liberties

One way to deal with crime is to restrict public freedom of movement in order to limit the opportunities for criminal behavior. Curfews may be instituted, certain areas placed off limits, prominently displayed identification required, and homes and persons routinely searched. The precedent for such measures exists in the concept of *martial law*—that is, rule by the military and suspension of civil liberties when civil authority fails. The implementing of such radical techniques may occur when the public (or, more precisely, its representatives) perceive crime as being wholly beyond normal means of control. In the United States at present, however, the situation is not perceived as being so desperate that it requires such drastic measures.

Still, there are several examples of *partial* restriction of individual freedom designed to combat crime. Searches of boarding airline passengers and their baggage testify to the gravity with which we view airplane hijackings. Controversy over gun-control laws represents a debate over the seriousness of violent crime and the merits of preventing it through eliminating the freedom of private gun ownership. Both the hijacking precautions and the proposed firearms regulations reflect the sentiment that conventional prevention mechanisms cannot combat crime. In both cases, restriction of individual liberties is seen as being undesirable but necessary in order to regain control of the crime situation.

Narrowing Procedural Rights

Measures that restrict the freedom of all citizens in order to curb the criminal behavior of a few are generally less acceptable than measures that will apparently affect only criminals and a few noncriminals. Hence, the demand for "law and order" often takes the form of proposals for altering those individual rights more directly linked to law enforcement and the administration of justice. To explore this theme, we must first examine criminal law and the public perception of it.

Criminal Law

Criminal law takes two forms, one clearly recognized by most people, the other less so. *Substantive law* defines acts (felonies and misdemeanors) that members of this society may not perform—for example, assault, use of heroin, corporate price fixing. Substantive law includes descriptions of specific penalties for violations. *Procedural law* governs actions of state officials in dealing with persons suspected or found guilty of criminal acts. This kind of law covers such phenomena as searches and arrests, the right to a fair and speedy trial, the right to counsel, admissibility of evidence, and the right to appeal. Through television crime shows, most people are familiar with at least one procedural law, the *Miranda* rule, whereby police must inform suspects of their legal rights at the time of the arrest. Generally, however, Americans are far less aware of and concerned about procedural than substantive law.

Law and Order

The oft-heard demand for "law and order" reflects society's current view of criminal law (see Skolnick, 1975:1–22). "Order" suggests control of law violations. The public, convinced that we are fast becoming a criminal society, is particularly concerned with such control. "Law" in this framework refers to substantive law that, it is argued, requires more stringent enforcement if crime is to be controlled. In addition to its dissatisfaction with substantive-law enforcement, the public—inspired by police and other agents of the criminal justice system—has come to view procedural law as being simply a set of "technicalities" that hinder law enforcement and encourage crime.

It is apparent there is an inherent tension between substantive and procedural law. Substantive law (the quest for order) strives for control of the population, but it is prevented from doing so by the rule of law (procedural law), which traditionally in the United States has been placed above the enforcement of substantive law. Hence, total order is beyond reach, and perhaps the popular phrase "law and order" should read, "law *or* order" (or, perhaps, "law *and a degree* of disorder"). We cannot presently have both total enforcement of substantive law and full protection of individual rights. Currently procedural law takes precedence, and until detection, prevention, and prosecution techniques are developed that work without violating individual rights, or until our priorities change, some apparent criminals will indeed go unpunished.

Eliminating "Technicalities"

Because laws, both substantive and procedural, are essentially social definitions of, or meanings given to, certain activities, they are always changeable. Thus, what is currently not considered a right may later be defined as such. Or current rights may be revoked or altered to become more liberal or more conservative. In addition, many laws are not clearly written and are therefore constantly open to changes in interpretation.

The way the public perceives a crime problem will affect how willing it is to affirm or deny individual rights. Depending on how serious the crime situation seems, rights may be totally affirmed (no restrictions), liberally affirmed (limited restrictions), conservatively affirmed (major restrictions), or abolished. The FBI's 1976 appeal for more liberal wiretap privileges to monitor suspected terrorist bombers is a plea for a restricted right to privacy.[3] It reflects the FBI's perception of bombings as increasing in number and becoming more difficult to prevent. Were bombings to escalate, we would hear calls for yet more conservative definitions of the right to privacy.

Because procedural law prevents substantive law from being applied to every offender, it is theoretically possible that the crime

---

[3] Former FBI director Clarence M. Kelley argued that wiretaps and bugs are extremely useful in criminal cases and that such techniques could yield equally successful results in gathering intelligence on suspected terrorists (New Orleans Times-Picayune, 1976a).

problem could become so uncontrollable that restriction of procedural law might occur as a "necessary evil." Indeed, the possibility may not be so theoretical after all, since our society has traditionally moved more readily in a conservative than in a liberal direction. However, because rights are not easily reinstated once forfeited, it is important that two precautions take place: first, consideration of more conservative definitions of procedural rights must be accompanied by accurate information about the scope of our crime problem; and, second, there must be relative certainty that restriction of a particular right will accomplish its end without undesirable side effects. Unfortunately, in the opinion of most experts, these precautions are rarely taken. Two examples will illustrate this point.

Example 1: The Organized Crime Control Act of 1970. Organized crime has been a source of major concern to the Justice Department since early in this century. Most efforts to deal with the problem involve attempts to jail major crime-syndicate figures, thereby depriving organized crime of its leadership and deterring potential leaders from assuming control. Before 1970, Justice Department efforts in this direction had been stymied by the refusals of underworld figures to divulge information when called before grand juries. Claiming their Fifth Amendment right to withhold testimony that might be self-incriminating, syndicate members had successfully avoided being indicted or providing information about their colleagues. In the minds of U.S. prosecutors, procedural law was hindering attempts to enforce substantive law. The important question was thus raised: Should procedural law be changed to deal with an apparent crime problem?

In 1970, the Justice Department, seeking a more efficient technique for combatting organized crime, convinced Congress to pass the Organized Crime Control Act (Public Law 91-452), which severely restricted the use of the Fifth Amendment by grand jury witnesses (see Cowan, 1973). The act introduced the concept of "use immunity," whereby witnesses might be granted immunity from prosecution on the basis of information they supplied the jury.[4] However, immunity did not provide freedom from prosecution on the basis of evidence independent of the immune witnesses' testimony. Thus, members of organized crime were trapped: On the one hand, testimony did not

---

[4] In the 1960s, prosecutors had developed the use of "transactional" immunity as a method of combatting organized crime. This form of immunity guaranteed freedom from all prosecution in return for testimony. Refusal to testify after the granting of immunity could result in a jail sentence. Transactional immunity was not widely used, however, because it appeared to most observers to overly compromise justice.

automatically guarantee freedom from prison, though it did guarantee the wrath of other underworld figures; on the other hand, refusal to testify meant a jail sentence of up to eighteen months for contempt.[5]

The example of the Organized Crime Control Act points up the urgent necessity for criminological research into the problem of crime control and procedural law. There has been considerable research into assessing the impact of organized crime in America, though our knowledge is still undoubtedly superficial.[6] The gathering of such information and, to some extent, its dissemination to legislative bodies and the public, are criminological problems. Whether the organized-crime problem merits consideration of a restricted Fifth Amendment is a legislative-political problem, and, unfortunately, the extent to which such political decisions rely on criminological data is suspect.

If we assume for the moment that the organized-crime problem is serious enough to require limitations on procedural rights, the next question is whether these limitations can indeed effectively combat organized crime. Before the Organized Crime Control Act was passed no effort was made to determine systematically whether investigation and prosecution of crime-syndicate figures were actually hindered by an overly liberal definition of Fifth Amendment rights. While the Justice Department strategy was based on its experience with organized crime, there was no hard evidence that harassment of syndicate figures would significantly alter the impact of organized crime on this society. To date, there is no published research on the effects of the Organized Crime Control Act on syndicate activity since 1970. Though no easy task, this empirical question seems researchable.

A final important problem that could and should have been addressed before the Organized Crime Control Act was enacted is the identification of possible less desirable effects that, if known, would have made the act less attractive to Congress. Again no easy task, historical and comparative research into similar attempts at crime control might have addressed this problem.

Critics contend that the Organized Crime Control Act was accompanied by at least one major drawback: It precipitated the use of the grand jury, originally developed to protect individuals from arbitrary state actions, as a Justice Department vehicle for gathering information about left-wing political activists of the early 1970s. Since grand-jury proceedings are less structured and controlled than trial proceedings, prosecutors simply subpoenaed witnesses and, under threat of citing

---

[5] The witness could be imprisoned for the duration of the grand jury proceedings or up to eighteen months. After release, the witness could immediately be recalled before the grand jury, granted immunity, and, if he or she still refused to testify, be reimprisoned for up to eighteen months.

[6] For a discussion of research on organized crime in America, see Chapter 2.

them with contempt, attempted to coerce them to reveal information not pertinent to the alleged crime being investigated.

Only when such "fishing expeditions" began to occur did activists decry the new use of the grand jury. Similarly, only when reporters were jailed for refusing to divulge news sources did editorials rail against the "misuse" of the grand jury. Earlier, activists and reporters had assumed the tactics developed in the Organized Crime Control Act would not be used against them, but against "crooks." Had the real facts been known, critics argue, the bill would not have been passed.

Example 2: Preventive Pretrial Detention. The situation above demonstrates the *need* for criminological research into the problem of fighting crime through restricting procedural rights. The following shows that such research can and in fact has been done.

In the late 1960s, public fear of crime as a serious social problem led to a rethinking of a number of earlier bail-reform acts. In an effort to restore to criminal suspects the full implications of the presumption of innocence, bail had been made easier to obtain and more persons had been released on their own recognizance. The result was a greater number of suspects free from jail pending trial. In 1970 the public began to be concerned that "dangerous criminals" (so defined by the fact of arrest) were free to commit other offenses while awaiting trial on their original charges.

The response of Congress to this fear was to include, in the 1970 District of Columbia Court Reform and Criminal Procedure Act, a provision for the pretrial detention (incarceration) of persons "likely" to commit crimes if free pending trial: persons charged with dangerous crimes such as rape, arson, burglary, heroin sale, and voluntary manslaughter or with obstructing justice. Passed with virtually no debate, the act required that persons who met certain criteria were to be kept in jail for up to sixty days before their trials. In deciding whether an individual should be detained, Congress ruled that judicial officials were to consider (1) the nature and circumstances of the alleged offense and weight of the evidence against the suspect and (2) the suspect's family ties, employment situation, financial resources, character and mental condition, past conduct, length of residence in the community, record of convictions, record of previous court appearances, attempted flights to avoid prosecution, and past failures to appear in court.

The pretrial preventive detention act basically subordinates the individual's right to pretrial release to the state's right to protect itself from possible criminals. The act assumes that pretrial crime is a problem, that much pretrial crime is committed by people charged with dangerous offenses, and that the criteria specified in the act can identify which among the dangerous offenders will commit pretrial crimes.

In an effort to determine the validity of these assumptions, a team of Harvard law students in 1970 studied Boston pretrial crime for a six-month period in 1968 (Angel et al., 1971). Their aim was to determine what impact the 1970 act would have had on 1968 pretrial crime.

An examination of official police and court records disclosed there were 427 individuals who could have been eligible for pretrial preventive detention at the time of their arrests. After reviewing these cases, the Harvard team concluded the following:

1. Pretrial crime is rather low. Only 17 percent of the potential offenders committed pretrial crime.
2. There is no correlation between the original alleged offense and the seriousness of the pretrial crime.
3. Most pretrial crime does not occur in the first 60 days following release, but during 120 to 240 days after release.
4. The criteria for determining who should be detained were not linked to pretrial crime, nor could the criteria be converted to scales to predict pretrial offenders.

A clearer example of the need and potential for criminological research in the area of crime prevention and procedural law could not have been invented. Had the Boston findings been known earlier, it is doubtful that the pretrial preventive detention provision would have been included in the District of Columbia Court Reform and Criminal Procedure Act. Thus, it appears that a basic individual right was forfeited for *no gain* in preventing crime. In fact, the pretrial crime problem that prompted the bill seems less serious than originally imagined.

As the demand for "law and order" increases, we will see more remedies like those described in these two examples. It is to be hoped that criminological research in this social policy vein will also become more visible.

The coming chapters are devoted to descriptions of various aspects of crime in this society. In Chapter 2 we will examine crime statistics to see how many and what types of crimes are occurring today. We will then analyze research on criminals and victims in order to present a picture of who commits crimes against whom. All this information is vital to sound decisions concerning crime prevention.

Summary

In this chapter we explored society's "crime problem" in terms of public definitions and fears of crime. We noted that during the past decade the crime problem has taken on a national, as opposed to community, flavor. Large segments of the public fear violent attacks from strangers and have altered their lives to cope with this fear. In addition, this fear has led to tremendous governmental and business anticrime expenditures. The increased fear of crime has led to the encouragement of anticrime proposals that call for restricted procedural rights, and many police and legislators have felt that crime can best be combatted through the elimination of the "technicalities" that supposedly block the arrest and prosecution of criminals.

In the introduction to this book, we suggested that criminology can make significant social-policy contributions by identifying and examining the accuracy of public assumptions about crime, and Chapter 1 has expanded on this theme. The Organized Crime Control Act and preventive pretrial detention illustrate the fact that legislatures are responding to public demands for law and order through conservative definitions of individual rights. The examples also demonstrate the urgent necessity for research about proposed crime solutions *prior* to passage of restrictive bills, to determine if the proposed measures will accomplish their goals. Such precautions are extremely important, given the fact that reinstatement of restricted rights is nearly impossible.

References

Angel, A. R., E. D. Green, H. R. Kaufman, and E. E. Van Loon
    1971   "Preventive detention: an empirical analysis." Harvard Civil Rights–Civil Liberties Law Review 6:289–396.

Arons, S., and E. Kalsh
    1977   "How TV cops flout the law." Saturday Review 4:10–18.

Conklin, John E.
    1975   The Impact of Crime. New York: Macmillan.

Cowan, Paul
    1973   "The new grand jury." New York Times Magazine, April 29:18 and *passim*.

Davis, F. James
    1952   "Crime news in Colorado newspapers." American Journal of Sociology 57:325–30.

Dominick, J. R.
    1973   "Crime and law enforcement on prime-time television." Public Opinion Quarterly 37:241–50.

Hindelang, M. J.
    1974   "Public opinion regarding crime, criminal justice, and related topics." Journal of Research in Crime and Delinquency 11:110–16.

Hindelang, M.J., M. R. Gottfredson, C. S. Dunn, and N. Parisi
    1977   Sourcebook of Criminal Justice Statistics—1976. Washington, D.C.: U.S. Government Printing Office.

Nettler, Gwynn
    1974   Explaining Crime. New York: McGraw-Hill.

New Orleans Times-Picayune
    1976a   "Kelley: tap use needed." March 22, sec. 1:1.
    1976b   "Noise, crime complaints rank highest." June 25, sec. 2:5.

The New York Times
    1974   "What New York thinks." January 20, sec. 4:5.
President's Commission on Law Enforcement and Administration of Justice
    1967a   The Challenge of Crime in a Free Society. Washington, D.C.: U.S. Government Printing Office.
    1967b   Task Force Report: Crime and Its Impact—An Assessment. Washington, D.C.: U.S. Government Printing Office.
Roshier, Bob
    1973   "The selection of crime news by the press." Pp. 28–39 in S. Cohen and J. Young (eds.), The Manufacture of News. Beverly Hills: Sage Publications.
Skolnick, J. H.
    1975   Justice Without Trial. 2d ed. New York: Wiley.
Sutherland, E. H., and D. R. Cressey
    1974   Criminology. 9th ed. Philadelphia: Lippincott.
Turner, R. H.
    1969   "The public perception of protest." American Sociological Review 34:815–31.
U.S. Department of Justice, Law Enforcement Assistance Administration, and U.S. Bureau of the Census
    1977   Expenditure and Employment Data for the Criminal Justice System: 1975. Washington, D.C.: U.S. Government Printing Office.

Suggested Readings

Though now somewhat dated, the 1967 reports by the President's Commission on Law Enforcement and Administration of Justice remain most enlightening analyses of the crime problem and responses to it. See especially the commission's *Task Force Report: Crime and Its Impact—An Assessment* and *The Challenge of Crime in a Free Society* (both Washington, D.C.: U.S. Government Printing Office, 1967). John E. Conklin also offers a more recent investigation of these same issues in *The Impact of Crime* (New York: Macmillan, 1975). James Garofalo's *Public Opinion About Crime* (Washington, D.C.: U.S. Government Printing Office, 1977), an analysis of victimization survey data, represents the best current source of information about citizens' attitudes toward crime.

In addition to the materials cited in the notes for this chapter, a number of readings point up the dilemmas of legal responses to the "crime problem." Herbert Packer's *The Limits of Criminal Sanction* (Stanford, Calif.: Stanford University Press, 1968) is widely considered one of the best descriptions of the competing interests of the due process and crime-control orientations. Jerome Skolnick examines the same law-and-order dilemma as it influences law-enforcement agencies in *Justice Without Trial*, 2d ed. (New York: Wiley, 1975).

2
Crime Facts and Figures

Official crime statistics are obviously important for governmental anticrime policies, but their importance in the everyday lives of the public is rarely considered. As we noted earlier, a realistic assessment of crime statistics is mandatory if sound decisions are to be made about crime prevention.

For most people, the "reality" of crime is, in great part, a matter of news media summaries of official crime statistics—crimes reported, arrests, convictions, persons imprisoned, and so forth. Most of these statistics, as we stated, are for "major" FBI-index offenses of homicide, assault, rape, robbery, burglary, larceny, and automobile theft. Statistics on organized crime, white-collar crime, and similar activities are available on a limited, less detailed basis.

Before we review current crime data, we should discuss certain problems with official statistics which, according to some critics, render these statistics worthless or at least suggest the need for cautious interpretation. Our present concern is with the FBI's *Uniform Crime Reports* (1976), the most frequently cited crime figures, although criticisms of these statistics are generally applicable to any official statistics for any form of crime.

The *Uniform Crime Reports* is a yearly FBI publication that presents the number of crimes committed in the United States during the previous year. Individual law enforcement agencies compile crime statistics based on definitions of crimes supplied by the FBI and report their figures to the FBI every month. Agencies currently reporting such statistics serve 95 percent of the U.S. population. "Crimes," in the *Uniform Crime Reports* context, refer to complaints or reports of crimes made to the police and determined through investigation to be legitimate.

The *Uniform Crime Reports* distinguishes between Part I or "Index" offenses and Part II offenses. Part I crimes are considered more serious. As we stated, they include crimes of violence (homicide, forcible rape, aggravated assault, and robbery) and property offenses (burglary, larceny, and automobile theft). Statistics for these offenses are generally detailed, providing volume, rates, characteristics of arrestees, and comparisons of national regions and cities. Part II offenses are generally considered less serious (though this is debatable) and receive very little statistical attention in the *Uniform Crime Reports*. They include such crimes as arson, forgery, fraud, embezzlement, vandalism, prostitution, gambling, possession of weapons, and buying, receiving, or possessing stolen goods. Most assessments of crime are based on analysis of Part I offenses. Hence, the problems with official crime figures pertain primarily to these crimes.

Uniform Crime Reports Problems

The problems we will discuss concern the competence of the data collection, the classification choices, and unreported crimes.

Competence

The reliability of a set of statistics rests on the competence of the agency compiling it. Unsophisticated data-collection methods will produce unsophisticated estimates of the incidence of crime. Police departments vary in the expertise with which they collect and assemble crime information. The "mark on the wall" method of the small department and the complex computerized methods of larger, urban departments both carry liabilities. Changes in crime statistics personnel or in procedures within police department statistics units will affect the crime rates in the communities they serve.

Classification Choices

Though legal definitions of crime might seem quite precise, police departments actually have considerable latitude in crime classification. For example, in a physical encounter between two citizens any number of possible charges may materialize—attempted murder, assault, disturbing the peace. An attempted rape may be labeled assault. A burglary may be called criminal trespassing. A purse snatching may be a robbery, an assault, or a theft. Multiple charges may also stem from a single act. Arrest charges are often made with the anticipated response of the district attorney's office in mind. Thus, it is clear that a police department's inclinations in classifying crimes will affect a community's crime rates.

It must also be remembered that crime statistics represent *political statements*. They may reflect on a political administration's promises to reduce crime and crimes may thus be classified as of a less serious nature. For example, Seidman and Couzens (1974), reviewing the results of a Nixon administration "law and order" campaign against crime in the District of Columbia, argue that though crime reductions appeared to reflect crime-control innovations, they actually reflected the police department's classification of offenses at less serious levels in order to protect the jobs of police officials. By the same token, a police department's request for more funds, personnel, or equipment may be given credence by the establishment of a "crime problem" in the community—in part a matter of classifying crimes as highly serious.

Unreported Crimes

Official crime statistics do not account for the "dark area" of crime—crimes that are unreported or undetected by police, observers, or victims. There are many reasons why citizens do not report crimes. First, observers may not realize they are witnessing an illegal act. Second, they may know it to be illegal but may feel the matter is of a private nature, such as a family fight. Third, they may believe reporting a crime may result in inconvenience, harassment, or even reprisals. Fourth, they may fear their insurance policies may be cancelled or premiums increased if a victimization is reported. Fifth, they may place a negative value on cooperation with the police or may view them as incompetent or uninterested in the crime in question. Sixth, they may simply be ignorant of the procedures for reporting a crime. Finally, they may be involved in other crimes that might be discovered if they reported the offense in question—for example, a person would probably be reluctant to report his car stolen if the backseat contained stolen goods.

Any rise in crime, it may be theorized, may simply represent increased citizen willingness to report crimes, and this problem makes interpretation of crime statistics particularly difficult. Thus, do currently increasing rape rates, for example, reflect more attacks on women, changes in women's attitudes about reporting rapes, or both? Perhaps the recent proliferation of rape crisis centers and the development of new police techniques for dealing compassionately with rape victims mean that rape rate increases represent, at least in part, changes in the reporting of rape. Similarly, are thefts on the rise? Or are theft reports on the rise, because more people now carry theft insurance and insurance companies require that property thefts be reported to the police before claims can be settled?

Not only witnesses and victims but police officers themselves often fail to report crimes, for a number of reasons. First, in some instances, unwritten departmental policy commands that certain violations be overlooked. For example, minor drug traffickers may be ignored, on the assumption that such arrests may frighten off the upper-level drug dealers the police are especially anxious to apprehend. Or police may apprehend but not formally arrest a lower-level drug user in return for his acting as an informant. Second, police graft—payoffs for overlooking illegal acts—is certainly a major source of underreported crime, especially for vice offenses (drugs, gambling, prostitution). Graft may vary from the acceptance of small conveniences (such as free coffee) and "discounts" for goods, to the extortion of money or goods, to large-scale bribery, and even to being given "a piece of the action" (share of the illegal profits) for "overlooking" violations. Most students of the police (see Sherman, 1974, for example) argue that as police officers are constantly encouraged by other officers, organized crime, and small businesses to grant small "favors," those favors eventually lead to more involved forms of corruption.

Third, much of the willingness to report crimes and make arrests is tied to police officers' perceptions of what their jobs are designed to accomplish. Recent studies (see Bittner, 1967, and Rubinstein, 1973, for example) indicate that police officers, especially those in urban areas, tend to view their jobs as "keeping order" within specific neighborhoods or "territories." Thus, "street justice" is often dispensed, with police harassing or punishing individuals and sending them on their way. Fourth, police officers may settle a dispute without making arrests, may escort a drunk home, or may bring a juvenile offender to his parents. Many of these various decisions depend on how the potential arrestee treats the police officer or the extent to which the individual fits the officer's stereotype of the criminal (Piliavin and Briar, 1964). Similarly, many decisions are linked to the way people who make complaints treat the police. Black (1970) found the legal seriousness of a complaint, the complainant's desire for police action, the relationship between the complainant and the suspected offender, the degree to which the complainant was civil to the police officer, and the social-class status of the complaint all factors related to the filing of an official report.

In sum, official crime statistics are highly dependent on citizen and police decisions to report crimes, and these decisions help shape public views of how much and what types of crimes are committed and by whom. In order to use official statistics for important inferences about crime, then, we must accept either of two questionable assumptions: (1) that the "dark area" of unreported crime is rather small and remains fairly stable over time, or (2) that known crime constitutes a representative sample of "real crime." Some are more willing than others to make such assumptions. One recent study (Skogan, 1977) suggests that the "dark area" is made up primarily of lesser crimes and that major ones are reported. However, most criminologists are highly skeptical of official statistics and, when possible, prefer to use alternative forms of crime data, as we will explain.

Two Alternative Ways of Estimating Crime Rates

The most popular methods that social scientists have developed to offset official statistics for estimating the amount of crime, both nationally and locally, are *self-reported crime studies* and *victimization surveys.* Like official police reports, both methods tell us something about crime, but both also have their own problems.

Self-Reported Criminal Behavior

One way to gain a sense of how many crimes are being committed is, simply, to *ask* people whether or not they have committed crimes. Obviously, this procedure creates problems since the true answer risks embarrassment and even legal penalties. To avoid this problem, most self-report studies employ self-administered questionnaires and guarantee anonymity to their respondents. No attempt is made to identify the persons reporting the crimes, and hence it is assumed that respondents will not over- or underreport their offenses.

But are respondents honest when they complete self-report questionnaires? Actually, probably more so than we might at first suspect. Using polygraph ("lie detector") tests, Clark and Tifft (1966) found that most responses to standard self-report items were truthful. Researchers (Hirschi, 1969) have also found that few respondents who report no offenses have police records, while a greater percentage confessing crimes do have police records. Other researchers (Gold, 1966) have established the fact that self-report data are generally free of dishonesty by questioning the respondent's peers and teachers about the veracity of their statements. Finally, researchers report a high degree of consistency in response when respondents are asked again at a later date to complete a self-report questionnaire (Dentler and Monroe, 1961). It is doubtful that respondents who were dishonest the first time would make an effort to report the same responses.

Despite the surprising degree of honesty in self-reports of delinquent behavior, we should not be lulled into accepting them as true measures of the extent of crime in this society. We cannot ignore the self-report technique's reliance on memory—and, honest or not, respondents will certainly have difficulty recalling offenses and the frequency with which they committed them. In addition, self-report research is hampered by its concentration on juvenile delinquency, and its lack of data on adult offenders. It has been assumed that adults risk greater losses in admitting to criminal behavior and are therefore unlikely to respond candidly to a self-reported criminality survey. Further, even the juvenile samples have not been representative of general juvenile populations, and the offenses studied were often of a less serious variety, indeed sometimes acts that are not really crimes, such as disobeying parents. In short, it is only with grave reservations that we can use self-report data to estimate the amounts and types of crime in this society.

Based on available self-report research, it *appears* that:

1. Nearly everyone violates the law at least once. In one of the few adult self-report studies conducted, Wallerstein and Wyle (1947) found that an astonishing 99 percent of a sample of upper-income respondents had committed at least one illegal act which, if detected and prosecuted, could have resulted in a fine or jail sentence. This and other self-report findings suggest that there is probably two or three times as much crime committed as is presently officially recognized.
2. Most people are not serious offenders. Even those committing less serious crimes seem to do so only occasionally. One self-report study (Silberman, 1976) of college student offenses reports that the most serious offense committed by most students is petty theft. The present author's own study of property crimes among young adults (Sheley, 1975) indicates that 28 percent of its respondents committed such offenses and that the majority were relatively minor crimes—thefts or property damage amounting to less than $10.

Victimization Surveys

Rather than ask individuals what crimes they have committed, some researchers prefer to ask their respondents about crimes committed against them. In this so-called "victimization survey," members of a large sample of the population are systematically interviewed to determine how many crimes have been committed against them. There are three advantages to the victimization survey, which make it superior to self-report studies and to the *Uniform Crime Reports*. First, it is assumed that people are less willing to discuss the crimes they have committed and more willing to discuss the crimes committed against them. Second, unlike the *Uniform Crime Reports*, victimization surveys also actively seek out information about crime rather than wait for victims to report crimes. Finally, victimization surveys have utilized more representative samples than either the *Uniform Crime Reports* or self-report studies. In these three ways, the "dark area" of crime seems more accessible through the victimization survey.

The first major victimization surveys were conducted in 1966. One, by the Bureau of Social Science Research (Biderman et al., 1967), interviewed residents of Washington, D.C. Another, conducted by the National Opinion Research Center (Ennis, 1967) (NORC), interviewed a sample of 10,000 drawn from the entire nation. Both studies suggested that *Uniform Crime Reports* estimates of the amount of crime in the nation should be *doubled*—and for some types of offenses, more than doubled.

Table 2-1 displays a comparison of the crime rates for 1965 as reported by the *Uniform Crime Reports* with the rates as estimated from the NORC victimization data for 1956-66. The NORC study indicates that forcible rapes are nearly four times more prevalent than the *Uniform Crime Reports* suggest. Aggravated assault is twice as prevalent. The *Uniform Crime Reports* seem to report only two-thirds of the robberies and burglaries that actually occur, and also vastly underreport larcenies. It should be noted that the NORC sample does not include crimes against businesses and other nonresidential establishments, while the *Uniform Crime Reports* does; thus, the differences between the two estimates are even more alarming. The only crimes that the *Uniform Crime Reports* may be relied upon to report somewhat accurately are homicide and automobile theft.

Since 1970, the U.S. Department of Justice, through the Census Bureau, has conducted victimization surveys for the nation and several major U.S. cities (see, for example, U.S. Department of Justice, 1976a; 1976b). These surveys consistently bear out the findings of the original studies with respect to the "dark area" of crime. The victimization studies are not wholly free of problems, however. They depend, like self-reported criminal behavior studies, on the recall and honesty of the respondents. That is, respondents may forget victimizations or specifics about them, may manufacture victimizations to "please the

Table 2-1
Comparison of Uniform Crime Reports *(UCR) and National Opinion Research Center (NORC) victimization survey estimates of crime in the United States, 1965-66*

Crimes	UCR for individuals (1965)[a]	UCR for individuals and organizations (1965)[b]	NORC for individuals (1965-66)
Homicide	5.1	5.1	3.0
Forcible rape	11.6	11.6	42.5
Robbery	61.4	61.4	94.0
Aggravated assault	106.6	106.6	218.3
Burglary	296.6	605.3	949.1
Larceny	267.4	393.3	606.5
Automobile theft	226.0	251.0	206.2

Rates per 100,000 population

[a] Does not include commercial establishments.
[b] Includes commercial establishments.

Source: Philip H. Ennis, *Criminal Victimization in the United States* (Washington, D.C.: U.S. Government Printing Office, 1967), p. 8.

interviewer" or gain attention, or may deny victimizations for any number of personal reasons.

The victimization survey technique is also limited to estimations of rates for offenses with specific victims who are willing to report them. Thus, information on "victimless" crime, such as prostitution, is not touched, nor are crimes such as embezzlement and shoplifting, both of which are not easily detected. In the final analysis, however, victimization surveys seem to be the most sensitive measure of the extent of crimes that the public fears most and that prompt much legislation—crimes of violence and property offenses.

How Much Crime?

Though both the *Uniform Crime Reports* and the victimization surveys have defects, they remain our best current means of estimating how much crime occurs in this society. Keeping in mind the cautions mentioned above, we may examine the amounts and trends of crime as they appear through these estimates. The figures reported below are taken from the 1975 *Uniform Crime Reports* and the 1976 Department of Justice report, *Criminal Victimization in the United States—1973*. These are the most recent statistics available at the time of this writing.

Table 2–2 displays *Uniform Crime Reports* estimates of the volume and rates (per 100,000 population) for the FBI index offenses in 1975. Table 2–3 presents the Department of Justice victimization survey estimates of the volume and rates for relatively the same offenses in 1973. Although the offense classification systems of the two estimates vary

Table 2–2
Estimates of crime in the United States: 1975 Uniform Crime Reports

Crimes	Volume	Rate per 100,000 population
Homicide	20,510	9.6
Forcible rape	56,090	26.3[a]
Robbery	464,970	218.2
Aggravated assault	484,710	227.4
Burglary	3,252,100	1,525.9
Larceny	5,977,700	2,804.8
Automobile theft	1,000,500	469.4
Total	11,256,000	5,281.7
Violent crimes	1,026,280	481.5
Property crimes	10,230,300	4,800.2

[a] 51 for females.

Source: 1975 FBI *Uniform Crime Reports*, p. 16.

Table 2-3
Estimates of crime in the United States: 1973 victimization survey results

Crimes	Volume	Rate per 100,000 population
Personal victimizations		(per 100,000 population)
Rape	159,700	100[a]
Robbery	1,120,100	700
Assault	4,213,800	2,600
Theft	15,160,000	9,300
Household victimizations		(per 100,000 households)
Larceny	7,590,700	10,900
Burglary	6,433,000	9,300
Automobile theft	1,330,500	1,900
Business victimizations		(per 100,000 businesses)
Robbery	264,100	3,900
Burglary	1,385,000	20,400

[a] About 200 for females.

Source: U.S. Department of Justice, *Criminal Victimization in the United States* (Washington, D.C.: U.S. Government Printing Office, 1976), p. 68.

somewhat,[1] comparison of the tables shows again that the *Uniform Crime Reports* grossly underestimate the amount of crime in our society. Even so, both sets of statistics tell much the same stories. The great majority of our crimes are property offenses. Rapes, robberies, and assaults constitute less than 15 percent of the crimes reported in either table. In general, ranking by frequency of occurrence of the offenses reflects the reverse of society's view of their seriousness (less serious crimes occur more often): larceny, burglary, automobile theft, aggravated assault, robbery, rape, and murder.

Trends in Index Crimes

Much is made of the fact that crime has risen tremendously over the past 15 years. Some of the increase undoubtedly is due to changes in crime-reporting practices of police departments and, perhaps, to a greater willingness by citizens to report crimes. As noted above, for example, there is certainly a change in women's attitudes toward reporting rape, so much so that it is difficult to determine how much of

---

[1] Victimization surveys do not collect information on homicides, nor are their rules for counting and classifying crimes identical to those of the *Uniform Crime Reports*. Further, victimization surveys do not include crimes against persons under 12 years of age, whereas the *UCR* set no limit on age of victims.

the 41 percent rise in rapes since 1970 reported by the FBI is a reporting increase and how much an actual increase. Overall, however, we deceive ourselves if we attribute rising crime rates wholly to altered reporting procedures. Crime has, in fact, increased.

The 1975 *Uniform Crime Reports* figures shown in Table 2–4 indicate about a 9 percent increase in the overall crime rate over 1974. The violent crime rate rose about 4 percent; the property crime rate increased about 9 percent. Comparing 1975 crime rates with those of previous years, it is easy to understand the nation's concern over crime. We have experienced an apparent *180 percent increase* in overall crime since 1960.

Increasing crime is also reflected in victimization rates in eight large American cities between 1971–72 and 1974–75 (U.S. Department of Justice, 1976b). Table 2–5 shows that victimization rates increased in most of these cities, with household larcenies up at least 11 percent and commercial robberies up greatly also. Though down in some cities, crimes of violence rose between 20 and 41 percent in others. Only two crimes displayed general downward trends: automobile thefts and commercial burglaries. In sum, two major estimates indicate that we have been experiencing a rise in crime over the past several years.

Somewhat optimistically, some experts have been arguing that we have begun to "turn the corner" on the crime problem. This claim is based on the fact that though crime has been increasing, recently it has been doing so more slowly (New Orleans Times-Picayune, 1977). The American public undoubtedly finds little consolation in such statements. Further, its concern with crime has increased because of recent attention given to other, non–FBI index offenses, such as white-collar

Table 2–4
Uniform Crime Reports estimates of crime rate changes—1975 over previous years

		Rate changes (in percent) over previous years		
Crimes	1975 rates	1974	1970	1960
Homicide	9.6	–2.0	+21.5	+88.2
Forcible rape	26.3	+.4	+40.6	+174.0
Robbery	218.2	+4.3	+26.8	+263.1
Aggravated assault	227.4	+5.4	+38.0	+164.1
Burglary	1,525.9	+6.1	+40.6	+200.0
Larceny	2,804.8	+12.7	+24.9	+171.1
Automobile theft	469.4	+1.6	+2.8	+156.5
Total	5,281.7	+8.9	+32.6	+179.9
Violent crimes	481.5	+4.4	+32.5	+199.3
Property crimes	4,800.2	+9.4	+32.6	+178.1

Source: 1975 FBI *Uniform Crime Reports*, p. 11.

Table 2-5
Victimization rate changes (in percent) for eight American cities—1971-72 to 1974-75

Crimes	Atlanta	Baltimore	Cleveland	Dallas	Denver	Newark	Portland	St. Louis
Personal								
Violence	−9	+41	+24	+13	+6	−10	+20	+15
Property (theft)	−7	+33	+20	+21	0	−11	+16	+26
Household								
Burglary	−2	+2	+10	+10	+5	−21	+15	+8
Larceny	+15	+24	+32	+21	+11	+11	+26	+16
Auto	−16	+20	−4	−4	−10	+8	+9	−2
Commercial								
Burglary	−30	−20	−4	+20	−2	−20	+18	−23
Robbery	−22	−9	+22	+14	+45	+9	+71	+52

Source: U.S. Department of Justice, *Criminal Victimization Surveys in Eight American Cities* (Washington, D.C.: U.S. Government Printing Office, 1976), p. 8

crime and organized crime. Though statistics for these offenses are limited, the increased law enforcement and media concentration on them has made them *seem* (perhaps justifiably) to be growing more problematic. For this reason, and because they carry important moral and sociological implications, they merit some discussion.

White-Collar, Corporate, and Political Crime

Consumerism interests and the Watergate scandal have broadened the public's conception of crime. Although most people are still fearful of personal and property offenses, they are now also concerned with *white-collar crime*. This term is somewhat ambiguous since it is in no way a legal term. Depending upon context and speaker, white-collar crime may refer to corporate crime such as price fixing, to occupationally-related illegal personal gain through such crimes as embezzlement or physician Medicare swindles, to illegal activity by public officeholders, or simply to any crime committed by persons generally considered members of the middle and upper classes. Given these possibilities, it is clear why white-collar crime is often referred to as "respectable crime."

Respectable or not, white-collar crime is costly for our society. Unlike standard property offenses, which harm specific individuals, white-collar crime penalizes the entire society economically. The costs of employee thefts and shoplifting are passed on to the consumer. Medicare fraud by patients and physicians is covered by tax increases. Corporate price fixing eliminates the industrial competition that keeps prices down for consumers. Income-tax evasion results in yearly government financial losses of more than $25 billion (President's Commission, 1967:103–104). Further, as Watergate demonstrated, the costs of white-collar crime are not only economic. Official corruption, when discovered, demoralizes the American public as much as the rise in traditional personal and property offenses.

Corporate Crime

Corporate crime is a special form of white-collar crime. The term refers to a number of business-related activities: defrauding stockholders (as with misreporting profits), defrauding the public (as with price fixing and product misrepresentation), defrauding the government (as with tax evasion), endangering the public welfare (as with industrial pollution), endangering employees (as with maintaining unsafe working conditions), and engaging in illegal political activities (as with making unlawful campaign contributions). Occasionally, corporate crime refers to misuse of a corporation position for personal gain. More often, it refers to practices performed for the financial benefit of a corporation.

A classic example of the latter form of corporate crime is the heavy electrical equipment case of 1961 (Smith, 1961; Geis, 1967). The case involved a number of antitrust violations by officials of twenty-nine corporations that produced and marketed electrical equipment. Representatives of the companies conspired to rig bids and set prices for their equipment. Meeting in secret, they sought to ensure that all the companies involved maintained their "fair" share of the market (that is, the share they held at the time the conspiracy was initiated). Nearly all the participants were "company men." Few sought personal gain from their actions; most were acting "in the company's best interests." That these interests countered consumer interests by limiting competition was, in the eyes of the conspirators, of lesser consequence.

The electrical equipment case is typical of corporate crime cases in that the offenders did not view themselves as criminals. Geis (1967:144–47) notes that the conspirators stated that they had not sought personal gain, had not harmed any individuals, and had violated only government "regulations" rather than important laws. In short, the offenders saw themselves as "respectable." Clinard and Quinney (1973:191) elaborate on this point:

> A major characteristic of occupational crime is the way in which the offender conceives of himself. Since the offenses take place in connection with a legitimate occupation and the offender generally regards himself as a respectable citizen, he does not regard himself as a criminal. At most, he regards himself as a "law-breaker." . . . The maintenance of a noncriminal self concept by the offender is one of the essential elements in the process leading to occupational crime.

The electrical equipment conspiracy is typical of corporate crime in yet another way. Such crimes are often seen as "good business," and good business often requires "cutting corners." Corporate legal violations are viewed by many as being part of our business system, much like industrial spying or psychologically suggestive marketing techniques. Basically, these activities are merely extensions of a capitalist ethic that stresses profit and a grudging semiadherence to the letter, rather than the spirit, of the law. That this is a pervasive view is in great part seen in the lack of both public outcry and governmental sanctions against offenders. Fines levied against the corporations involved in the electrical equipment case were negligible (though civil suits stemming from the case were more costly). Of the forty-five company officials charged in the case, almost all of whom pleaded guilty, most received fines or were given probation. Seven drew jail terms of thirty days, though none actually served more than twenty-five days.

How much corporate crime actually exists? Sociological studies have documented offenses by retail pharmacists, landlords, the wholesale meat industry, and automobile manufacturers and dealers (Quinney, 1963; Ball, 1960; Hartung, 1950; Leonard and Weber, 1970). A pioneering study of violations by seventy large corporations in the earlier part of this century (Sutherland, 1949:20–25) found that all of the corporations had encountered adverse court decisions concerning such activities as restraint of trade, infringement, unfair labor practices, and misrepresentation in advertising; 60 percent of the corporations had been convicted in criminal court. However, it is clear that we see only the tip of the iceberg. Corporate crimes take so many forms, are committed in such secrecy, and have victims so generally unaware of their losses, that sound estimates of the extent of corporate crime are impossible.

A number of factors place the possibility of control of corporate crime in doubt (Kadish, 1963; Geis, 1973). First, legal definition of specific corporate offenses is problematic. That is, it is difficult to define exactly what constitutes such offenses as "illegal monopolies" and "manufacture of unsafe products." Second, even were these crimes well specified, it is difficult to determine whom to charge with an offense—a corporation or the individuals within it? How, for instance, does the state prosecute a corporation? Third, intent to commit a crime is generally difficult to prove in corporate crime cases.

Fourth, and probably most important, while the public grows increasingly aware of corporate crime, it remains relatively unperturbed about the situation and places little pressure on the government to solve the problem. Concern with corporate offenses rests primarily with a few consumer-protection groups. Policing corporations adequately would require a massive bureaucracy. As it is now constituted, law enforcement in this country cannot assume the task. A public that is not outraged by corporate crime would seem unwilling to fully finance adequate government surveillance of big business.

Political Crime

A similar analysis applies to political crime. Traditionally, we have thought of political crime in terms of corrupt politicians embezzling government funds or accepting bribes (Gardiner, 1967). Or we have envisioned political crime as treason or spying. However, recent events have caused us to expand our definitions (Heidenheimer, 1970). Our view of political crime now includes such acts as misuse of public office for political or personal ends; misuse of government agencies to cover up unethical or criminal acts; unauthorized, secret, and relatively indiscriminate gathering of intelligence on U.S. citizens; misrepresentation of a government agency's activities to higher authorities such as the Congress; and government violation of both substantive and procedural laws during the investigation of suspected law violators or "threats to national security." Watergate and other recent political embarrassments suggest that far more political crime and unethical conduct occur than is generally imagined by the public.

Political crime differs somewhat from corporate crime, however, in that control of political crime is hampered by the direct or indirect involvement of the offenders in the control process. That is, we expect violators to police and prosecute themselves. This problem became most clear in President Nixon's attempt to suppress the Watergate scandal through his control of the Justice Department. It became apparent as well in revelations that the FBI has been virtually free to violate laws during investigations because no agency actively investigates the FBI.

Wilson and Rachal (1977) suggest that government regulation of government agencies is far more complicated than government regulation of private business. Government agencies now have many more laws by which to abide (for example, laws governing affirmative action and access to files on citizens), and therefore regulatory agencies face a more complex task. Further, most regulatory agencies are at best semipowerful. That is, control of other agencies and their personnel is primarily a matter of reporting offenses to a higher command rather than of initiating criminal proceedings. Since the higher command (such as a mayor, a governor, a president) cannot afford the scandal that often accompanies disclosure of governmental improprieties and, for that matter, cannot risk alienating large numbers of government personnel, he or she will likely handle the matter privately and informally (for example, through the forced resignation or reassignment of the major offenders). This structure of command obviously makes control of the higher command nearly impossible.

In the final analysis, however, two problems are the most crucial in the failure to prevent political deviance. First, regulation of political agencies and officers requires massive bureaucracy and financing—far more than that required to control street crime. Second, and related, is the problem of public resignation to political crime. While public outrage over political crime exceeds public anger over corporate crime—especially when high-level political leaders are involved—political crime is generally seen as "expected," occasionally expedient, and sometimes necessary. As if paraphrasing Merton's (1957:72–82) classic analysis of the functions of the political machine, the average citizen undoubtedly finds some positive features in political violations. This is evidenced by the frequent assessment of Justice Department "excesses" in investigating political radicals as the lesser of two evils (the greater evil being the success of the radical politics). Until the public becomes as indignant about political crime as about street crime, little will be done to control violations by politicians and government agencies.

White-Collar Crime Wave?

In sum, white-collar crime encompasses a multitude of offenses in the private, business, and political sectors. It is difficult to know whether the white-collar crime problem represents a crime wave or an "awareness wave." That is, we do not know whether various forms of white-collar crime have increased significantly or public knowledge and concern about such offenses have grown. Perhaps both possibilities have prevailed.

Whether or not grounded in real offenses, the general increase in the reporting of "respectable crime" has resulted in greater (though still relatively limited) government action against white-collar offenders. As governmental activity increases, the perception of white-collar crime as a social problem will increase and spur further government activity (Douglas, 1977). If the above analyses of corporate and political crime are correct, those concerned about these offenses can look forward to frustrating times. White-collar crime is rational and calculated and some offenders have much to lose if caught; therefore, white-collar crime *should* be deterrable through increased criminal sanctions. However, there is no evidence that penalties and apprehension rates for white-collar offenders will increase dramatically in the future. General public apathy and the enormity of the bureaucracy needed to control white-collar crime ensure its continued existence.

Organized Crime

For nearly eighty years, the American public has been intermittently concerned with organized crime. Eleven Italians were lynched in New Orleans in 1891, for example, in an outburst of public hostility toward alleged Mafia activities.

Basically, "organized crime" refers to a group of persons organized to commit an offense. However, some people use the term to refer to involvement in vice activities—gambling, prostitution, drugs—and others limit their definition to a supposed *national* syndicate that controls vice activities and invests profits in legitimate business concerns. This latter definition more clearly approximates the public stereotype of organized crime.

There is considerable disagreement about the structure and extent of organized crime in America. On the one hand, we are offered the picture of a national—perhaps international—Mafia "family." The family is militarily organized, with bosses, underbosses, lieutenants, and soldiers. The national family is allegedly divided into twenty-four groups in various major American cities. A "commission" composed of the more powerful syndicate figures in the United States oversees the activities of the twenty-four subgroups. The commission settles disputes and enforces treaties within the family. The organization is protected from external government threats by a strict code of loyalty to and silence regarding the activities of family members (President's Commission, 1967b).

Countering the picture of a national Mafia is the view that organized crime is less formally structured and more local in nature.[2] The key to this view is the notion that any supply-and-demand organization, whether legal or illegal, can survive only if it is flexible enough to withstand pressures and changes in its environment. The situation in Seattle, for example, may differ greatly from that of Miami or Detroit: political processes, historical acceptance of syndicate activity, demand for illegal services, and opportunities to enter illegal enterprises all may vary. The rigidity that characterizes the alleged national Mafia would prohibit the flexibility necessary for an organization to meet these dynamic situations. As Joseph Albini (1971) points out, persons who are patrons in one area may be clients in other areas. Those in power in one place are powerless in other places. Patron-client relationships are often symbiotic, each participant holding some measure of power over the other. In sum, organized crime is integrated into local social structures and cultures.

There is little disagreement about the activities of organized crime. The syndicate has interests in gambling, narcotics, prostitution, pornography, loan sharking, labor racketeering, and stolen securities. In addition, through investment of illegally earned profits or by "muscling in," organized crime has developed interests in vending machines, restaurants and taverns, real estate, the garment industry, trucking, food processing, and other legitimate businesses. Gambling activities alone are said to net at least $7 billion yearly. Narcotics worth over $350 million dollars on the street net tremendous sums for organized crime annually (President's Commission, 1967b:1–15).

---

[2] For a collection of writings in this vein, see Ianni and Reuss-Ianni (1976).

Organized crime is best understood when placed in a historical and social context. Organized crime has always been economically tied to the community. It has traditionally been linked to the immigration and social mobility of various ethnic groups into the United States. As Irish, Jews, and Italians moved into American cities and, in succession, faced relatively blocked socioeconomical mobility, they moved into illegal endeavors. As each group, in succession, found more legitimate opportunities, its involvement in organized crime decreased. Presently, organized crime is increasingly being controlled by blacks and Puerto Ricans, current inhabitants of our society's socioeconomic cellar.

It must also be realized that organized crime requires a demand for its services and alliances with government and law-enforcement groups in order to operate relatively freely. Most observers currently view organized crime as a moderate-sized business. As such, it is concerned with limiting the supply of vice services. Like any business, it thus attempts to eliminate competition. In the case of illegal services, this is accomplished by society when it outlaws "vices." While many forms of organized-crime interests can be thwarted (for example, labor racketeering), organized crime will exist as long as a demand for illegal services exists. The resistance to legalization of vices is more than moral; organized crime is so pervasive that economic involvement in it stretches to nearly every socioeconomic corner of the society. Put simply, benefits from organized crime are not limited to members of gangs. Large and small businesses, politicians, labor leaders, and other respectable citizens share in its profits and therefore resist decriminalization of its services.

As with white-collar crime, it is difficult to know whether organized crime grows stronger or weaker or if the public's concern about it rises or falls. Either way, interest in it enlarges the scope of the "crime problem."

Crime Statistics: Taking a Critical Approach

Three major points have surfaced in the preceding pages:

1. Crime statistics suffer from problems of representativeness and accuracy.
2. Despite these problems, we cannot ignore the fact that FBI-index crimes have increased.
3. The scope of the crime problem has grown with increased public concern about white-collar and organized crime.

In the previous chapter, we noted that precisely these conclusions sometimes have prompted drastic changes in the personal habits of citizens, increased government anticrime spending, and a greater societal willingness to surrender individual rights to combat crime.

Are these sensible responses to our crime situation? Rather than answer this question directly, let us note that if they represent correct responses, it is quite by accident. We stated in the introduction that solutions to any problem necessitate as thorough an understanding of the nature and scope of the problem as possible. Few people move beyond hearsay in assessing the crime problem. Those who do tend to rely on official statistics concerning the volume, rate, and rate changes for particular crimes.

Statistics, even accurate ones, can be misleading. Examples of reporting insufficiencies are numerous. Percentages are often cited without base figures. (A 50 percent increase in crime may mean little if the base figure is small. For example, three thefts in 1975 as opposed to two the previous year constitute a 50 percent rise in theft.) Crime statistics are usually reported for the nation or, at best, for a community. In either case, averages can be deceiving. One should consider whether a national high crime rate is due to nationally pervasive crime or simply to a great deal of crime in certain areas or cities. Similarly, high crime rates in a city may be confined to a few neighborhoods, while the remainder of the city may be relatively safe.

Too little attention is given by the public, government, and some criminologists to the characteristics of crimes beyond the broad categories used to define and distinguish them. To say that property offenses are increasing is to say very little. Are they minor or major thefts? Do they occur at night or during the day? Who is victimized? To note that robberies are on the rise is to leave much to the imagination. Before we can prevent robberies or protect ourselves, we must know what forms the robberies take: bank holdups, muggings, household robberies, and so forth. It is important to understand when and where the robberies occur and against whom; the kind of weapon used also is important.[3] Similarly, assaults committed by strangers in the streets carry different governmental and personal policy meanings from assaults committed during domestic or barroom quarrels among non-strangers.

In sum, the public must become more critical of the crime statistics it receives. In essence, every statistic should be challenged with the question, "How are these figures distorted or misleading?" In terms of personal adaptations to crime, individuals should also ask, "How does this affect me?" That is, what are the individual's chances of being the victim of a particular form of crime, given his sphere of social interaction—his home, neighborhood, and areas of work, shopping, and entertainment? In terms of support for government anticrime programs, people must ask if the solution is based on a misleading interpretation of crime statistics.

---

[3] For a discussion of possible answers to such questions, see the examination of robbery in the coming chapter and see Conklin (1972).

The consequences of uncritical acceptance of crime figures are easily seen in two examples.

Example 1: Homicide in New Orleans. The politicians and citizens in New Orleans were both frightened and embarrassed by the FBI *Uniform Crime Reports* for 1974, for the statistics placed the city third in the nation in homicide rates: 22.7 per 100,000 people. Residents of the greater New Orleans metropolitan area were statistically more likely to be murdered than citizens of such larger metropolitan areas as Detroit, New York, or Los Angeles. Editorials denounced the increasing lawlessness. The police department called for more funds and more officers. It was generally agreed that the "streets must be made safer."

It was clear from the reactions of the people of New Orleans that they envisioned homicides in the city as street attacks by strangers. In such situations, government policy responses are predictable: Police departments are restructured; officers are added to the homicide detail; street patrols are increased; bills calling for capital punishment are reintroduced in the legislature. In terms of personal adjustments, fears increase: people stay indoors more often, especially at night; strangers are scrupulously avoided; public places and public transportation are not used.

Research published by Marvin Wolfgang (1958) some time ago cautioned against hastily stereotyping homicides as attacks by strangers and consequently hastily supporting policies based on such stereotypes. In a study of 588 homicides committed in Philadelphia between 1948 and 1952, Wolfgang found that 65 percent involved close friends, relatives, and acquaintances. Fifty-one percent of the slayings occurred in the home. Alcohol was involved in 64 percent of the cases. Most startling, 26 percent of the deaths were *victim precipitated;* that is, the victim was the first one to use physical force in the homicide encounter. Homicides generally resulted from lovers' quarrels, family disputes, and barroom disturbances.

The 1975 FBI *Uniform Crime Reports* suggest that Wolfgang's findings were not extraordinary. As Table 2–6 indicates, 68 percent of the nation's homicides occurred between people who knew each other, often very well. Over 22 percent involved relatives. Felony-related homicides (killings due to robberies, rapes, gang wars, and the like) accounted for only one-third of the 1975 murders. It is also worth noting that, though 1975 homicide figures indicate a 28 percent rise in volume over 1970, felony-related homicides are up in volume less than 3 percent. Most of our increase in murders, then, represents a rise in dispute-related killings, generally labeled "crimes of passion."

New Orleans homicides in 1974 were little different from the homicides described in Table 2–6. An Orleans Parish coroner's report (Minyard and Niklaus, n.d.) notes that New Orleanians were killed by strangers in only 4 percent of the homicides in which the killer was

Table 2-6
1975 homicide circumstances

Type of killing	Percent of total
Spouse killing spouse	11.5
Parent killing child	3.0
Relative killing relative	7.9
Romantic triangles and lovers' quarrels	7.3
Other arguments	37.9
Known felony-related killings	23.0
Suspected felony-related killings	9.4

Source: FBI *Uniform Crime Reports*, p. 19.

identifiable. Most of New Orleans murders could be labeled "dispute homicides." Nearly half of the killings in the city occurred in homes and bars rather than on the streets. Another 28 percent happened near places where alcohol was served or where drug "rip-offs" had occurred. Alcohol was, in fact, involved in 44 percent of the slayings; drugs were implicated in 20 percent. Most of the alcohol- and drug-related deaths resulted from drunken arguments or "settling the score" among drug dealers and users.

Regarding apparent motives for homicide, predatory felonies were again in the minority. Revenge governed 27 percent of the New Orleans murders; sudden anger accounted for 20 percent; jealousy and hate, 8 percent; mental illness, 2 percent; armed robbery, 23 percent; and other unknown motives, 20 percent. Of double murders (two victims), 64 percent were drug related, 18 percent stemmed from jealousy, and 18 percent resulted from robberies.

The coroner's report provides a rather different picture of homicides from that produced in New Orleanians' minds by the bald statistic, 22.7 murders per 100,000 population. Most killings are dispute oriented rather than predatory. The chances of the average citizen, who would generally not be placed in lethal dispute situations, being a homicide victim are quite low. Changing personal habits because of the homicide statistics seems unreasonable. Further, it is difficult to conceive of any governmental program that could effectively reduce homicides. Most experts concede that the police are relatively powerless to combat the crime, given the circumstances of most murders. Nor is capital punishment likely to reduce dispute-related murders. Yet, few people are given the opportunity or take the time to evaluate critically homicide statistics so that these conclusions become implemented in personal and government anticrime policies.

Example 2: Indecent Assault in Toronto. If the public were told that indecent or sexual assaults on females were becoming a problem, we could easily imagine proposed solutions to deal with it. On the less radical side, there would be demands for increased street lighting and police patrols. Judges would be asked to deal more harshly with convicted offenders. Public-awareness programs, some including courses in self-defense techniques, would be tried. On the more radical side, curfews might be suggested. Preventive detention of all known sex offenders might be encouraged.

These proposed solutions would indicate a public stereotype of indecent assault as a violent attack on a woman, probably at night. If the stereotype approximated reality, the public would indeed have cause for worry. Yet few citizens would stop to question the accuracy of the public view. Were they to do so, both their fears and their proposed solutions for the indecent assault problem might change drastically.

To illustrate this point, J. W. Mohr (1973) studied official cases of indecent assault in the city of Toronto. His report noted, first, the broadness of the legal definition of indecent or sexual assault. (Canadian and American law on this point are pretty much the same.) The term applies not only to actual injurious attacks but also to unauthorized touches and even to threats and gestures. Reviewing Toronto's indecent assault cases, Mohr then observed that most involve female children as victims. Of these, only a few involved violence, none particularly serious. As the age of victims increased, so did the seriousness of the offenses, yet truly violent attacks were rare.

A rather large number of indecent assaults, Mohr found, occurred in August and September during the Canadian National Exhibition. In most of these cases, the victims did not complain. Instead, arrests followed police observation of assaults. The "indecent assaults" that inspired these arrests were cases in which men took advantage of crowded situations to move close to and rub against females, a familiar occurrence on the subways of large cities. Mohr referred to a "crime wave" of indecent assaults that appeared when fifty-three extra cases were reported as the result of increased police activity along a crowded parade route.

The purpose of this illustration is not to minimize the seriousness of child molesting nor to condone the liberties taken by some men in crowds. Rather, we wish to demonstrate the importance of a critical approach to crime statistics. We are often given statistics for a form of crime without being told *exactly* what behaviors the legal definition of the act encompasses. Nor are we told the proportions of the total violations of a statute represented by each type of act covered by the statute. The dangers in these forms of ignorance are clear in the Toronto indecent-assault example. The solutions proposed if the assaults were assumed to be rapes would be both costly and, perhaps, drastic. They would also be needless if investigation of the Toronto statistics indicated that most cases of indecent assault were of a less serious variety.

In sum, personal and government policy decisions should not be made without a critical review of all aspects of the problems they address.

Summary

In this chapter we tried to accomplish two tasks: first, to provide an overview of the extent of crime in our society—and by most estimates, we have more crime now than in the past—and, second, and more important, to raise a number of red flags concerning crime statistics.

Crime statistics may not be representative of actual crime. Even if they are, the statistics still do not meaningfully convey to the average citizen his or her actual chances of being victimized. Knowledge of what a definition of a criminal act actually includes and what a "rise" in crime actually means is mandatory if we are to make sound personal and governmental anticrime decisions. As we suggested earlier, incautious decisions regarding crime are often more costly than crime itself.

References

Albini, J. L.
    1971   The American Mafia: Genesis of a Legend. New York: Appleton-Century-Crofts.

Ball, H. V.
    1960   "Social structure and rent-control violations." American Journal of Sociology 65:598–604.

Biderman, A. D., L. A. Johnson, J. McIntyre, and A. Weis
    1967   Report on a Pilot Study in the District of Columbia on Victimization and Attitudes Toward Law Enforcement. Field Survey I: President's Commission on Law Enforcement and Administration of Justice. Washington, D.C.: U.S. Government Printing Office.

Bittner, E.
    1967   "The police on skid row: a study of peace keeping." American Sociological Review 32:699–715.

Black, D. J.
    1970   "Production of crime rates." American Sociological Review 35:733–48.

Clark, J. P., and L. L. Tifft
    1966   "Polygraph and interview validation of self-reported deviant behavior." American Sociological Review 31:516–23.

Clinard, M. B., and R. Quinney
    1973   Criminal Behavior Systems: A Typology. 2d ed. New York: Holt, Rinehart & Winston.

Conklin, J. E.
    1972   Robbery and the Criminal Justice System. Philadelphia: Lippincott.

Dentler, R. A., and L. J. Monroe
    1961   "Social correlates of early adolescent theft." American Sociological Review 26:733–43.

Douglas, J. D.
    1977   "A sociological theory of official deviance and public concerns with official deviance." Pp. 395–407 in J. Douglas and J. ·M. Johnson (eds.), Official Deviance. Philadelphia: Lippincott.

Ennis, P.
    1967   Criminal Victimization in the United States: A Report of a National Survey. Field Survey II of the President's Commission on Law Enforcement and Administration of Justice. Washington, D.C.: U.S. Government Printing Office.

Federal Bureau of Investigation, U.S. Department of Justice
    1976   Crime in the United States: Uniform Crime Reports, 1975. Washington, D.C.: U.S. Government Printing Office.

Gardiner, J. A.
    1967   "Wincanton: the politics of corruption." Pp. 61–79 in President's Commission on Law Enforcement and Administration of Justice, Task Force Report: Organized Crime. Washington, D.C.: U.S. Government Printing Office.

Geis, G.
    1967   "White collar crime: the heavy electrical equipment antitrust cases of 1961." Pp. 139–51 in M. B. Clinard and R. Quinney (eds.), Criminal Behavior Systems: A Typology. 1st ed. New York: Holt, Rinehart & Winston.
    1973   "Deterring corporate crime." Pp. 246–58 in R. Nader and M. J. Green (eds.), Corporate Power in America. New York: Viking Press.

Gold, M.
    1966   "Undetected delinquent behavior." Journal of Research in Crime and Delinquency 13:27–46.

Hartung, F. E.
    1950   "White-collar offenses in the wholesale meat industry in Detroit." American Journal of Sociology 56:25–34.

Heidenheimer, A. J.
    1970   Political Corruption: Readings in Comparative Analysis. New York: Holt, Rinehart & Winston.

Hirschi, T.
    1969   Causes of Delinquency. Berkeley: University of California Press.

Ianni, F. A. J. and E. Reuss-Ianni
    1976   The Crime Society. New York: New American Library.

Kadish, S. H.
    1963   "Some observations on the use of criminal sanctions in enforcing economic regulations." University of Chicago Law Review 30:423–49.

Leonard, W. N., and M. G. Weber
    1970   "Automakers and dealers: a study of criminogenic market forces." Law and Society Review 4:407–24.

Merton, R. K.
    1957   Social Theory and Social Structure. 2d ed. New York: The Free Press.

Minyard, F. E., and K. C. Niklaus
    n.d.   New Orleans Murder Scene. New Orleans: Simmons Press.

Mohr, J. W.
　1973　"Facts, figures, perceptions and myths—ways of describing and understanding crime." Canadian Journal of Criminology and Corrections 15:39–49.

New Orleans Times-Picayune
　1977　"Violent crime dips 4 per cent during 1976." September 28, sec. 1:3.

Piliavin, I., and S. Briar
　1964　"Police encounters with juveniles." American Journal of Sociology 70:206–14.

President's Commission on Law Enforcement and Administration of Justice
　1967a　Task Force Report: Crime and Its Impact—An Assessment. Washington D.C.: U.S. Government Printing Office.
　1967b　Task Force Report: Organized Crime. Washington, D.C.: U.S. Government Printing Office.

Quinney, R.
　1963　"Occupational structure and criminal behavior: prescription violations by retail pharmacists." Social Problems 11:179–85.

Rubinstein, J.
　1973　City Police. New York: Random House.

Seidman, D. and M. Couzens
　1974　"Getting the crime rate down: political pressure and crime reporting." Law and Society Review 8:457–93.

Sheley, J. F.
　1975　An Empirical Assessment of Neutralization in Control Theories of Deviance. Ph.D. dissertation, Department of Sociology, University of Massachusetts.

Sherman, L. W.
　1974　"Becoming bent: moral careers of corrupt policemen." Pp. 191–208 in L. W. Sherman (ed.), Police Corruption. Garden City, N.Y.: Anchor Books.

Silberman, M.
　1976　"Toward a theory of criminal deterrence." American Sociological Review 41:442–61.

Skogan, W. G.
　1977　"Dimensions of the dark figure of unreported crime." Crime and Delinquency 23:41–50.

Smith, R. A.
　1961　"The incredible electrical conspiracy." Fortune 63:132–37 and *passim*; 161–64 and *passim*.

Sutherland, E. H.
　1949　White Collar Crime. New York: Holt, Rinehart & Winston.

U.S. Department of Justice
　1976a　Criminal Victimization in the United States—1973. Washington, D.C.: U.S. Government Printing Office.
　1976b　Criminal Victimization Surveys in Eight American Cities: A Comparison of 1971/72 and 1974/75 Findings. Washington, D.C.: U.S. Government Printing Office.

Wallerstein, J. S., and C. Wyle
　1947　"Our law-abiding lawbreakers." Federal Probation 25:107–12.

Wilson, J. Q., and P. Rachal
　1977　"Can the government regulate itself?" The Public Interest 46:3–14.

Wolfgang, M. E.
    1958   Patterns in Criminal Homicide. Philadelphia: University of Pennsylvania Press.

Suggested Readings

As this chapter has indicated, the primary sources of our knowledge about crime trends in the United States are the FBI *Uniform Crime Reports* and various Justice Department victimization surveys. Readers are encouraged to examine these documents, since they are generally written in language the public can easily understand.

Critiques of official police statistics are, of course, numerous. Among the better ones are Sophia Robinson's, "A Critical View of the Uniform Crime Reports," *Michigan Law Review,* April 1966, pp. 1031-54, and Harry M. Schulman's, "The Measurement of Crime in the United States," *Journal of Criminal Law, Criminology, and Police Science,* December 1966, pp. 483-92. A similarly effective review of the problems in victimization surveys is found in James P. Levine's "The Potential for Crime Overreporting in Criminal Victimization Surveys," *Criminology,* November 1976, pp. 307-30.

Don C. Gibbons's *Society, Crime, and Criminal Careers,* 3d ed. (Englewood Cliffs, N.J.: Prentice-Hall, 1977) and Marshall Clinard and Richard Quinney's *Criminal Behavior Systems: A Typology,* 2d. ed., (New York: Holt, Rinehart & Winston, 1973) offer detailed classifications and descriptions of various types of crime. Recent collections of reading on white-collar, political, and corporate crime are available in J. Douglas and J. M. Johnson's *Official Deviance* (Philadelphia: Lippincott, 1977) and M. D. Ermann and R. J. Lundman's *Corporate and Government Deviance* (New York: Oxford University Press, 1978).

Part Two   *Criminals and Victims*

If crime really is a problem for our society, its solution must be grounded in available knowledge about it. ☐ We must find out who is committing crimes and under what circumstances, what seems to be causing criminal behavior, and who are the targets of criminal activity. ☐ Chapters 3, 4, and 5 summarize thoughts on these issues.

3

Patterns of Criminal Behavior

Though self-reported criminality research indicates that most people violate laws, there are different patterns in this society in the types of laws violated and the frequency of violation. For example, those who commit the offenses we seem to fear most—"serious" personal and property crimes—are predominantly young, lower-class males. This high-crime group also contains a greater proportion of blacks than chance alone would suggest. Crimes about which this society is showing increasing concern—white-collar offenses—are more often committed by middle- and upper-middle-class, white males over the age of twenty-five.

Delineating such correlates of criminality is very important for the formulation of crime-prevention programs. This is true whether we are seeking target groups for implementation of immediate preventive measures or engaged in long-term causal analysis aimed at more permanent answers to crime questions. Research that seeks out patterns of crime and criminal behavior is called *epidemiology*, and it is essential, since little else can be said about crime until its dimensions are accurately assessed.

It is important to stress that epidemiological analysis, although the starting point of the search for causes of crime, does not itself represent causal analysis. Throughout the history of both criminological and public thought on crime, *patterns* of criminality have been confused with *causes* of crime. For example, high crime rates among blacks have led many to assume that being black *causes* criminal behavior. However, it is not race itself that determines behavior patterns, but the social factors that accompany race—for example, economic deprivation. To interpret the situation otherwise is to fall victim to the type of muddled thinking that argues that fire engines must cause fires because they are so often found at fire scenes. The goal of epidemiological analysis, then, is not to find causes of crime but to point the way for the search for causes.

In this chapter, we will first present an overview of the factors influencing differences in criminal involvement among various groups in society. Next we will discuss four basic correlates of criminality: gender, age, socioeconomic status, and race. We will conclude the chapter with an epidemiological examination of two forms of taking other people's money: robbery and embezzlement.

Overview of Criminality Patterns

Official statistics that indicate that some groups or categories of people are more criminal than others reflect combinations of three important differences among these populations. First, there are differences in the manner in which members of various groups are treated when caught committing crimes. That is, members of two groups may commit the same number of crimes, but members of one of the groups, owing to discrimination in the administration of justice, may be more apt to be arrested and processed by criminal justice agencies. Thus, the apparent differences in criminal behavior are, in fact, unreal. Second, members of various groups may commit crimes but differ in the types of crimes committed. Some types of crime are more easily detected than others and thus may lead to greater arrest rates for groups committing such crimes. Finally, the official statistics may be signaling *real* differences in criminal behavior among groups; some may actually commit more crimes than others.

Differential Processing of Suspects by the Criminal Justice System

Discretionary arrest, prosecution, and sentencing practices are built into our criminal justice system. Chapter 7 explores this theme in detail, but it is worth noting here that apparent differences among groups in officially tabulated crime rates may as easily reflect biases in the criminal justice system as actual behavioral patterns. Once detected, crimes are more likely to result in criminal justice actions if the suspect is lower class, black, and young rather than middle class, white, and older (Piliavin and Briar, 1964). Thus, the former may appear to be more criminal than the latter. When faced with official statistics indicating that one group is more criminal than another, we must first assume that the differences are manufactured, the product of criminal justice system bias. Only after we have tested this hypothesis can we proceed to others.

Differential Likelihood of Detection

Some groups are watched more closely than others. Blacks are watched more than are whites, youths more than are older persons, males more than are females. It is possible, then, that apparent criminal-behavior differences between these various groups actually reflect only greater detection rates. Thus, it may not be that males commit more crimes than females but that males are more often caught.

Similarly, some offenses are less visible than others. Child abuse is a case in point. The victim is unlikely to complain; any visible bruises can be falsely attributed to accidents. Other "hidden" crimes include embezzlement, blackmail, and various vice offenses—gambling, narcotics, prostitution. These crimes will likely go undetected. The victim may be reticent or even a willing party to the offense; or perhaps the victim is an organization that cannot afford the publicity accompanying a crime report. Robbery, theft, rape, and assault, on the other hand, are less likely to go undetected. Here, the victim can be more vocal in calling attention to the offense. Observers of the crime are also more likely to report its occurrence.

It stands to reason that if various groups engage in different forms of offenses, those committing "hidden" crimes will appear less criminal than those engaging in more visible crimes. It is theoretically possible, for example, that corporate executives violate the law as often as slum dwellers. Yet, corporate crimes such as price fixing are so much more difficult to detect than cruder offenses such as burglary that slum dwellers will always appear to be more criminal. We must always test this hypothesis before we examine the hypothesis that general crime-rate differences among groups are real.

Differential Criminal Involvement

If we are unable to account for apparent differences in criminal involvement among various groups solely as a function of criminal justice system biases or commission of hidden versus visible offenses, we must assume that the criminal-involvement differences are real. In accounting for these differences, we should examine the four primary ingredients of any offense behavior:

1. *impetus*, motivation to commit the offense;
2. *freedom* from various social constraints which hinder criminal activity;
3. the *skill* necessary to commit the criminal act; and
4. the *opportunity* to employ the freedom and skill when impetus occurs.

Impetus. Since groups within this society differ in their economic situations and cultural views of right and wrong, we may expect differences in the extent to which members of these groups are pushed toward or encouraged to commit crimes. All else being equal, for instance, the poor person would seem to have greater impetus to rob a bank than would the rich person. Similarly, all else being equal, members of segments of society that encourage tax evasion would seem more likely to evade taxes than members of segments that condemn the practice. The study of the impetus toward crime is generally referred to as *causal analysis*. It will be covered in depth in the next chapter.

Freedom. The impetus toward crime is not enough to ensure its commission. Most of us are tempted to violate the law at times, yet only some of us do so. This difference is due to certain social hurdles or constraints that stand between impetus toward and actual commission of an offense. These constraints must be circumvented or removed before a crime can take place. Groups in this society differ in the extent to which they are faced with social constraints. Assuming equal impetus, we may expect groups with fewer constraints to have higher crime rates.

Social constraints take two basic forms: external and internal. *External* constraint may take the form of strong ties to conventional members of one's social groups or high investment in valued material objects. The greater the value a person places on either of these social or material ties, the less likely he or she will be to risk their loss by engaging in criminal behavior (Hirschi, 1969:16–21). Thus, some college students may desire to smoke marijuana but not feel free to do so if they feel that their parents, whom they respect, will learn of their actions. Or the minister with much to lose in terms of socioeconomic status in the community will be less free to risk visiting a prostitute than will the laborer who has little to lose.

Internal social constraint on criminal behavior results from the socialization process by which the member of a conventional group internalizes its rules—that is, becomes morally committed to the rules and derives self-esteem from "doing what is right." Hence, the individual who defines theft as morally wrong will generally not violate his or her conscience by stealing. The individual who grants no moral validity to theft laws will not be faced with this same constraint and will be free to steal. Although this society is not sharply divided in its moral beliefs, there is evidence that its members do vary somewhat in their views of right and wrong (Hirschi: 23–26; Sheley, 1977). This variation may account for differences in criminal involvement among various groups in this society.

Regarding social constraint and criminal behavior, low crime and delinquency rates among Oriental Americans have traditionally been attributed to strong familial ties within that subculture.[1] Higher crime

---

[1] For a contrasting view, see Light and Wong (1975).

rates among the lower classes than among the upper classes may reflect, among other things, the fact that the lower classes have less to lose in terms of status and wealth and are therefore freer to engage in crime. There are, as well, differences among the classes and subcultures of this society in the degree to which members are socialized into "conventional" moral values. The South's consistently higher homicide rates are often attributed to its different view of violence as an appropriate response to certain dispute situations (Gastril, 1971). Accounts of youth gangs suggest their value systems eliminate conventional moral values as constraints against criminal behavior.

Opportunity and Skill. In addition to freedom from social constraints on criminal behavior, a potential law violator must possess the necessary opportunity and skill to commit a crime. This fact seems relatively obvious on the face of it, but opportunity and skill are variables that are often overlooked in discussions of differential crime rates among various groups. For instance, the fact that embezzlement is more a middle-class than a lower-class crime is in great part connected to the fact that lower-class persons are rarely placed in situations of financial trust in which embezzlement is a possibility. Nor is everyone who has the opportunity to embezzle able to capitalize on it. Not everyone possesses the knowledge necessary to "juggle the books" successfully (see Cressey, 1953). Even the seemingly most basic of crimes—mugging, robbery, theft—require opportunity and expertise that not everyone has. Undoubtedly, few people reading this book could successfully commit a mugging without practice or the advice of a competent mugger.

In sum, we have seen that reported differences in crime rates among various groups in society may be due to a number of factors. They may represent criminal justice system biases or the involvement of some groups in more "hidden" offenses. The differences may also be real, the result of differences in impetus toward crime, freedom from social constraints on criminal behavior, or opportunity and skill necessary for criminal behavior. With these factors in mind, we may examine four variables often correlated with criminal behavior: gender, age, socioeconomic status, and race.

Gender and Criminality

Of all the variables that appear related to crime, the sex or gender variable displays the most consistent, uncontaminated relationship. In this and most other cultures, males have higher rates of involvement in most forms of criminal behavior than do females. This is the case whether official or self-reported criminal acts are considered. Table 3–1 displays 1975 *Uniform Crime Reports* arrest figures for males and females. For most crimes, male arrests outnumber female arrests about four to one. Even the crimes we might call "female offenses"—larceny, forgery and counterfeiting, fraud, and embezzlement—are still primarily committed by males. The only offense that is truly characteristically female is prostitution (and male participation in this offense seems to be growing).

Since these are official arrest statistics, we cannot know for certain the extent to which they reflect actual male-female criminal behavior patterns. Undoubtedly, women often receive preferential treatment from the criminal justice system, yet it is difficult to believe that this occurs frequently with regard to more serious offenses. It is also possible that women's crime rates for property offenses are underestimated because women engage in crimes that are harder to detect. For example, Cameron (1964) reports that amateur shoplifters are more often females and that female shoplifters steal more items than do males. This aside, self-report studies of criminal behavior suggest that official arrest statistics *do* mirror reality somewhat. One study of college-

Table 3–1
1975 U.S. arrests by sex of arrestee

Offense	Total arrests	Percent male	Percent female
Criminal homicide			
murder and nonnegligent manslaughter	16,485	84.4	15.6
manslaughter by negligence	3,041	88.8	11.2
Forcible rape	21,963	99.0	1.0
Robbery	129,788	93.0	7.0
Burglary—breaking or entering	449,155	94.6	5.4
Larceny—theft	958,938	68.8	31.2
Motor vehicle theft	120,224	93.0	7.0
Other assaults	352,648	86.2	13.8
Arson	14,589	88.7	11.3
Forgery and counterfeiting	57,803	71.1	28.9
Fraud	146,253	65.8	34.2
Embezzlement	9,302	68.9	31.1
Stolen property—buying, receiving, etc.	100,903	89.3	10.7
Weapons—carrying, possessing, etc.	130,933	92.0	8.0
Prostitution and commercialized vice	50,229	25.7	74.3
Narcotic drug laws	508,189	86.2	13.8
Gambling	49,469	91.2	8.8
Disorderly conduct	632,561	82.4	17.6
Total (all offenses)	8,013,645	84.3	15.7

Source: 1975 FBI *Uniform Crime Reports*, p. 183.

student property crimes reports that 14 percent more males than females admit to committing the offenses (Sheley, 1975). Numerous self-report studies of juvenile delinquency support this finding (see, for example, Clark and Haurek, 1966; Hindelang, 1971).

Despite its obvious primary relationship to criminal behavior, the gender variable has until recently attracted little attention among criminologists. At the root of the lack of interest are some basic assumptions about the "nature" of females and about sex roles in our culture. For the most part, women have been viewed as passive creatures who are relatively incapable of aggressive (criminal) acts and whose natural role is that of homemaker. Further, from a policy point of view, there has seemed no reason for a concern with female crime; most crime has been committed by males.

Older crime theories clearly reflect this position. At the turn of the century, Caesare Lombrozo (1903), a biological criminologist (see also Chapter 4), argued that women naturally lack the initiative to break laws, and that men possess this initiative. Female crime was therefore seen as a deviation from the basic female nature. This theme was also present in the writings of Freud. Noncriminal women were viewed as being naturally passive, and criminal women supposedly deviated from the norm as a result of an inability to repress a natural envy of males (Simon, 1975:2–9; Klein, 1973). Such views of female crime portrayed the female offender as "sick," a notion that still forms the basis of most female corrections programs (Smart, 1977).

One earlier theory of female crime stood apart from the rest. Rather than viewing female offenders as deviating from basic natural female inclinations, Otto Pollak (1950) argued that women are naturally inclined toward crime. He viewed women as being far more devious and cunning than men. Women are, he argued, biologically and socially better equipped for certain forms of crime. In fact, he felt women commit as many crimes as men but that they simply commit offenses that are more difficult to detect, offenses in keeping with their supposedly deceitful nature. Further, he stated, they receive preferential treatment from the criminal justice system.

Through the 1950s and 1960s, criminologists showed almost no interest in female crime. Anthony Harris's (1977) review of the major criminological theories of crime causation indicates that most would have to be severely altered in order to explain female crime rates. Yet, the 1970s have fostered a new interest in the gender difference. Discussions of female crime are appearing with greater frequency in journals and textbooks, due in part to the growth of the women's movement and its focus of attention on all aspects of female behavior and, in part, to some recent, very noticeable changes in female crime patterns, as indicated by these crime statistics (Simon, 1975; Noblit and Burcart, 1976):

1. The percentage of females arrested for most crimes has increased greatly since 1960 (see Table 3–2).
2. The increase in arrests has been greater for females than for males (see Table 3–2).
3. For adolescent females, both violent and property crime rates have increased (see Table 3–3).
4. For adult females, the major increases have occurred in rape, robbery, and property offenses; murder, manslaughter, and assault show less dramatic increases (see Table 3–3).

Some observers are quick to conclude that the women's movement has caused the increase in female crime rates. This conclusion should not be too readily accepted, however. Simon (1975:Chap. 3) points out that although more women are working than ever before, women still remain blocked from all but lower-level jobs. In fact, their participation in professional and managerial occupations has barely changed in more than twenty years. Female incomes are also still much lower than male incomes. Increased crime rates for women are therefore not simply a matter of increased opportunity to enter the economic and occupational world. Further, there is no evidence that female criminals have been influenced by women's movement ideology. Indeed, it can be argued that those who commit crimes are the least conscious of oppression.

Table 3–2
U.S. arrest change by sex, 1960–75

Offense	Percent change, males	Percent change, females
Criminal homicide		
murder and nonnegligent manslaughter	+138.2	+105.7
manslaughter by negligence	−20.2	−4.8
Forcible rape	+98.1	+633.3
Robbery	+214.3	+380.5
Aggravated assault	+130.6	+118.8
Burglary—breaking or entering	+116.9	+288.8
Larceny—theft	+129.6	+464.6
Motor vehicle theft	+35.6	+163.2
Other assaults	+58.3	+137.6
Forgery and counterfeiting	+30.8	+192.3
Fraud	+91.1	+488.5
Stolen property—buying, receiving, etc.	+515.1	+727.2
Weapons—carrying, possessing, etc.	+154.3	+291.1
Prostitution and commercialized vice	+65.2	+74.4
Narcotic drug laws	+1,028.0	+1,011.9
Gambling	−64.9	−65.5
Disorderly conduct	−20.6	+51.0
Total (all offenses)	+22.8	+101.7

Source: 1975 FBI *Uniform Crime Reports*, p. 183.

Table 3-3
U.S. female arrest changes by age group, 1960-75

Offense	Percent change, adolescents	Percent change, adults
Violent crimes		
Murder and nonnegligent manslaughter	+275.0	+99.8
Manslaughter by negligence	+333.3	−21.9
Forcible rape	+466.7	+716.7
Robbery	+646.8	+293.4
Aggravated assault	+438.0	+88.8
Total	+503.5	+115.0
Property crimes		
Burglary	+327.5	+258.0
Larceny	+457.3	+469.8
Auto theft	+140.3	+204.1
Total	+420.4	+441.8

Source: 1975 FBI *Uniform Crime Reports*, p. 183.

Whether or not the women's movement has caused it, there does appear to have been a significant change in sex roles in American society since 1960. It may be linked to changes in female crime patterns.[2] Sex-role changes for adult women have resulted in a partial drift from the traditional female role into which they have been socialized. Adult women are now not totally homebound. They have the opportunity to commit occupationally related crimes—even if the opportunity is limited to minor offenses related to lower-level jobs. More importantly, adult women may have recently undergone a partial change in view of self (Harris, 1977:11-14). In addition to viewing themselves as workers, they may also now view themselves as capable of committing *some* acts traditionally thought to be performed only by males. The statistics in Table 3-3 suggest that they now see themselves as capable of committing property offenses and robbery. Yet the sex-role change for adult women has not been great enough to allow for the view of self as one who commits assaultive violent crimes (not including rape).

The changes in traditional female sex roles may have affected female adolescents to a greater degree. They have not been faced with a new set of values and expectations that conflict with those stressed in their earlier socialization. Rather, they have inherited from the student-movement days of the 1960s a view of women able to work, to use drugs, and to protest politically. Further, a major socialization in-

---

[2] For a discussion of the link between traditional sex roles and female criminal involvement, see Hoffman-Bustamante (1973). Adler (1975:5-30) provides a discussion of the links between the women's movement, changing sex roles, and changing female crime patterns.

stitution, the school, is no longer stressing the traditional feminine role. Female adolescents are given role values and expectations that do not differ greatly from those given males. We can, therefore, expect young females to view themselves as capable of engaging in most of the behaviors performed by young males. Table 3–3 suggests that these behaviors include both violent and property offenses.

Age and Criminality

Figure 3–1 indicates the age distribution of people arrested for crimes in the United States in 1975 according to the FBI *Uniform Crime Reports*. Examining the graphic trends for all offenses, we see that most arrestees are under thirty years of age. In fact, 9 percent are under fifteen, 32 percent under nineteen, 42 percent under twenty-one, and 47 percent under twenty-five. For major index offenses alone, 43 percent of arrestees are under eighteen.

Some interesting contrasts appear when violent offenses are viewed apart from property offenses. Although almost 65 percent of

Figure 3–1
Percentage of total arrests for all offenses, violent offenses, and property offenses by age group, 1975.

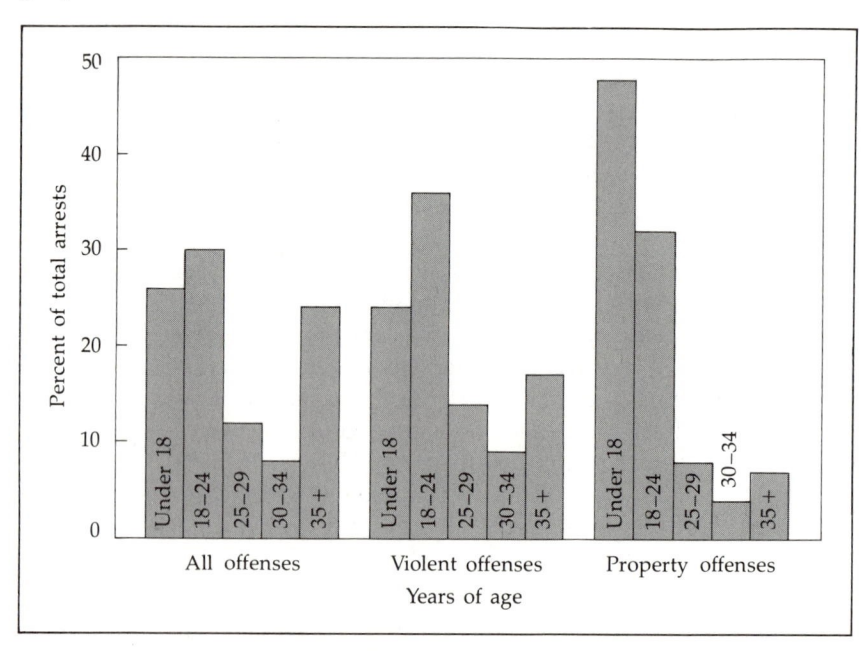

Source: 1975 FBI *Uniform Crime Reports*, pp. 188–89.

the violent offenses are committed by persons twenty years or older, only about 40 percent of the property crimes are committed by this age group. Yet we cannot simply say that property crime is youthful crime while violent crime is more characteristic of adults. If we were to separate robbery from other violent offenses, we would find it committed primarily by persons under twenty years of age. The common violent crimes of people over twenty are homicide and aggravated assault. Hence, we may argue that predatory property crimes (robbery, theft, auto theft, and burglary) are youthful crimes, while older persons have higher percentages of "crimes of passion" and dispute crimes (homicide and aggravated assault).

A number of factors may account for the fact that predatory crime appears to be an activity of youth. It is possible that crimes are committed equally by all ages but that youth are more likely to be arrested for their offenses. Perhaps the difference lies in the types of crimes committed by various age groups. Older persons may commit more "hidden" offenses, younger persons more visible crimes. It is also possible that, since youth tend to associate more with peers, the number of youths arrested for a given crime may be larger than that for older persons, who are more likely to be arrested alone.

While these explanations suggest that the age differences in criminal behavior are apparent, not real, one recent article argues that older persons are indeed less criminal than younger persons. Rowe and Tittle (1977) studied "criminal propensity," an individual's estimate of the likelihood of his or her engaging in criminal behavior. They found that for four types of crime (thefts of $50, illegal gambling, physical assault, and cheating on income taxes), criminal propensity declined steadily with age.

Though Rowe and Tittle were unable to account for the age differences in criminal propensity, they did suggest a number of possible explanations, most of which centered around differences in freedom from social constraints and the opportunity and skill necessary for criminal behavior. Youth are not only traditionally more adventurous but also freer than older persons to engage in deviant activities. Younger people have developed fewer stakes in conventional behavior; that is, they have not yet been burdened with the time-consuming responsibilities of work and family. They have less to lose in risking apprehension for a crime. They lack the maturity to comprehend fully the potential consequences of their crimes.

Opportunity is one possible factor governing "youth crimes"—property offenses and violent crimes such as robbery. Youth are seldom in a position to commit any other than standard offenses. Physical prowess may also influence crime-rate differences among age groups. The absence of older persons in the population committing the seven index crimes may reflect the fact that many of these offenses require the strength, agility, and stamina of youth. We find few sixty-year-old burglars, for instance, because burglary often demands physical agility.

Some observers link the relationship between youth and high crime rates to urban industrialization. Friday and Hage (1976) argue that industrialization in urban societies has decreased the need for unskilled labor, emphasized skilled jobs requiring training, and thus increased the time period between childhood and first major job. In essence, industrialization has lengthened adolescence. In the past, persons approximately fifteen years old were exposed to the diversity of the adult world through employment. Employment also served to build in the youth a commitment to conventional goals and values. Today this process has not simply been postponed, it has been replaced by longer exposure to the undiversified world of the youth peer group. Although youths have been delayed from joining the work force, they have not become less interested in the material rewards that are thought to result from work. For those who see these rewards as unattainable, especially those in the lower classes, frustration is likely to occur. Increased exposure to the youth peer group in this deprived setting will likely cause violent crimes of frustration and predatory crimes in the pursuit of the "good life."

The above theory is supported by the fact that crime rates for most offenses drop dramatically after age twenty-five. Although most adult felons were juvenile delinquents, the majority of juvenile delinquents—including some rather serious offenders—do not become adult felons. Criminologists refer to this phenomenon as *maturational reform*, the decrease of illegal activity after adolescence (Matza, 1964:22). Reckless (1973:81–82) attributes the change in behavior to a "settling-down" process fostered by the acquisition of adult responsibilities. A clear example is seen in the process by which some college students decrease marijuana use after graduation. J. W. Brown et al. (1974) studied various marijuana use patterns among college graduates. They found that decreases in or cessation of marijuana use are tied not so much to changes in attitudes regarding the drug but to the constraints imposed by family and job situations and changes in friendship patterns after graduation. In short, the former users were experiencing the "settling-down" process implied in the concept of maturational reform.

The age of persons committing crimes is highly important in policy planning for the future. Although we are concerned that crime has increased in volume faster than our population during the past fifteen years, we generally fail to consider the role of the age composition of the population in the crime rise. If crime is, in fact, an activity of youth, we can expect more crime when we have a younger population. A review of population trends over the past century indicates that never before have we had so many people between the ages of twenty and thirty. The 1946–57 "baby boom" that followed World War II ensured an unusually high number of youthful offenders in the 1960s through the mid-1970s (Chilton and Spielberger, 1971). Indeed, crime became a "national problem" in 1967 as the bulk of the postwar babies reached the "crime-prone" years. As the last of this population moves into their thirties—about 1980—crime should decrease, for the trend toward population control will have resulted in fewer babies and therefore fewer young offenders.

Our optimism about declining crime rates in the future is best tempered with caution, however. We assume that general socioeconomic conditions will remain relatively stable. Yet changes in these conditions can alter the age–crime rate pattern. If the economic situation worsens dramatically in the early 1980s, for example, members of the baby-boom population might be expected to continue their criminal activity into their thirties. Further, some observers feel that post–baby boom groups (now fifteen to seventeen years of age) seem to be committing more crimes than was the norm for previous generations. If this is true, and not simply a change in arrest or crime-reporting practices, crime rates may remain high in the 1980s.

In the final analysis, we must wait several years before the baby-boom crime-rate theory can be fully evaluated. Interestingly, many population experts predict a new, though smaller, increase in the birth rate in the 1980s as many people who have so far postponed having babies begin to have them. Thus, we may be faced with increased crime rates around the turn of the century.

Socioeconomic Status and Criminality

Despite the importance of socioeconomic status (SES) as a major variable in criminological theory and research (see Chapter 4), the link between SES and criminality is hotly contested among criminologists. At the source of the disagreement is the fact that most criminological conclusions about SES and criminal behavior have been based on problematic data and have concentrated on juvenile delinquency. Official crime statistics (police, courts, corrections) consistently show the lower classes to be more criminally involved. Yet official crime statistics so often reflect biases by the criminal justice system toward the lower classes that they cannot readily be trusted.

Self-reported criminality studies have not shed much more light on the problem. They have generally been unable to gather information about adult violations and more serious juvenile offenses (see Chapter 2). Even with regard to more standard, less serious juvenile offenses, self-report studies have obtained mixed results. Some have found differences by social class; some have not. Almost all are flawed by the fact that they have relied on unusual samples—often unrepresentative samples of rural youth. Better quality self-report studies that included urban youth have found contradictory results and are themselves not problem-free (Box and Ford, 1971; Harry, 1974).

Lack of hard evidence notwithstanding, criminologists generally feel that criminal justice system bias alone cannot account for SES differences in criminal involvement. There are very real differences in types of crimes committed, if not in frequency of commission. Middle- and upper-class persons generally commit "white-collar" offenses— that is, less visible and less violent forms of theft. Much nonprofessional shoplifting is committed by middle-class offenders, for example (Won and Yamamoto, 1968; Cameron, 1964). However, those who commit *Uniform Crime Reports* index offenses, usually considered more serious crimes, are more often lower class. Victimization studies (see, for example, U.S. Department of Justice, 1976) indicate that the poor, especially the black poor, have high victimization rates for both personal and property offenses. They report also that central-city residents—predominantly lower class—have consistently higher victimization rates (see Chapter 5). It is unlikely that members of higher-SES groups enter lower-SES areas and victimize lower-SES individuals. Rather, we may assume that lower-class victimizations are perpetrated by lower-class criminals.

SES-related patterns of criminal behavior are linked to three factors: opportunity, moral validity granted the law, and conditions conducive to crime. Clearly, lower-SES groups do not have access to situations of white-collar crime. One indicator of the upward mobility of lower-SES groups is increasing involvement in such offenses. We find few lower-SES persons engaged in illegal rebates, violations of import laws, or copyright violations, for example.

Opportunity alone, however, cannot account for class differences in crime patterns. Although the lower classes are blocked from white-collar crime, the middle and upper classes are not blocked from traditional index offenses. Yet the middle- and upper-class commission rates for these crimes are lower than those of the lower classes. The difference may be, in part, a matter of definitions of right and wrong and the extent to which the law is viewed as being sacred. Perhaps the lower classes do not place the severe moral connotations on theft and receipt of stolen goods, for example, that the middle and upper classes place on these acts. This is not to say that lower-SES groups encourage these behaviors. Rather, they condemn them less than do their nonlower-SES counterparts. Thus, the lower-SES individual is morally freer to engage in such offenses.

The moral freedom to commit more serious crimes combines with crime-conducive conditions to raise the crime rates for lower-SES groups. Low economic status and little opportunity to alter that status in a consumption-oriented society fosters property crime. A low stake in the economic structure of society also supplies the freedom ("nothing to lose") to commit such crimes. Living conditions that are both relatively and actually substandard create an atmosphere of despair and frustration, leading to the violent offenses that characterize inner cities.

Race and Criminality

The 1975 *Uniform Crime Reports* concerning characteristics of arrestees show blacks to be disproportionately involved in most offenses. Although they comprise about 12 percent of the general population, blacks represent 25 percent of our arrest population. Table 3–4 indi-

Table 3–4
1975 U.S. arrests by race of arrestee

Offense	Total arrests	Percentage white	Percentage black
Criminal homicide			
Murder and nonnegligent manslaughter	15,173	43.4	54.4
Manslaughter by negligence	2,971	78.0	18.7
Forcible rape	19,920	52.3	45.4
Robbery	110,411	39.5	58.8
Aggravated assault	180,668	58.2	39.5
Burglary—breaking and entering	422,032	69.8	28.4
Larceny—theft	923,129	67.2	30.6
Motor-vehicle theft	110,320	70.7	26.4
Other assaults	338,441	64.3	33.6
Arson	13,667	79.3	19.2
Forgery and counterfeiting	53,692	66.3	32.5
Fraud	141,866	70.5	28.5
Embezzlement	8,809	68.5	30.5
Stolen property—buying, receiving, etc.	93,148	64.9	33.8
Vandalism	165,846	83.3	15.2
Weapons—carrying, possession, etc.	123,114	56.7	41.4
Prostitution and commercial vice	46,727	45.0	53.6
Sex offenses (except forcible rape and prostitution)	47,901	78.6	19.3
Narcotic drug laws	487,287	78.7	19.8
Gambling	47,798	25.0	72.0
Offenses against family and children	52,199	70.4	28.0
Driving under the influence	893,798	84.0	13.1
Liquor laws	263,051	88.6	8.1
Drunkenness	1,161,140	76.1	19.3
Disorderly conduct	578,630	67.4	30.2
Vagrancy	58,228	58.4	39.3
All other offenses (except traffic)	986,652	70.6	27.1
Suspicion	27,133	59.4	39.3
Curfew and loitering law violators	111,167	72.4	25.6
Runaways	186,314	87.8	10.1
Total (all offenses)	7,671,230	72.2	25.2

Source: FBI *Uniform Crime Reports*, pp. 192–94.

cates the proportion of blacks among arrestees for various crimes. "Black crimes," those for which blacks are more often arrested, appear to be gambling, prostitution, robbery, and homicide. Although still predominantly white offenses, a few crimes have arrest rates for blacks considerably higher than the proportion of blacks in the general population: possession of weapons, rape, and aggravated assault.

Other studies of the racial factor in crime seem to buttress the *Uniform Crime Reports*. Studies of juvenile delinquency often report higher violation rates for blacks. A study of 10,000 male juveniles born in Philadelphia in 1945 notes that 29 percent of white boys and 50 percent of nonwhite boys had police contacts by their eighteenth birthdays (Wolfgang et al., 1972).

Much of the disproportionately high black official crime rate is due to differential treatment of blacks by the criminal justice system. Yet arrest and reporting practices alone cannot explain black crime rates. A reexamination of Table 3–4 suggests one answer. Black crimes are more *visible*. They are the types of offenses that more likely have complaining victims (such as robbery) or toward which police direct more of their resources (such as vice offenses). Whites, on the other hand, show higher levels of involvement in less conspicuous crimes (such as sex offenses and fraud). The result is a never-ending cycle. Black crime patterns—commission of visible "dangerous" offenses—have drawn attention to black crimes. This, in turn, has led to increased police surveillance of blacks. Increased surveillance has caused higher levels of detection and, in turn, even higher levels of surveillance. Whites, on the other hand, are not only watched less closely but are, because of this lack of surveillance, in many ways *encouraged* to enter into and continue traditional white crimes.

It seems, then, that it is at least theoretically possible that white crime rates equal black crime rates. The races may simply differ in the types of offenses they commit. Self-reported delinquency studies add some support to the "visibility" argument. They tend to show that differences in delinquency involvement between the races are much smaller when self-report data are examined in place of official statistics (Hirschi, 1969:75–81; Chambliss and Nagasawa, 1969). As with self-report data concerning SES and criminality, however, problems of reliability plague self-report studies of race and crime. The offenses examined are often of low seriousness; the samples are often not generalizable; and, again, we have no data on adult offenders.

Given official criminal justice system biases and lacking reliable self-report data on racial differences in crime rates, it is difficult to know with certainty that blacks commit proportionately more crime. Victimization survey data have helped in this regard since they are generally free of the biases found in official and self-report data. One recent study (Hindelang, 1978) used national victimization survey results to analyze offender characteristics in rape, robbery, and assault cases. Blacks were represented in the offender population far in excess of their representation in the general American population. Findings such as these have led many experts to concede that blacks commit more serious offenses more frequently. The same experts also caution us against concluding that race is in any way causally connected to criminal behavior. Rather, they suggest that black crime is high because blacks are overly represented among the lower classes, which do have the higher crime rates. According to the President's Commission on Law Enforcement and Administration of Justice (1967:44–45):

> Many studies have been made seeking to account for these differences in arrest rates for Negroes and whites. They have found that the differences become very small when comparisons are made between the rates for whites and Negroes living under similar conditions. However, it has proved difficult to make such comparisons, since Negroes generally encounter more barriers to economic and social advancement than whites do. Even when Negroes and whites live in the same area the Negroes are likely to have poorer housing, lower incomes, and fewer job prospects. . . . If conditions of equal opportunity prevailed, the differences now found between the Negro and white arrest rates would disappear.

Thus, the social environment in which blacks are found is seen as the cause of their higher crime rates. Economic pressures encourage property offenses. Frustration, disorder, and weak social ties foster crimes of violence (Gibbons, 1977:203; Curtis, 1975). Urban lower-class life seems conducive to many offenses. Although in rural and suburban areas black crime rates closely resemble black population rates, in urban areas, blacks accounted for 28 percent of crime in 1975, yet they constituted only about 13 percent of urban populations.

The crime-rate gap between whites and blacks has been decreasing in recent years, but rate differences will probably remain as long as blacks are disproportionately represented among lower socioeconomic groups in this society. In viewing the difference in rates, however, we must realize that, on the average, crime is *not* a black phenomenon in this society. Although the black crime *rate* is higher, the vast majority of crimes, including more serious offenses, are committed by whites.

Two Examples of Epidemiological Analysis: Robbery and Embezzlement

The primary goal of epidemiological analysis is the accumulation of as much information as possible about the extent, distribution, and characteristics of offenses and offenders. It is hoped that such knowledge will aid causal and policy research. In an attempt to illustrate some aspects of epidemiological research, the remainder of this chapter will examine two forms of theft: robbery and embezzlement.

Some points about these crimes are particularly noteworthy. First, there are considerable differences in the characteristics of persons committing these crimes. Second, surprisingly little is known about either offense. Third, much less is known about embezzlement than about robbery. Regarding this last point, we might also note that embezzlement is a much less visible crime than robbery, that the public perceives embezzlement as the less serious offense, and that embezzlers tend to enjoy higher socioeconomic status—and presumably have greater influence in criminal justice matters—than robbers do.

Example 1: Robbery Patterns and Characteristics

Definition. According to the FBI *Uniform Crime Reports* classification, robbery is the stealing or taking of anything of value from the care, custody, or control of a person by force or by violence or by putting the person in fear, such as strong-arm robbery, stickups, armed robbery, assault to rob, and attempts to rob.

Statistical Dimensions. The *Uniform Crime Reports* indicate that 464,970 robberies were known to have been committed in the United States in 1975. This number represents a rate of 218 per 100,000 population. Robbery has risen 33 percent in volume since 1970, 5 percent since 1974, and robbery rates have shown similar increases. The crime constitutes about half of the total violent offenses reported in the *Uniform Crime Reports*.

Recalling the tendency of FBI statistics to underreport offenses, we are also able to learn something about robbery through the 1973 Department of Justice (1976) national victimization survey. By this study's estimate, 1,120,100 robberies of individuals and 264,100 commercial-establishment robberies occurred in 1973. This represents about 700 robberies per 100,000 individuals and 3,900 robberies per 100,000 commercial establishments. Although the survey's definition of robbery may be slightly broader than the FBI's, these figures suggest that robberies are, in fact, substantially underreported in the *Uniform Crime Reports*.

Crime Characteristics. Robbery appears to be an urban (especially center-city) crime. Seventy percent of the robberies reported by the 1975 *Uniform Crime Reports* were committed in cities of over 100,000. Half of the robberies reported in 1975 were committed in the streets. With the rapid spread of banking establishments throughout greater metropolitan areas, bank robberies have been rapidly rising—up 79 percent since 1970.

According to the 1973 victimization survey results, robberies—especially those in which the victim was injured—were more likely to occur at night, usually on the street. Robberies of commercial establishments were evenly divided between night and day. Most robberies (55 percent) were committed by two or more persons. Weapons (most often firearms or knives) were used in half of the personal robberies and most of the commercial robberies. Although the presence of a weapon had little bearing on the likelihood of injury to the victim, firearms greatly enhanced the success rate of business-establishment robberies. In general, the more professional the robber, the more likely the preference for a firearm over a knife. The firearm facilitates the robbery by better intimidating the victim (it can also be used as a club), by keeping the victim at a safe distance, and by aiding in the escape (Conklin, 1972:108–112).

Offender Characteristics. Robbery is committed almost exclusively by males. Fifty-nine percent of those arrested in 1975 were black. For the most part, robbery is intraracial. When race lines are crossed, however, whites are more often the victims of blacks than vice-versa. Black offenders seem responsible for most multiple-offender robberies perpetrated on both black and white victims. Conklin (1972:29–37) attributes black robberies primarily to the socioeconomic frustration suffered by that race. Increases in living standards in the past fifteen years have been greater for whites than for blacks. Black expectations have risen, but socioeconomic attainment has not. The result is a sense of deprivation that encourages crime.

Most of those arrested in 1975 for robbery were under twenty-five years of age. Victimization research indicates that in 1973, victims under twenty years old were more likely to be robbed by persons of their own age. The proportion of offenders under twenty increases as the victim's age increases beyond twenty.

In a major study of robbery, John E. Conklin (1972:29–78) classified robbers into four categories. *Professional robbers* tend to be white and to be strongly committed to robbery as an occupation designed to support pleasurable life styles. Their robberies are well planned and the take is larger. The professional usually operates with accomplices, though seldom with a well-organized gang. Most often a firearm is used in the offense. The *opportunist robber*, the most common type in Conklin's opinion, is not committed to robbery as a way of life but will rob if in need of money and an opportunity occurs. Opportunists choose targets who are easy prey and generally get only small sums. Opportunist robbers tend to be black, young, and lower class and their robberies are generally done for a little spending money. The crimes are generally committed with the help of other robbers and usually do not involve weapons.

The *addict robber* commits drug-related robberies. Robbery is viewed as the least preferable of a number of methods of obtaining money for drugs. Addict robbers plan their crimes somewhat, though they are often careless in the robberies. The crimes are designed to produce enough money for the next drug fix. Weapons vary; however, the addict prefers not to use loaded firearms. The *alcoholic robber* steals to buy alcohol or sometimes robs while under the influence of alcohol. Robberies by alcoholics often occur on the spur of the moment. They are rarely planned and are sometimes simply the conclusion to a fight or an assault. Weapons are rarely employed by alcoholic robbers.

Victims and Losses. According to the 1973 Department of Justice victimization survey, robber and victim are strangers in the vast majority of cases. As noted earlier, most robbery victims are city dwellers. In cities, black males have the highest victimization rate (31 per 1,000), followed by white males (16 per 1,000), black females (10 per 1,000), and white females (6 per 1,000). Overall, males are victimized twice as often as females. Regarding age, the higher rates are for people under twenty-five. Males over sixty-five and females over fifty have the lowest rates.

For both whites and blacks, the income group most victimized by robbers is that under $3,000 per year. Those in the highest income group in both races have slightly lower robbery rates than do members of other income groups. Overall, however, the income levels of robbery victims differ relatively little. Blacks have higher rates in all income categories than whites do.

Most robberies do not result in injury to the victim. Few victims incur expenditures for medical services or receive hospital treatment. However, most robbery victims do lose money. Most losses amount to less than $50. Only 10 percent exceed $250. In most cases, robbery losses are never recovered, even through insurance reimbursement. In most commercial robberies economic losses occur; but in 20 percent, the robber gains nothing. Most commercial robbery losses exceed $50; in one-third of the cases, losses total more than $250. In most cases, no recovery of losses occurs.

The majority of commercial robberies are reported to police, but interestingly, only half of the personal robberies are. Even when serious injury is involved, only 71 percent of the personal robberies are reported.

Example 2: Embezzlement
Patterns and Characteristics

Definition. The FBI *Uniform Crime Reports* classify embezzlement as the misappropriation or misapplication of money or property entrusted to one's care, custody, or control.

Statistical Dimensions. It is generally conceded that official statistics for embezzlement reflects only the tip of the iceberg. Only 9,032 cases were reported in the *Uniform Crime Reports* for 1975. Rather than estimate cases or numbers of people committing embezzlement, most experts tend to estimate economic losses caused by embezzlement. By extremely conservative estimates, employee thefts and embezzlement total at least $4 million per day (Gibbons, 1977:337). Victimization research is unable to aid in assessing the extent of embezzlement. Employers are often either unaware of or unwilling to report embezzlement. Overall, the crime is said to cost companies more money than all other forms of theft put together.

Crime Characteristics. Embezzlement may occur in any situation in which an individual is given control of another party's money. Stock investment agents may use an investor's money illegally for personal gain. Sales representatives may systematically pocket portions of a store's income. Research into compulsive gambling provides examples of bowling-alley managers using business weekly receipts to pay gambling debts and treasurers of bowling leagues using trophy and prize money for gambling (Lesieur, 1977:191). The major limitation on the crime is the extent to which the owner of the money takes precautionary measures to discourage embezzlement. Banks, for example, conduct regular audits to determine whether such offenses are committed. City governments, on the other hand, are notoriously lax in this regard.

Offender Characteristics. Since few lower-class persons are given positions involving financial trust, it is not surprising that embezzlement is more often committed by "respectable" people—working or middle class, better educated. Cressey (1953) has noted that embezzlers are often people who have become involved in problems that have no conventional solutions and cannot be shared with conventional persons. Cressey also argues that few embezzlers view themselves as "criminals" in the sense that they are morally evil or dangerous to society. In fact, in order to embezzle, the offender must be able to rationalize the theft as "borrowing." He is further encouraged by the fact that he is stealing from an organization rather than an individual. As Smigel (1956) has noted, it is more difficult to commit a crime against an identifiable individual victim than it is to victimize a nonperson, an organization.

Victims and Losses. The primary victims of embezzlement are businesses and government agencies. Yet few people realize that most citizens become secondary victims, in the sense that organizational losses are passed on to consumers and taxpayers.

Few embezzlers go to prison. Those who do receive rather lenient sentences. This is in part because they are not viewed as being in need of rehabilitation. It is also because this society traditionally has not shown a condemnatory interest in this offense. Employers of embezzlers often do not report the offense, to avoid potential company embarrassment or insurance problems. Many times embezzlers are simply dismissed from their jobs; occasionally they agree to make partial restitution for the offense.

Implications for Causal and Policy Analysis

As noted in the introduction to the discussion of robbery and embezzlement, our knowledge of these offenses is rather limited. As a result, only limited, "containment-oriented" policies can be directed at these crimes. Thus, the knowledge that robberies tend to peak in the evenings on city streets suggests the need for increased police patrols on city streets at that time. However, it is doubtful that this action will dramatically decrease robberies. Instead, it will probably only alter the robbery patterns for the community as robbers change the locations and times of their crimes. (Interestingly, one study [Kelling et al., 1974] has found that neither increases nor decreases in preventive patrols influenced the robbery rates in a large urban area.)

The known characteristics of embezzlement suggest that this offense may be somewhat controlled by increasing audits of company financial records. This action may be too costly for small businesses, however. The fact that most embezzlers do not view themselves as criminals points to a need for public education concerning the criminal nature of this offense. Certainly, this is an effective strategy with respect to preventing new embezzlements by apprehended embezzlers. In a similar situation, Cameron (1964) found that once amateur shoplifters were forced to face the fact that they were indeed violating the law, they did not repeat their offenses.

The policies described above are aimed at limiting the freedom or opportunity for the commission of certain crimes. They are not aimed at eliminating the causes of these crimes. A review of our epidemiological information concerning robbery and embezzlement indicates that we are very far from such policies. At best, the correlates of robbery—its urban nature, the fact that it is committed disproportionately by blacks and young males—suggest directions for causal analysis. Yet, even here, care must be taken not to confuse correlates with causes. The fact that robbery is an urban crime, for example, may be less reflective of a causal relationship than the fact that urban areas provide greater opportunity for robbery.

Summary

In this chapter we reviewed some basic correlates of criminal behavior generally and with reference to the specific crimes of robbery and embezzlement. Groups in this society appear to vary in involvement in crime. Some of the differences are real and are due in large part to group differences in freedom from various social constraints on criminal behavior and in the opportunity and skill necessary for the commission of crimes. However, some of the differences in crime rates are only apparent, the result of differential detection and processing by the criminal justice system.

The inventory of facts about robbery and embezzlement demonstrates both how little and how much we know about these crimes. That is, though a considerable amount of information has been gathered about the offenses, its usefulness in policy planning and causal analysis is limited. At the moment, we tend to use the information we have to formulate short-term policy decisions and to initiate the search for the more basic causes of the offenses. The next chapter comments on the present state of the search for causes of crime.

Finally, we return to a major theme in this book: What is the impact of knowledge about patterns of criminal behavior on the average citizen's everyday life? The patterns discussed in this chapter are as crucial to our making sound anticrime decisions as was the information on crime trends discussed in Chapter 2. Again, a critical approach to stereotypes about criminals and their behavior patterns is needed if we are to avoid unnecessarily restrictive personal responses to crime and ill-conceived government anticrime policies. For example, the knowledge that youths are increasingly becoming involved in crime may suggest a number of harsh policies to reduce their involvement. A more critical look at the statistics suggests that the effects of the baby boom may soon decrease; hence, the need for harsh policies seems less pressing. If this chapter has accomplished anything, we hope it has shown that crime patterns are complicated and dynamic. Our responses to crime must be equally sophisticated and flexible.

References

Adler, F.
    1975   Sisters in Crime. New York: McGraw-Hill.

Box, S., and J. Ford
    1971   "The facts don't fit: on the relationship between social class and criminal behavior." Sociological Review 19:31–52.

Brown, J. W., D. Glaser, E. Waxer, and G. Geis
    1974   "Turning off: cessation of marijuana use after college." Social Problems 21:527–38.

Cameron, M. O.
    1964   The Booster and the Snitch: Department Store Shoplifting. New York: The Free Press.

Chambliss, W. J., and R. H. Nagasawa
    1969   "On the validity of official statistics: a comparative study of white, black and Japanese high school boys." Journal of Research in Crime and Delinquency 6:71–7.

Chilton, R., and A. Spielberger
    1971   "Is delinquency increasing? Age structure and the crime rate." Social Forces 49:487–93.

Clark, J. P., and E. W. Haurek
    1966   "Age and sex roles and their involvement in misconduct: a reappraisal." Sociology and Social Research 50:495–508.

Conklin, J. E.
    1972   Robbery and the Criminal Justice System. Philadelphia: Lippincott.

Cressey, D. R.
    1953   Other People's Money. New York: The Free Press.

Curtis, L.
    1975   Violence, Race, and Culture. Lexington, Mass.: Lexington.

Federal Bureau of Investigation
    1976   FBI Uniform Crime Reports, 1975. Washington, D.C., U.S. Government Printing Office.

Friday, P. C., and J. Hage
    1976   "Youth crime in postindustrial societies." Criminology 14: 347–68.

Gastril, R. D.
    1971   "Homicide and a regional culture of violence." American Sociological Review 36:412–27.

Gibbons, D. C.
    1977   Society, Crime, and Criminal Careers. 3rd ed. Englewood Cliffs, N.J.: Prentice-Hall.

Harris, A. R.
    1977   "Sex and theories of deviance: toward a functional theory of deviant type-scripts. American Sociological Review 42:3–16.

Harry, J.
    1974   "Social class and delinquency: one more time." Sociological Quarterly 15:294–300.

Hindelang, M. J.
    1971   "Age, sex, and delinquency." Social Problems 18:522–35.
    1978   "Race and involvement in common law personal crimes." American Sociological Review 43:93–109.

Hirschi, T.
    1969   Causes of Delinquency. Berkeley: University of California Press.

Hoffman-Bustamante, D.
    1973   "The nature of female criminality." Issues in Criminology 8:117–36.

Kelling, G. L., T. Pate, D. Dieckman, and C. E. Brown
    1974   The Kansas City Preventive Patrol Experiment—A Summary Report. Washington, D.C.: The Police Foundation.

Klein, D.
    1973   "The etiology of female crime: a review of the literature." Issues in Criminology 8:3–30.

Lesieur, H. R.
    1977   The Chase. Garden City, N.Y.: Anchor.

Light, I., and C. Wong
    1975   "Protest or work: dilemmas of the tourist industry in American Chinatown." American Journal of Sociology 80:1342–68.

Lombrozo, C.
    1903   The Female Offender. New York: Appleton.

Matza, D.
    1964   Delinquency and Drift. New York: Wiley.

Noblit, G. W., and J. M. Burcart
    1976   "Women and crime: 1960–1970. Social Science Quarterly 56:651–57.

Piliavin, I. and S. Briar
    1964   "Police encounters with juveniles." American Journal of Sociology 70:206–14.

Pollak, O.
    1950   The Criminality of Women. Philadelphia: University of Pennsylvania Press.

President's Commission on Law Enforcement and Administration of Justice
    1967   The Challenge of Crime in a Free Society. Washington, D.C.: U.S. Government Printing Office.

Reckless, W. C.
    1973   The Crime Problem. 5th ed. Englewood Cliffs, N.J.: Prentice-Hall.

Rowe, A. R., and C. R. Tittle
    1977   "Life cycle changes and criminal propensity." Sociological Quarterly 18:223–36.

Sheley, J. F.
    1975   An Empirical Assessment of Neutralization in Control Theories of Deviance. Ph.D. dissertation, Department of Sociology, University of Massachusetts.
    1977   "The need for neutralization in the commission of adult crime." Paper presented at the annual meeting of the American Sociological Association, Chicago.

Simon, R. J.
    1975   Women and Crime. Lexington, Mass.: Heath.

Smart, C.
    1977   "Criminological theory: its ideology and implications concerning women." British Journal of Sociology 28:89–100.

Smigel, E. O.
    1956   "Public attitudes toward stealing as related to size of victim organization." American Sociological Review 21:320–27.

U.S. Department of Justice
    1976   Criminal Victimization in the United States—1973. Washington, D.C.: U.S. Government Printing Office.

Wolfgang, M., R. M. Figlio, and T. Sellin
    1972   Delinquency in a Birth Cohort. Chicago: University of Chicago Press.

Won, G., and G. Yamamoto
    1968   "Social structure and deviant behavior, a study of shoplifting." Sociology and Social Research 53:44–55.

Suggested Readings

Material on various correlates and patterns of criminal behavior is relatively scattered throughout the criminological literature. The reader who wishes to pursue the topics raised in Chapter 3 would do well to examine the data on characteristics of arrestees presented in the FBI *Uniform Crime Reports* and the characteristics of prisoners presented in such documents as the U.S. Department of Justice, Law Enforcement Assistance Administration's *Survey of Inmates of State Correctional Facilities, 1974—Advance Report* (Washington, D.C.: U.S. Government Printing Office, 1976). However, these reports should be read with all the biases of official crime data firmly in mind.

Among the better summaries of the sociological literature concerning correlates of criminal behavior are E. H. Sutherland and D. R. Cressey's *Criminology*, 10th ed. (Philadelphia: Lippincott, 1978), pp. 118–55; 229–37, and G. Nettler's *Explaining Crime*, 2d ed. (New York: McGraw-Hill, 1978), pp. 118–62. H. D. Barlow's *Introduction to Criminology* (Boston: Little, Brown, 1978) offers a good summary of epidemiological literature for a number of specific forms of crime.

4

Theories About the Causes of Crime

Why is there crime? Why are crime rates so high? Why do people commit crimes? These questions are popular variations of the criminologist's query: How can we scientifically discover the causes of criminal behavior? The criminologist's search for an answer to this question differs from the lay person's, and the difference is primarily a matter of method. Most people have "theories" about crime, but the criminologist's theories are supposed to be more logically formulated and scientifically scrutinized and tested. In this chapter we will examine some popular thoughts on the causes of crime, outline the scientific approach to causal analysis, explore traditional attempts at explaining crime, and examine the implications of causal analysis for anticrime policy.

Popular Guesses About the Causes of Crime

A survey of the American public concerning the causes of crime would undoubtedly uncover a set of "evil causes evil" ideas. That is, some of the evils of society (such as poverty, family breakdowns) result in other evils (such as crime, mental illness, drug use). According to popular opinion, it is the social environment—either past or present—of criminals that is the cause of their illegal behavior. Urban life, poverty, bad companions, weakened family ties, and the mass media are often cited as causes of crime.

The fact that these ideas about crime causation are "popular guesses" does not mean they should be dismissed as invalid. Indeed, they have fostered a great deal of insightful criminological research. However, they have been studied primarily as crime-related variables rather than tested within a more formal theoretical framework. For this reason, we will now discuss them separately from the more formal causal theories covered later in the chapter.

Urbanization and Poverty

Generally, urban areas experience higher crime rates than suburban and rural areas do. Crime rates also vary by type of urban pattern:

older versus newer cities, sprawling versus concentrated cities, ethnically and racially mixed cities versus homogenous cities, industrial versus frontier cities, and so on. Further, crime rates differ within cities; some areas—most often those closest to the central city—have higher crime rates. Yet we do not know with certainty exactly what aspects of urbanization are related to crime, causally or otherwise. Some argue that population density (urban overcrowding) is at fault. By itself, density cannot explain crime; in 1974, for example, Jacksonville, Florida, and Gadsden, Alabama (not New York or Detroit), had the highest homicide rates in the country, though they are not high density cities. Simply crowding people together does not produce crime. For example, Tokyo, one of the world's largest, most crowded cities, has a low crime rate.

Cultural and class variation, so apparent within most cities, is definitely linked to crime. Crimes of violence and most property offenses are concentrated in the lower class, especially in lower-class black and ethnic groups. Urbanization concentrates poverty into ghettos and makes class distinctions more apparent. Absolute and relative poverty certainly cause the kinds of frustration that can lead to violent outbursts. Yet rural areas also have high levels of poverty but lower crime rates.

Clearly, the reasons for higher crime rates in urban areas are complex. So are the differences between and within cities in physical deterioration, migration patterns, population density and composition, and historical and cultural features. No one can say which factors, individually or jointly, account for crime. In the final analysis, we may discover that urbanization does not *cause* crime so much as provide greater opportunity for it. Cities offer more targets for crime as well as greater degrees of anonymity for the criminal.

Bad Companions

"Getting in with the wrong crowd" is often viewed as a source of criminal behavior. This theme is most pronounced in theories of juvenile delinquency. It occurs infrequently in theories of adult crime. In one sense, it is clear that if one interacts only with persons who encourage law violations, one will probably favor such behavior. Yet few people are fed such a socialization diet. Instead, they receive a number of definitions of morality, conventional and unconventional. The key question is: What governs the choice of definitions by the individual?[1]

---

[1]This is the essential question of what is known as the theory of differential association, which is discussed in greater detail later in this chapter.

We really do not know at present whether bad companions cause delinquency or vice versa. That is, which comes first, the commission of a crime or the affiliation with evil people? Some argue that delinquents seek out and join other delinquents more often than innocent people are corrupted by evil ones. Others suggest (Hirschi, 1969:135–61) that juveniles caught committing delinquencies are, by virtue of the structure of juvenile justice, forced into the company of other delinquents.

Whether or not they spawn or simply attract delinquents, bad companions are often associated with juvenile delinquency. Yet we have not really established a causal relationship between the two. In searching for cause, we must answer some other questions: What causes groups of "bad companions" to form? Is the "bad companion" syndrome simply an intervening process between a causal factor (for example, poor parental supervision) and delinquency, or is it a cause in and of itself (Jensen, 1972)? Finally, as we pointed out in Chapter 3, most delinquents do not become adult criminals. Thus, we need to know what effect the delinquent peer group has on the movement of the minority from delinquent to criminal acts.

Weakened Family Ties

Members of societies that are undergoing social change characteristically perceive social-control institutions to be failing. Thus, perceived changes in the status of the family as an informal mechanism of social control are often viewed as being causes of criminal behavior, especially among the young. The "broken home" has often been credited with placing a juvenile on the path to delinquency and, for some juveniles, to adult crime. However, evidence regarding this relationship, especially its causal aspects, is contradictory. While many studies (Glueck and Glueck, 1950:122; Nye, 1958:43–48) have claimed that higher proportions of delinquents than nondelinquents come from broken homes, a smaller number argue persuasively that there is little support for such a claim (Rosen, 1970). Toby (1957) states that the broken home is not related to the delinquencies of older male juveniles but is associated with female and preadolescent male delinquency.

If home situation is related to delinquency, the question is: How? Among the possible answers is the socialization of the child by the family into criminal values. This seems among the least likely occurrences, however, since, as Hirschi (1969:97, 108) points out, even criminal parents will not teach their child to be a criminal. A second possibility is that parents simply do not prepare the child to function conventionally in society. As we shall see later, the poor socialization theme is at the heart of many formal theories of delinquency. Yet if we are to believe the evidence cited in Chapter 2, that most juveniles at some time commit delinquencies, and we wish to attribute the acts to poor family socialization, then we must also accept the unlikely fact that poor family socialization is highly characteristic of most of this society. (This is not to deny the possibility that it is related to the commission of serious offenses by a smaller number of juveniles.)

Some argue that juvenile delinquency is an attention-getting device employed by the child in an unhappy home; others claim that delinquency is a means of punishing or hurting parents in the unhappy-home situation. There is little evidence to support either claim. The most plausible of the possibilities relating home life to delinquency is that which concerns parental supervision of juveniles. This thesis reflects the popular sentiment that some parents "let their kids get away with anything." Indeed, there is evidence that poorer parental supervision is linked to delinquency (Hirschi, 1969: 83–109). If the broken home also means weakened supervision of juveniles, then the higher delinquency rates among children from broken homes are somewhat understandable.

Strictly speaking, the parental supervision thesis is not causal. Instead, it speculates that causal factors are allowed to operate on an individual because he or she is free from parental control. To illustrate, we may imagine two boys who enter a store and see an item they wish to have but cannot afford. The owner of the store is not watching them, and the risk of being caught shoplifting is very low. Both boys know shoplifting is wrong. However, one chooses not to shoplift; the other shoplifts the item. How are we to explain the different behaviors of the two boys, whose desires and opportunities to steal were the same and whose beliefs about the morality of shoplifting were alike? One possible answer is that the boy who stole is not as closely tied to his parents as the boy who did not. That is, the "good" boy may be more fearful of what his parents' reaction would be if they learned that he shoplifted. He may also be more highly supervised by his parents and more likely made to explain how he obtained an item he could not afford. Thus, we may say that poor parental supervision did not *cause* the "bad" boy to shoplift; it *permitted* him to shoplift.

If we assume that family supervision is a key to delinquency, we may also extend the control thesis to adult crime. It would seem that the more attached the adult is to the family—in the sense that he or she is responsive to family pressures, has little opportunity to be secretive, and fears losing the family's respect or hurting the family if caught in a criminal act—the less that person is free to commit a crime. Again, this thesis views family situations not as a causal but as an intervening variable. At this date, we lack a definitive test of this line of explanation.

Mass Media and Crime

Recently, there has been considerable popular concern that the mass media, particularly motion pictures and television crime dramas, have influenced juveniles to commit crimes. Most of the criticism is directed at the impact of mass media portrayals of violence, since, on the whole, property offenders are usually not glorified and are usually caught by "supercops" (Dominick, 1973). The argument concerning violence is stated thus:

1. Mass-media emphasis on violence—murder, rape, robbery, assault, arson—desensitizes the public, especially youth, to the reality of violence. In short, people are not shocked by it.
2. The mass media provide knowledge and techniques for violent crime to youth who are already in some way predisposed to violence. (A 1978 lawsuit against a major television network claimed that an explicit rape scene in a crime drama inspired a group of youths to imitate the rape with a young girl. The suit was dismissed by the courts.)

That the mass media dwell on violence is well documented. As a special committee report noted in 1972, not only crime dramas, but almost all children's cartoons and many situation comedies as well contain violent episodes (Surgeon General's Scientific Advisory Committee, 1972a). Less documented is the effect of entertainment violence on viewers. A recent review of the literature pertaining to media violence and crime and delinquency produces two conclusions:

1. Public fears about the issue are not groundless.
2. Yet there is no hard evidence to support the claim of a causal relationship.

These two conclusions are not as contradictory as they may at first seem. There is *some* evidence that television violence has a short-term impact on viewing youngsters. In controlled experiments, some children viewed "aggressive" programs, some viewed "nonaggressive" programs. In tests immediately after the viewing, those children who viewed the "aggressive" films showed higher levels of aggressive attitudes and play (Surgeon General's Scientific Advisory Committee, 1972b; 1972c). Researchers are cautious regarding such findings, however. Most involve laboratory situations that impose aggressive-potential situations on the subjects. The link between aggressiveness and actual violence or other forms of delinquency has yet to be shown. In sum, critics seem willing to accept the fact that media violence *may* have short-term effects on some violence-prone individuals but harbor strong reservations pending more sophisticated research findings (see Nettler, 1974:227–30; Schur, 1969:77–78).

There is very little evidence that media violence has any lasting effects on viewers. One panel study (Eron et al., 1972) interviewed 427 youths as third-grade students and again, ten years later, as teenagers. At both times the subjects reported their television-viewing preferences. Among the third-grade students, children who chose violent shows also exhibited higher levels of aggressiveness. Ten years later, the same relationship was discovered, but for males only. Although the researchers attach much causal significance to this finding, we cannot really know the causal order: Did the aggressiveness lead to the viewing preferences or vice versa? Or are both aggressiveness and viewing preference manifestations of some other factor that only makes them seem related?

In short, we know very little about television violence and crime. For this reason we can neither confirm nor disconfirm hypotheses regarding the relationship between the two. Nor can we allay the fears of the public.

More Formal Theories About the Causes of Crime

Although popular guesses about the causes of crime have fostered much research, certain more formal causal theories have captured the attention of the majority of criminologists. Before we examine these theories, however, some attention should be devoted to the general assumptions, principles, procedures, and problems of causal analysis. Too often, theories of crime causation are presented to readers without an accompanying attempt to describe the process that produces these theories. Many causal theories fail to adequately explain delinquency not because they are flawed in themselves but because basic principles and methods of causal analysis are violated in testing the theories. In short, causal analysis is extremely difficult.

Two basic assumptions underlie a scientific approach to causal analysis of crime. First, we assume that every social phenomenon has a cause (if there is a B, there must be an A that caused it). Every social phenomenon is, therefore, an effect. Further, most phenomena are both causes and effects. That is, they exist in a causal chain, influenced by some phenomenon and, in turn, influencing others. This point is best understood if we imagine the commonly occurring "chain-reaction" collisions on our highways. In these accidents, most cars are propelled forward by one car and, in turn, propel another car forward. The movement of any given car is, then, both the effect of one car's movement and the cause of yet another car's movement.

Second, we assume that if we can identify various social phenomena related to a form of crime and correctly establish the order

Figure 4–1
Causal analysis of explanatory variables linked to crime: the domino-theory model

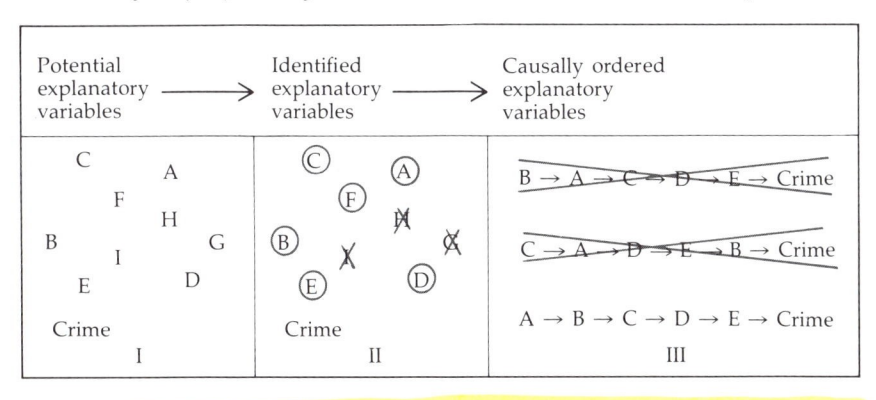

Potential explanatory variables →	Identified explanatory variables →	Causally ordered explanatory variables

C A
  F
    H
B   G
  I
E   D
Crime
	Ⓒ Ⓐ
	   Ⓕ
	      H̷
	Ⓑ X G̷
	   Ⓔ Ⓓ
	Crime
		B → A → C → D → E → Crime
		
		C → A → D → E → B → Crime
		
		A → B → C → D → E → Crime

I	II	III

in which these phenomena influence each other, we can predict the occurrence of crime. Figure 4–1 illustrates this basic process. In square I are a number of explanatory variables possibly linked to crime. Square II displays those identified as actually linked to crime and those not. Square III suggests a few possible orderings of the explanatory variables and the eventual successful ordering.

Needless to say, this "domino-theory" model is uncomplicated. However, few explanations of social phenomena fit this model. Instead, more complicated models attempt to capture some of the more intricate interrelationships among sociological variables—how a variable is both directly and indirectly influenced by other variables, for example. Figure 4–2 displays a more complicated causal model, in this

Figure 4–2
A causal model of the adoption of the "gay role"

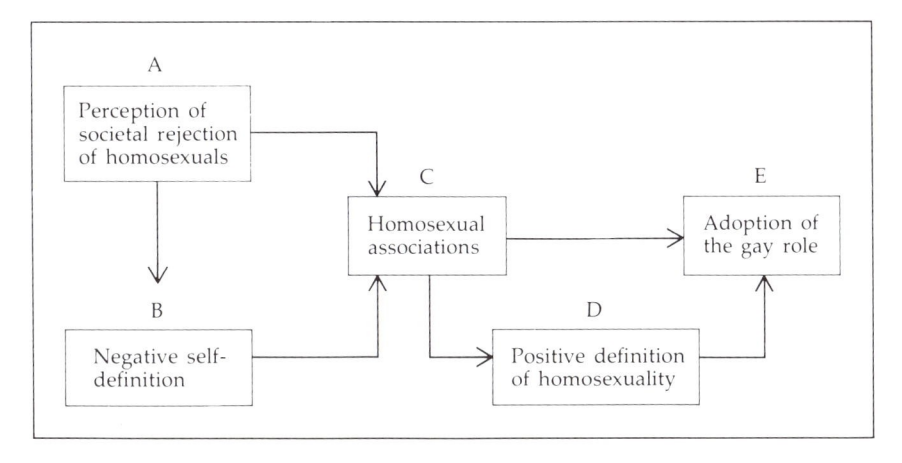

```
        A
 ┌──────────────┐
 │ Perception of│
 │ societal rejection├──────────┐
 │ of homosexuals│          │
 └──────┬───────┘          │
        │              C           E
        │         ┌──────────┐  ┌──────────┐
        │         │Homosexual│→ │Adoption of│
        │         │associations│  │the gay role│
        │         └────┬─────┘  └──────────┘
        ▼              ↑              ↑
        B              │       D      │
 ┌──────────────┐      │  ┌──────────┐│
 │Negative self-│──────┴─→│Positive definition├┘
 │definition    │         │of homosexuality│
 └──────────────┘         └──────────┘
```

Source: Adopted and modified from R. A. Farrell and J. F. Nelson, "A Causal Model of Secondary Deviance: The Case of Homosexuality," *Sociological Quarterly*, Winter 1976, p. 111.

instance, one that tries to explain an individual's adoption of the "gay role"; that is, behavior and attitudes somewhat in line with society's stereotypes of homosexuals (Farrell and Nelson, 1976). As the model suggests, the process begins with the individual homosexual's perception of society's rejection of homosexuals (A). This perception leads to association with other homosexuals (C)—either directly because the individual feels uncomfortable with heterosexuals or indirectly because the perception leads to a negative self-image (B), which causes the individual to seek the company of others like him or her. Association with other homosexuals (C) leads both to pressure to conform to the gay role (E) and to a positive definition of homosexuality (D), which leads to acceptance of the gay role (E).

Although the gay-role model is more complicated than the domino-theory model in Figure 4–1, it is also undoubtedly only a rough approximation of reality. Surely other variables are implicated in a person's adoption of this role, both directly and indirectly. It will be a long while before our models and measurement techniques allow us to incorporate them.

The immediate goal of causal analysis is understanding and prediction. That is, criminologists hope to understand the interrelationships of a number of variables to such an extent that they can predict the outcome of any given arrangement of those variables. The ultimate goal of this venture is intervention in and control of particular social processes. Thus, criminological causal analysis has traditionally attempted to locate the causes of crime (in general or with reference to specific offenses) so that "something can be done about it." Causal research has always been policy oriented. It seeks to discover ways by which a society—or, more specifically, governmental agencies—can break the causal chain of crime.

A review of criminological literature on causes of crime indicates that the search has not been particularly successful. Although we have often established what *does not* cause criminal behavior (for instance, criminal ancestors), we cannot say with any certainty what *does* cause it. Many factors impede the search for causes. Our basic theories about crime remain relatively unsophisticated. We are also dealing with concepts and variables that do not easily lend themselves to precise measurement. Our earlier discussion of estimates of the amount of crime in this society (see Chapter 2) provides a fine example of a measurement problem: How are we to begin to explain crime when we have so much difficulty determining how much we have and who commits it?

Aggregate Data

A persistent problem for criminological research is its frequent reliance on *aggregate data*—pieces of information about groups of people (such as a society, a city, a neighborhood, a racial or ethnic group) as opposed to information about specific individuals within those groups. Aggregate data are often secondary data; that is, information collected for one use and later adopted for criminological research. Such research generally involves the analysis of *rates*—that is, the number of persons for some unit of the population (usually 10,000 or 100,000) who share a particular characteristic at a given time. Thus, we note, for example, that low-income areas have higher delinquency rates than higher-income areas do. The lower-income areas are also marked by higher rates of overcrowded and poor housing. Pending further research, it may be inferred from these findings that overcrowding and substandard living conditions influence delinquency rates (see Chilton, 1964).

The criminologist must be very careful in drawing conclusions from correlations found in aggregate data. It is possible that correlations found in aggregate data will disappear when data collected from individuals within the aggregation are examined. Figure 4–3 provides a hypothetical example. Using census data and FBI statistics (both forms of aggregate data), a researcher may find that crime rates climb as the proportion of blacks in given areas grows. Should the researcher conclude that blacks are more crime prone than whites? This conclusion may be unwarranted. If we were somehow to obtain self-reported criminality information and the race of all the individuals in the three areas (nonaggregate data), we could determine how much of the crime

Figure 4–3
Problems in interpreting crime correlations in aggregate data

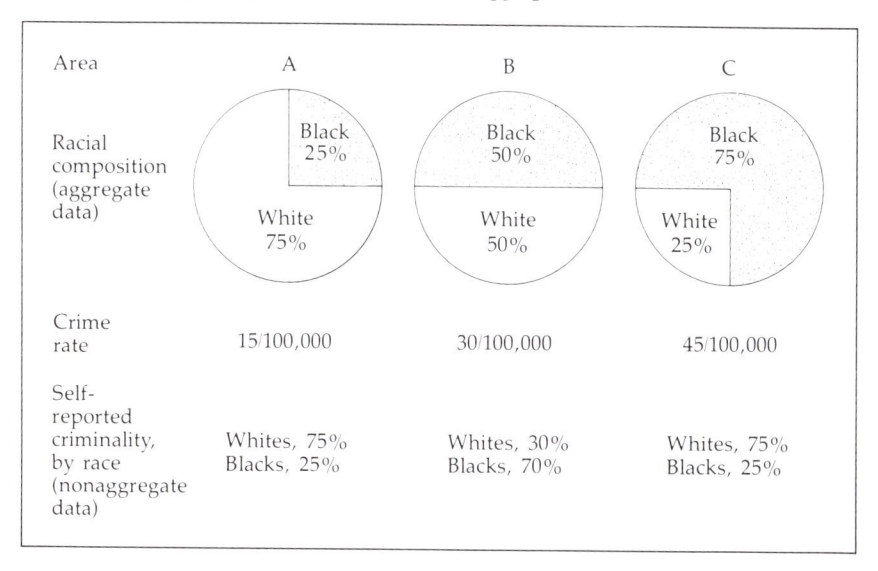

Area	A	B	C
Racial composition (aggregate data)	Black 25% / White 75%	Black 50% / White 50%	Black 75% / White 25%
Crime rate	15/100,000	30/100,000	45/100,000
Self-reported criminality, by race (nonaggregate data)	Whites, 75% Blacks, 25%	Whites, 30% Blacks, 70%	Whites, 75% Blacks, 25%

in each area is committed by whites and how much by blacks. As Figure 4-3 indicates, the results could seriously challenge our earlier conclusions based on aggregate data. In area A, the percentages of crimes committed by both races is the same as the percentage of both in the population. In area B, blacks commit more of the crimes than do whites, though they are equal in the population. A look at area C tells us that the small number of whites in the area commit the majority of crimes. Thus, though we may say that the amount of crime in a given area is correlated with the size of its black population, we *cannot* say that blacks are more crime prone. The hypothetical results in Figure 4-3 suggest that we study some other aspect of the geographic areas in question—economic conditions or transient criminals, for example—to explain their crime situations.[2]

Nonaggregate Data

Given the weaknesses encountered in the use of aggregate data, most criminologists prefer to use nonaggregate data whenever possible. More often than not, these data are collected by survey methods. The survey utilizes questionnaires or interviews to gather information about members of a population. Using this information, researchers attempt to explain variation among respondents with respect to a particular behavioral or attitudinal characteristic (such as amount of theft behavior) by linking this variation to differences regarding other behavioral, attitudinal, or biographical variables (such as socioeconomic status).

In 1966, for instance, the National Opinion Research Center conducted a survey of victimization in the United States during the previous year (Ennis: 1967). Over 10,000 randomly selected individuals were interviewed to determine how many had been the victims of crime in 1965 and to gain a sense of citizen attitudes toward police, neighborhood security, and crime. Victims were interviewed in depth about the crimes they experienced. Among the findings of the study are those concerning patterns of victimization. A person's race affects his or her likelihood of being a victim of crime, for example. Blacks are consistently more victimized than are whites (see Chapter 5).

Criminologists also occasionally attempt controlled experiments to find answers to questions about crimes and criminals. Generally, a group of individuals is subdivided into two (or more) smaller groups. The researcher is careful to ensure that each of the subgroups is similar either by randomly assigning individuals to the subgroups or by carefully matching an individual in one group with a similar individual in

---

[2]Sociologists refer to the assumption that we may infer individual correlation on the basis of a group correlation as the *ecological fallacy* (See Galtung, 1967; Robinson, 1950).

the other group. This accomplished, the researcher applies a stimulus to the members of one group only. The extent to which this group now differs from the other may be attributed to the effects of the stimulus.

Experimental research is less common in criminology than survey research because experimenters face many methodological and ethical problems when engaging in such research. Nonetheless, good examples of criminological experiments are available. One such piece of research is Kassebaum, Ward, and Wilner's (1971) evaluation of a group counseling program in a California prison. As inmates arrived at the prison, they were randomly assigned to various group counseling situations. After six years, the experimenters found no differences with respect to adjustment to prison and later recidivism between those inmates subjected to various counseling stimuli and those without group counseling.

Constraints on Criminological Research

Criminologists must constantly cope with their personal biases in choosing research topics and methods, interpreting research results, and publishing those results. As social beings, researchers themselves have inherited many of the attitudes and biases of their society. Graduate-school training also gives them a set of ideas by which to make sense of what they see. Sometimes researchers begin to take their views of the world for granted. Rather than challenge their ideas, they distort or "bend" their research findings to fit those ideas. Unquestioned assumptions about the "natural" inclinations of women, for instance, could heavily influence a criminologist's research on prostitution.

The base of operations of the criminologist will also greatly affect his research. Generally, criminologists conduct research as members of an academic institution, as researchers in governmental or private research organizations, or as employees of business concerns. Within the academic setting, which is the most common base of operations, the criminologist is fairly autonomous regarding choice of research topics, research designs, and publication of research results. But as the academician turns to funding agencies for research support, some autonomy is sacrificed, particularly with respect to choice of topic and research design.

Nonacademic criminologists generally lack autonomy and are, in fact, under considerable pressure to produce certain kinds of results. Often the agency-affiliated criminologist's ability to publish research results rests on the extent to which the funding organization defines the results as threatening to its existence. At times, the business-affiliated criminologist's job is at stake if his or her research results do not bode well for the organization's financial future. Such pressures work to hamper sound criminological research.

More than most sociological subfields, criminology faces a number of ethical and legal research constraints. That is, certain forms of research may provide answers to key criminological questions but may also present ethical or legal dilemmas. Much as the police officer must work within a framework of rules protecting the rights of crime suspects, so also must the criminologist honor the rights of research subjects. For instance, to ascertain the effects on trial outcomes of the U.S. Supreme Court's *Miranda* ruling (stating that suspects must be informed of their legal rights upon arrest), the criminologist cannot legally or ethically conduct an experiment whereby some suspects are informed of their rights and others are not. Gaining information about the customers of prostitutes by spying on them also raises ethical questions. Determining the effectiveness of police patrols on crime rates by overpatrolling one area and underpatrolling another is to engage in legally and ethically problematic research.

A classic example of legal constraints on criminological research is what has come to be known as the Wichita Jury Study (Vaughn, 1967). In 1954, a group of social scientists interested in how juries arrive at verdicts proposed secret recording of jury deliberations. They were granted permission by a Wichita, Kansas, judge to "bug" jury deliberations in his trials, provided that the judge maintain complete control of the research, that only civil cases be studied, and that counsel for each party consent to the research. Despite these precautions, members of Congress who learned of the research argued that it violated the safeguard of secrecy by which jurors could feel free to state their opinions without fear of public scrutiny. Were future jurors to suspect that their jury-room conversations were being recorded, they might impose restraints upon their participation in deliberations to the extent that the fairness of the trial would be jeopardized. As a result, a law was passed that forbade jury recordings. For this reason, most jury studies today take the form of mock trial deliberations.

In sum, the search for causes of crime is very difficult. As noted earlier, it has not met with tremendous success. As we shall see in the coming pages, we have progressed very little in many ways during the past seventy-five years. Yet when we take time to examine the theories, we find them surprisingly rich and suggestive. Given the problems encountered in formulating and validating causal theories, they bear witness to the considerable perseverance of many criminologists. The following section describes some of these theories.

Directions of Causal Analysis

The search for the roots of crime has traditionally taken three forms. The first states that criminality is an inherent individual trait. Variations of this theme have stressed biological and genetic explanations of crime; supporters argue that criminal behavior is a symptom of a congenitally flawed individual. The second form, which also stresses the problematic individual, views criminality as the result of acquired individual predispositions toward crime. Many such theories stress the role of personality development and glandular malfunctions in criminal behavior. The third form places the weight of explanation on sociological variables; supporters claim that crime originates in problems with the institutional structure of society or subcultural definitions of forms of law violations as morally acceptable.

Some of the more sociological theories treat the individual criminal passively. That is, they make little attempt to explain the manner in which societal factors influence the individual to commit crimes. Instead, they deal simply with variations in societal crime rates as they relate to variations in other societal conditions. Others (a smaller number) attempt to establish the link between societal conditions and individual perceptions in trying to account for criminal behavior.

The approach to causal explanations chosen by the criminologist is, of course, a matter of training and personal preference. The approach of the majority will tend to dominate the field of criminology. The dominant approach will influence, at least to small degrees, public perceptions about the causes of crime and, to a greater extent, crime prevention and criminal-corrections policies. The wide range of policy possibilities dependent on beliefs about the causes of crime will be discussed later in this chapter.

Biological Explanations

Historically, much emphasis has been placed on the notion of a "born criminal" in attempts to account for criminal activity. Theories have varied in sophistication, but all have assumed that the difference between criminals and their conventional counterparts is a difference brought into this world. Some early biological theories assumed that criminals were throwbacks to more primitive species of man (Lombrozo, 1911). Hence, researchers attempted to establish that criminals differed from noncriminals in such features as body type, skull shape, length of arms, hair texture, and facial characteristics—features felt to mirror primitive man.

Body-Type Theories

"Body-type" theories of criminal behavior were popular as late as the 1950s. Two of the better known theories were offered by Hooton and Sheldon. Hooton (1939) published the results of thousands of measurements of physical characteristics of criminals (in prisons) and noncriminals. He claimed to have found differences between criminals and noncriminals and differences among the various criminal types. He noted, for example, that criminals tended to have thicker, straighter, and more reddish hair. They tended as well to have low, sloping foreheads; thinner lips; long necks; and sloping shoulders. First-degree murderers, Hooton further found, had an abundance of the characteristics described above, assaultists had an excess of olive skin color and broad noses, burglars had concave noses, and arsonists had protruding ears.

In a series of books in the 1940s, Sheldon (1942 and Sheldon et al., 1940; 1949) attempted to attribute temperament to body type and body type to criminality. In essence, he believed that physical constitution shaped personality and that certain personality types were more crime prone. Sheldon, and in later years, the Gluecks (1956), claimed to have discovered links between delinquency and, especially, a more athletic build, which, they argued, signaled a more aggressive temperament.

Body-type theories have diminished in popularity during the past two decades. Part of this decline is attributable to the strong methodological criticisms directed at the studies cited above. Generally, most have not taken care to define clearly delinquents and criminals. Hooton, for instance, relied on institutionalized prisoners as his "criminals." Prisoners are certainly not a representative sample of criminals —indeed, they may have been imprisoned because they fit judges' stereotypes as to what dangerous persons look like. Sampling in the studies was also generally poor. Overall, we may say that the purer the methods employed in these studies, the weaker the link found between physical characteristics and criminal behavior.

Beyond their methodological flaws, however, the body-type and "throw-back" theories lacked content. That is, the theories paid little attention to the question of *how* physical characteristics are linked to social acts. How, for instance, does a "primitive" man become inclined toward law violations rather than some other acts? How is it that some people who are inherently "aggressive" become football players or shrewd businessmen rather than criminals?

Biogenetic Theories

While research like the above has lost favor, biogenetic research is still very much alive. Some scholars approach criminality as an inherited trait, passed on from generation to generation. The more sophisticated of research attempts to test the "bad seed" hypothesis have centered on studies of identical and fraternal twins. If criminality is, in fact, inherited, it is assumed that identical twins, the product of a single fertilized egg, will be more alike in their criminal behavior than fraternal twins, the products of two separately fertilized eggs. Again, it is generally argued that the more methodologically rigorous of studies into the matter have found few differences between the types of twins. Further, if differences existed, it would be impossible to determine the extent to which they were inherited and the extent to which they were environmentally transmitted. We need only view the extent to which so many identical twins are treated alike to realize the difficulty of attributing like behavior purely, or even partially, to heredity.

The best known of recent biological research into criminality concerns the alleged relationship between the XYY chromosomal pattern and violent criminal acts. Briefly, scientists have observed that some males are genetically abnormal in the sense that they possess an extra Y sex chromosome (XY is the normal male sex chromosomal arrangement; XYY is an abnormal pattern). A rare occurrence, the extra Y pattern has appeared with slightly higher regularity in incarcerated populations of mentally retarded and criminal persons than it has in the greater population. Some persons have speculated that the extra Y chromosome is linked to antisocial, especially violent, behavior.

Although the news media have given considerable coverage to this hypothesis, there is, in fact, little evidence to support it. Quite the contrary, some argue, XYY individuals are less prone to aggression than chromosomally normal persons are. Most reviewers of XYY research conclude that the studies done so far are methodologically inadequate and not generalizable. We really know very little about the XYY pattern in general, much less about how it influences behavior (Fox, 1971). Again, current theories involving the phenomenon lack content in terms of spelling out *how* the genetic condition influences social actions. And given the rarity of the pattern, it is felt that, at best, the XYY pattern could account for only a small amount of violent behavior.

Interestingly, social scientists have recently softened somewhat in their opposition to theories espousing biological causes of behavior. They now seem more willing to conclude that some forms of aggression and crime may indeed be in some way biologically influenced. Yet the influence is seen as secondary to that of the social and psychological environment. They argue that some forms of crime (for instance, a sudden violent outburst) may be explained by environmental situations acting in conjunction with the influence of individual biogenetic factors. Only when the correct environmental influences occur, they assert, will the genetic features bring their influence to bear (Shah and Roth, 1974).

Psychological Explanations

A second strain of causal analysis focuses on the psychological makeup of individuals as the source of criminal behavior, or, in popular jargon, "People who do such things must be crazy." In more scientific terms, crime is attributed to mental, emotional, or personality disturbances. The noncriminal is one who is psychologically sound enough to control impulses to commit crimes and to appreciate the moral and social implications of criminal behavior.

Intellectual and Mental Impairment Theories

Once a popular scientific notion, the claim that most criminals are somehow intellectually or mentally impaired is no longer generally accepted. While occasional offenses may be related to mental retardation, there is no evidence that criminals are any more or less intellectually endowed than noncriminals are. Indeed, many forms of crime require high levels of intelligence—embezzlement, for example, requires considerable mental skill. Although unpopular among criminologists, the question of mental and intellectual capacity remains open for the present since the measurement of intelligence remains problematic. Only when the measurement problem is resolved and the measures applied to representative samples of criminals and noncriminals will the question be laid to rest.

A 1977 article by Hirschi and Hindelang argues that the problem cannot be ignored any longer. Their examination of recent research concerning delinquency and IQ indicates that intelligence is at least as strongly related to delinquency as class and race. The link is not direct but indirect; they argue: IQ influences school performance; low IQ produces school failures; school failures produce delinquency. However, Hirschi and Hindelang have drawn heavy criticism, particularly for failing to stress that IQ is not inherited but rather environmentally formed, that standard IQ measurement cannot be trusted, and that other orderings of variables are possible (Simons, 1978; see also Hirschi and Hindelang, 1978). Regarding this last point, rather than IQ being directly or indirectly implicated in the causes of delinquency, low IQ scores and delinquency may both be the effects of the same cause: a negative attitude toward teachers and school and a resultant lack of motivation to excel in school or in conventional behavior. Whether or not correct, the Hirschi and Hindelang article performs a needed service. It forces criminologists to better specify the presence or absence of a relationship between intelligence and crime.

Psychoanalytic Theories

Today theories that emphasize emotional or personality disorders as causes of criminal behavior are in greater favor than mental inferiority explanations. One variation of this theme is the psychoanalytic approach. Current versions of this approach are modifications of Freudian psychoanalytic theories, which posit that behaviors and feelings are overtly symbolic of unconscious conflicts between three supposed components of every human personality—the id (the biological drives component), the superego (the socially responsive component), and the ego (the component that attempts to subdue the id to minimize conflict with superego). According to psychoanalytic theory, most people are viewed as being able to keep these components somewhat in harmony (at least most of the time), usually through repression of the id. However, some are not able to produce this harmony, and the imbalance may create problematic or even antisocial behavior.

Thus, in the psychoanalytic framework, crime is viewed as antisocial behavior that is symptomatic of unconscious conflicts. A crime may be the result of a lack of repression of the id or symbolic of unfulfilled impulses. Since the superego is continually present, the ego may feel guilty. Further crimes may be committed in order to bring about punishment to eliminate the guilt feelings. The only resolution to criminal-behavior syndromes such as this, these theorists suggest, is psychoanalysis, a highly individualistic, long-term therapy program in which a patient comes to recognize his or her unconscious conflicts under the guidance of a therapist or analyst.

The major criticism of the psychoanalytic approach is that it is scientifically untestable. Although *all* theories are essentially acts of faith, some hold more promise of verification than do others. Psychoanalytic theory holds none. The various components of the personality are neither observable nor measurable. The result of psychoanalysis is an analyst's interpretation of a patient's interpretation of what is occurring in the subconscious. We are left with a small number of highly individualistic, nongeneralizable accounts of behaviors and events (Vold, 1958).

Personality-Disorder Theories

Less problematic than psychoanalytic ideas are theories that view personality or emotional problems as the source of crime but do not assume any unconscious motives or symbolism in criminal behavior. Basically, this viewpoint asserts that personality flaws contribute to criminal behavior. Some theories have stated this thesis in rather extreme terms, attributing crime to *psychopathic* (or sociopathic) personalities, terms that refer to chronic antisocial behavior. Psychopaths are generally seen as being callous persons with problematic social relationships who have few ties to society, and as relatively amoral and unafraid of sanctions against crime.

Most social scientists are distrustful of the psychopath concept, however, noting that its vagueness prevents any meaningful attempts to link it to criminal behavior. Some argue that there is no such thing as a psychopath, that the concept was created to deal with otherwise unclassifiable personality disorders, or that if psychopaths do exist, their numbers are so small that they could not account for much crime.

Less extreme versions of personality-disorder theories point to such problems as overaggression, insecurity, paranoia, emotional instability and immaturity, and egocentrism as possible causes of delinquent or criminal behavior. The social science literature in this area is divided. On the one hand, there are reviews of most studies done through 1965 that fail to find a conclusive link between personality disorders and criminality (Waldo and Dinitz, 1967). On the other hand, some criminologists argue that there is promise in personality-disorder research (Gibbons, 1977:177). They view the problem of low correlations as a measurement problem and suggest that the relationship of crime to personality will appear stronger when we are better able to define and measure personality attributes.

The general position of most criminologists regarding personality-disorder research seems to be one of cautious encouragement. This research may discover certain personality traits that, when combined with certain social and environmental stimuli, may foster criminal behavior.

Sociological Explanations

The biological and psychological causal theories discussed above have generally viewed criminal behavior as the result of individual abnormalities or defects. However, the sociological approach to explaining crime tends to view criminal behavior as somewhat more "normal," an expected response to social and cultural events and situations. There are a number of sociological crime theories, but three have been the most popular: (1) that the roots of crime lie within structural problems encountered by a social system, (2) that crime reflects inherent flaws in the capitalist economic system, and (3) that the roots of crime lie within cultural or subcultural acceptances of behaviors that counter the law. This section examines these three theoretical orientations.

Structural Theories

Social systems are generally organized or structured to maximize the chances of their continued existence. Societies develop institutions (religion, law, government, family, and so on) to cope with system-maintenance problems. The family, for example, is the major mechanism for population growth or control; religion serves to explain and allay fears about the unknown as well as to control individuals through moral codes. As social systems grow more complex, their institutions become more complex and distinct.

No society is so well structured that it has no problems. That is, social institutions are imperfect. At times they fail to accomplish their designated tasks; religion, for example, may fail to obtain allegiance to traditional norms. At times, institutions may conflict with each other. For example, a consumption-oriented economic system will not be compatible with a religious system stressing thrift and moderation. Moreover, when a society is undergoing rapid social change, so that its institutions lag, break down, or conflict with other institutions, social problems such as racial strife, unemployment, and mental illness will likely arise. Thus, the sociologist who adheres to the above ideas (the structuralist) tries to understand social problems by examining social institutions for disruptions, conflicts, or weaknesses.

Traditionally, structuralists have looked to three institutions as the sources of criminal behavior: the family, religion, and the economic system. Crime, especially juvenile delinquency, has often been viewed as the result of a decline of the family and religion as strong mechanisms of social control. However, the best-known structuralist explanations of crime have emphasized the economic system as the key problematic institution. Changes in the economy, for example, have long been thought to be associated with homicide and suicide trends. Henry and Short (1954) suggest that suicide increases with economic depression and homicide rises during economic prosperity. They also believe that suicide is an upper-class phenomenon, that will rise during depression times because the upper-class then suffers more financial hardship, and that homicide is a lower-class phenomenon, that is more likely to occur during economic good times when the lower class experiences intense frustration at standing still in prosperous times.

The structuralist formulation that inspired the majority of theory and research into the economic system and crime was Robert Merton's (1957:Chapters 4 and 5) theory. He argued that while our culture strongly encourages all members of society to pursue relatively the same goal, material success, the economic system does not provide equal access to the culturally prescribed means to attain success—sufficiently lucrative employment. The greater the discrepancy between success goals and access to the means to attain them, he felt, the more problematic the life situation of those caught in the discrepancy.

Merton outlines a number of possible responses or adaptations to the means-ends discrepancy. The responses most relevant for a discussion of crime are innovation and retreatism. *Innovation* represents a creative response to the problem of blocked means to goal attainment. When legitimate means are not available, individuals will create or turn to illegitimate means. Organized crime is often viewed as an innovative avenue of socioeconomic mobility for newly arrived lower-class immigrant groups (Light, 1977). Merton argues that, overall, much of the lower-class high crime rates, especially for property crimes, represents illegitimate attempts to get ahead in a system that denies the lower classes legitimate avenues of success.

Retreatism involves a drop-out response to the means-ends discrepancy, with individuals rejecting both the goals and the means and searching for nonproblematic situations in drugs, alcohol, transiency, and the like. In addition to fostering drug violations, retreatism is also implicated in secondary offenses such as robbery or theft committed to support a drug habit.

Merton's theory has been criticized for its apparent overemphasis on lower-class offenses, especially theft. Critics argue that his scheme fails to account for nonutilitarian crimes such as murder during an argument and for the offenses of those who are not denied access to the means of success attainment—for example, the bank vice-president who embezzles. Further, the theory is not explicit concerning what governs the choice of adaptation to blocked means. Merton has attempted to respond to some of these criticisms by suggesting that *most* people are relatively deprived—that is, blocked from attaining some desired end—and must adapt. Yet this seems to make the theory too loose, too easily applied to any situation. The strength of Merton's theory, however, lies more in the criminological work it has inspired and the policy implications it has had. These will be reviewed later in this chapter.

Marxist Theories

In recent years, some criminologists have developed a renewed interest in the writings of Karl Marx and their implications for the study of crime (Quinney, 1975; 1977; Taylor et al., 1973). Called "the new criminology" or "radical criminology," the new Marxist criminology has devoted most of its attention to exploring the economic interests behind legislation and criminal justice activities (see "The Interest-Group Conflict Perspective" in Chapter 6). However, some attention has been turned to the use of a Marxist framework to account for criminal behavior. Within this framework, criminal behavior is viewed, in somewhat a structuralist mode, as resulting from inherent self-destructive flaws within the capitalist economic system. The following discussion is drawn from the work of Richard Quinney (1977:31–62), a leading advocate of a Marxist approach to the study of criminality and crime control.

Quinney argues that crime in the capitalist society reflects an inherent tension between its two primary economic classes: the owners (those who own the wealth and industry) and workers (those who supply the labor for industry). To maintain and increase their wealth, the owners must exploit the workers; that is, get the workers to accept less in wages than the full market value of the products they manufacture.

The lower the workers' wages, the greater the profit realized by the owners. Capitalist-system history, Quinney asserts, is the history of the attempts by owners to structure the world view of the workers so that they readily accept their unequal economic position. These attempts are made through owner control of the major social institutions that shape ideas—law, education, government, religion—and the use of the criminal justice system to suppress attempts to alter the owners' favored position.

The Marxist analysis of capitalism suggests that problems within that system will eventually cause its destruction. In order to keep workers dependent on the owners and willing to work for low wages, the capitalist system generates a labor surplus—that is, more workers than available jobs—so that workers compete with each other for jobs and do not unite against the owners. Further, to increase profits, owners constantly seek to mechanize industry and cut production costs and to create monopolies and reduce competition. The result is an ever-growing population of unemployed or poorly paid workers who face a rising cost of living. This, in turn, leads to worker disenchantment and discontent with the economic system. When the workers begin to examine the roots of their situation and understand how the system operates, they have begun to gain a class consciousness, Marxists argue, an awareness of the fact that their interests as a unified group are opposed to those of the owners.

According to Quinney, crime is a manifestation of the struggle between classes and a symbol of the slow erosion of dominance by the owner class. Some crimes, he argues, are crimes of *domination and repression*. These are offenses committed by the owners and the state as they attempt to maintain the economic status quo (crimes such as corporate price fixing and state use of illegal wiretaps to monitor political radicals). Some crimes are crimes of *accommodation and adaptation*, offenses committed by the workers and the poor as they seek to deal with the deprivations stemming from their class position. These crimes include predatory acts (stealing from others) and personal violence stemming from anger and frustration. Quinney feels that, even when these crimes are committed against other workers, they represent unconscious rebellion against the capitalist system. Finally, Quinney writes of *crimes of resistance* committed by workers and the poor who have gained a class consciousness and seek to disrupt and bring down the system. These are "political" crimes—illegal strikes, civil disobedience, sabotage, and terrorism.

In Quinney's view, crime can only increase in the capitalist system as it plunges further toward its own destruction. Increasingly, owners must commit crimes of dominance and repression as they try to hold the line against a growing worker-class consciousness. Crimes of accommodation and adaptation will increase as the plight of workers and the poor worsens. And crimes of resistance will increase as more workers gain a class consciousness. Quinney (1975:61–62) writes:

> Variations in the nature and amount of crime occur in the course of developing capitalism. Each stage in the development of capitalism is characterized by a particular pattern of crime. . . . The contradictions and related crises of capitalist political economy are now a permanent feature of advanced capitalism. . . . The dialectic between oppression by the capitalist class and the daily struggle by the oppressed will continue—and at an increasing pace. . . . The *ultimate meaning* of crime in the development of capitalism is the need for a socialist society.

In the final analysis, the Marxist approach to crime causation is open to much the same criticisms as those leveled at structuralist explanations. The approach is not amenable to testing, for we cannot test the "intentions" of the system and the paths it takes. Like Merton's theory of crime causation, Quinney's theory lacks content. That is, it is not explicit as to how the workers actually come to gain a class consciousness, how they interpret their crimes, and why they choose crime rather than some other adaptive or resistant response. Nor does Quinney deal with the vast stratification in this society and the types of crimes tied to it. How, for instance, does he account for shoplifting by the economically comfortable middle-class person or embezzlement by the bank vice-president? To attribute these to unconscious rebellion is fo employ a very convenient escape valve.

Whether or not Quinney and other radical criminologists are correct in their theory of crime causation and their predictions of increasing crime, they must be credited with stimulating criminological theory and more vigorous investigation of the relationship between crime and our political and economic system. As with Merton's work, perhaps the real value of the Marxist approach lies in the debate and research it is sure to foster.

Cultural Transmission Theories

A third variety of sociological crime theory stresses that criminal behavior, like any form of behavior, is learned—that is, transmitted from one person to another, from a group to its individual members. E. H. Sutherland's major version of this theme is the theory of differential association (see Sutherland and Cressey, 1974:71–93).

Differential Association. Basically, Sutherland argues that we are all exposed to numerous definitions of acceptable and unacceptable behavior, since the United States is a complex society made up of groups or subcultures that view the world differently. Some of these groups will favor law violations of certain types; others will not. A person who commits a criminal act is one who has received more positive definitions than negative definitions of that act. Thus, the key to understanding differential crime rates among groups is to understand their differing views about violating the law. And the key to understanding an individual's criminal acts is to understand the duration, frequency, and intensity of the associations by which he or she came to view the acts as acceptable.

Similar views of the source of criminal behavior can be found before and after the work of Sutherland. Gabriel Tarde (1912) suggested in the late 1800s that many criminal ideas and techniques are learned through close contact with others. In the 1920s and 1930s, the notion of *cultural pluralism*, the idea that American society is composed of diverse subcultures, formed the basis of many social problems and crime theories. Ethnic subcultures introduced into this society during peak immigration periods were viewed as the transmitters of values that clashed with mainstream conventions. Thus, immigrants and their offspring, by learning and adhering to values stressed by their subcultural ties, would often find themselves at odds with American law, which reflected more traditional values.

Among more recent formulations of the cultural transmission approach is Walter Miller's (1958) theory of lower-class delinquent subcultural values as reflections of general lower-class values. Miller argues that there is a distinctive lower-class cultural system in this society that differs from middle- and upper-class cultures in its emphasis on imminent trouble (usually legal), toughness (masculinity, bravery), smartness (shrewdness, capitalizing on opportunities), excitement (pursuit of risk, danger, adventure), fate (favored or unfavored by fortune), and autonomy (independence). Miller claims that lower-class juvenile concern with peer-group status leads to behavior reflecting virtues implicit in the lower-class culture. Thus, lower-class boys pick fights to show toughness and steal to demonstrate shrewdness and daring. Often, simply living up to lower-class standards will place a juvenile in violation of the law; certainly, pursuit of these standards increases the likelihood of legal violations.

Techniques of Neutralization. Yet another variation of the cultural transmission thesis is Sykes and Matza's (1957) notion of techniques of neutralization. These authors suggest that American society is really not as culturally diverse as many observers believe. Instead, they argue that societal norms are more or less universally honored in spirit but that greater levels of violation exist for some groups than for others. Sykes and Matza feel that this is because some groups have developed "techniques of neutralization"—that is, rationalizations that allow an individual to violate a norm without denying its legitimacy. For example, a person may agree that theft is generally wrong yet feel that it is acceptable if the victim will never miss the loss (as in shoplifting from a large department store). Similarly, an individual may disavow attacks on others—unless the victim is not a "full-fledged" citizen (as in the case of youth gangs beating up homosexuals).

The rationalizations take many forms: denial of responsibility for an act, denial of injury to anyone, denial of an actual victim of an act, denial of the moral character of those who condemn the act, and appeal to higher loyalties. Sykes and Matza suspect that the use of techniques of neutralization is distributed unequally by age, sex, social class, ethnic affiliation, and so on. Also, they feel that these techniques are learned, passed on to individuals by family and peer group. Whatever their source, the learning of such values would seem to increase the likelihood of criminal behavior.

Cultural transmission explanations of criminal behavior have been severely criticized. Some argue that they are nearly if not totally untestable: how is the researcher to trace the number and strength of various influences on an individual's beliefs? Others note that cultural-transmission theory seems unable to explain impulsive crimes (unless, of course, impulsiveness is also somehow learned). Studies of other forms of crime have also found a lack of positive reinforcement for the act in the criminal's social background and environment. Such is the case, Cressey (1953:149–50) found, with embezzlers. Finally, to say that all behavior is learned is similar to saying that all water is wet. Just as the more important questions concerning water are those that ask what governs its chemical content, its temperature, and so on, so we must ask about learned behavior: What accounts for the positive definitions of law violation attributed to some groups? What governs the transmission of subcultural ideas to members of those groups? In what situations do these ideas come into play?

However problematic they may be, cultural transmission theories can be credited with calling our attention to the fact that in a complex society we can expect some variation in world views. The typical city represents a large array of socioeconomic situations and cultural beliefs. It seems highly unlikely that the middle-class businessman and the ghetto dweller will view welfare fraud or shoplifting in exactly the same way. Although subcultural ideas that support crime and, perhaps, even teach crime techniques cannot be said to *cause* criminal behavior, they definitely make it more likely to occur.

Three Prominent Sociological Crime Theories

The notions of differential economic opportunity and learned criminal values inspired much criminological theory in the late 1950s and early 1960s. Three theories gained special prominence. All reflect aspects of the various sociological approaches discussed above. They are discussed briefly in this chapter because they represent the last, rather elaborate causal theories to gain popular recognition. Even though formulated nearly two decades ago, they are still often cited.

Reaction Formation and Gang Delinquency. In 1955, Albert Cohen published *Delinquent Boys: The Culture of the Gang*, a highly provocative causal theory that attempted to tie together structural and cultural phenomena with individual motivations for delinquent acts. Cohen traces delinquency to status problems among lower-class youth. The status problems arise from the fact that the social institutions to which the youth are exposed (education, work, religion) emphasize middle-class values somewhat foreign to the lower-class youth. Middle-class values include deferment of gratification, ambition, responsibility, control of aggression, wholesome use of leisure time, and respect for property. Middle-class children have been well socialized into these values and are likely to succeed in institutions that emphasize them. Lower-class youth, on the other hand, are not well socialized into these values and will likely fail in institutional settings, such as school, that measure the youth's worth by such middle-class standards. The result is a low level of self-esteem for the lower-class child and withdrawal from the institutional setting.

Youths who fail and withdraw are drawn into each others' company. Together, they develop standards by which they can succeed and thereby raise their self-esteem. The resulting delinquent subculture represents what Cohen calls a "reaction formation." The lower-class juvenile develops a set of behaviors and values in direct opposition to middle-class values. Status and self-esteem are derived from violating middle-class rules. To buttress his argument, Cohen argues that the delinquency (even thefts) of lower-class gangs is nonutilitarian—that is, done not for profit but for the thrill or simply out of meanness. The lower-class gang is oriented toward immediate pleasure. Courage, shown through toughness and violence, is paid off in status in the eyes of peers. Delinquent youth have simply switched social systems, moving from one in which they were failures to one in which they are successes. The ultimate causes of delinquency, then, are structural failures of the system: the failure of the lower-class family to prepare the youth for success in institutional settings, and the failure of the institutional settings, primarily educational, to accommodate the lower-class youth.

Although Cohen is to be credited with turning our attention to the possible role of the school in delinquency, his work is open to criticism (Bordua, 1961). For one thing, it focuses exclusively on subcultural or gang delinquency and is inapplicable to the offenses of individual delinquents. Further, it is limited to lower-class delinquency and so is unable to offer insight into the offenses of middle- and upper-class juveniles. In Cohen's defense, however, we must note that he has never claimed that his theory is directed to any other than lower-class gang delinquency; that is, he has not attempted to formulate a general theory of delinquency.

The more serious problem with Cohen's thesis lies with the reaction-formation concept. Miller (1958) argues that Cohen fails to recognize that lower-class values differ from those of other classes and that what Cohen sees as "reactive" gang values are in reality simply extensions of general lower-class values (see the above discussion in "Cultural Transmission Theories"). Beyond this, we find no evidence that lower-class delinquents directly reject middle-class values. In the final analysis, the reaction-formation concept is not able to be validated, since it refers to a social-psychological process about which, presumably, even the delinquent is unaware. We also cannot help but wonder why delinquents must gain status and self-esteem from negativistic acts. Why does their reaction to school failure not include an attempt to succeed through illegal *utilitarian* acts—that is, crimes committed for profit?

Blocked Opportunity and Juvenile Delinquency. In 1960, Cloward and Ohlin presented a theory of lower-class gang delinquency primarily influenced by Merton's structuralist scheme but reflecting elements of Marxism and the cultural transmission approach as well. Like Merton, these authors begin with the premise that material-success goals are pervasive, though the legitimate means to attain them are not equally available to everyone. The response to the situation of blocked opportunity is governed by the amounts and types of illegitimate opportunities available to the potential delinquent. That is, it should not be assumed that the social structure provides equal access to illegitimate means of goal attainment any more than it does to legitimate means.

According to Cloward and Ohlin, there are three basic subcultural responses to blocked opportunity. The first is the *criminal subculture*. This response is primarily a neighborhood phenomenon, reflecting the presence of a stable, relatively organized adult crime pattern. Juveniles observe and are inducted into the neighborhood crime structure, mainly property crimes; learn the neighborhood criminal values; and work, in apprenticeship fashion, into the adult crime structure.

The second response pattern is the *conflict subculture*. This pattern arises in neighborhoods that have neither legitimate nor stable illegitimate opportunities for success. Because the community is devoid of the criminal subcultural values and structure, there is no apprenticeship in organized crime. The result is a more violent form of gang delinquency, perpetrated on members of the neighborhood as well as on strangers. Robberies, assaults, and gang fighting are the primary crimes in this subcultural setting.

The third form is the *retreatist* pattern. Juveniles who are blocked from or fail to capitalize on legitimate and illegitimate opportunities are prone to withdrawal from the community into drug usage. In essence, this response is the same as that postulated by Merton in his reference to retreatism—an abandonment of or withdrawal from both the goals and means of the society.

In sum, the major contributions of Cloward and Ohlin's blocked-opportunity theory are its emphasis on the failure of the economic system as the source of criminal behavior, its claim that illegitimate means to offset blocked opportunity are not open to all, and its notion that responses to blocked opportunity will reflect the structure and culture of the neighborhood.

Cloward and Ohlin's theory may be criticized in much the same fashion as Cohen's was—that is, it is limited to lower-class gang delinquency and leaves us searching for answers concerning individual offenses and those of middle- and upper-class youth (Bordua, 1961). However, like Cohen, Cloward and Ohlin were not attempting to construct a general theory of delinquency. Unlike Cohen, though, they picture lower-class gang delinquents as youths who have succeeded, not failed, in their preparation for life in the American economic system. The delinquency results not from limited preparation but from limited opportunities to which to apply it.

We must wonder, given current criticism of inner-city education, whether lower-class youth are indeed well prepared for conventional economic success. If they are not, perhaps "blocked opportunity" is not so much a cause of delinquency as an espoused justification for it. In sum, though Cloward and Ohlin have succeeded in focusing our attention on potential links between the lower-class opportunity structure and crime, they have left many important questions unanswered.

Containment, Self-Concept and Delinquency. Through the 1950s and 1960s considerable attention was directed toward Walter Reckless's (1967:444–83) theory of juvenile delinquency. Reckless argued that social structure by itself was not sufficient to account for crime. That is, a variety of social pressures (poverty, blocked opportunity, bad companions) might serve to encourage individuals to commit delinquent acts but these pressures do not explain why they actually commit them. Reckless feels that the encouraging factors must interact with certain social-control or containment factors to produce a juvenile delinquent. One such factor is external containment: delinquency is less likely if the juvenile is effectively pressured to conform by family and other conventional persons. Similarly, delinquency is influenced by effective or ineffective internal containment, the extent to which the individual has internalized and is committed to society's norms. Internal containment is reflected by a healthy self-concept and self-control.

Of all these variables, the key to juvenile delinquency, Reckless argues, is internal containment—a strong self-concept. In a complex, rapid-paced society, we can expect individuals to be stimulated toward crime by a number of factors. Similarly, modern society seems characterized by a weakening of external constraints—family and community ties. In the final analysis, the variable that separates juvenile delinquents from nondelinquents is the extent of internal constraint. The strong self-concept acts as a buffer against the causal factors and weak external constraints that encourage delinquency.

Unlike other theorists, Reckless has received little criticism for his theory. Instead, most critics have attacked methodological weaknesses in the research he and his associates performed in testing parts of the theory. Some have argued that self-concept has been poorly measured and its link to internal containment and delinquency poorly demonstrated in these studies. The studies are also considered flawed for their dependence on official court records as indicators of delinquency, for their faulty sampling procedures, and for their lack of control groups (Tangri and Schwartz, 1967; Orcutt, 1970).

These problems aside, Reckless's theory itself poses some difficulties. It is vague about the interrelationships of the various inducements to commit crimes and the internal and external inhibitors of criminal behavior. It gives little information about how these variables are originally developed in and around the youth. The reliance on the self-concept variable seems too strong, since we cannot know whether poor self-concept is influentially or simply incidentally linked to delinquency.

Still, the containment thesis represents an improvement over most theories of delinquency in that it more closely examines the types of variables that may offset initial causal factors in delinquency.

In sum, none of the three theories can escape criticism. Although subjected to partial testing, none has been fully researched, in part owing to the vague definitions of many of the concepts each employs. Despite their problems, however, these theories represent milestones in causal analysis, for they are far more elaborate and sophisticated than the simplistic, single-variable views of crime causation, and, most importantly, are detailed and elaborate enough to stimulate criticism. The critical flurry that has pursued each of these theories has served as much as the theories themselves to sharpen our understanding of the problem of crime and the difficulty of causal analysis.

Sociological Crime Theories Appraised

We began this chapter by discussing the possible sources of criminal behavior. We reviewed—and dismissed as sound explanations—the concepts of biological and psychological flaws. What about the sociological approach, with its emphasis on social structure and the cultural transmission of criminal attitudes? Is it any better? In some ways, yes.

The sociological theories have turned our attention away from the traditional view that criminal behavior is abnormal and have suggested instead that it may be *quite* normal. Blocked opportunity theories basically ask: What are we to expect from people who are given a goal and then denied the opportunity to seek it? In this light, criminal attempts to reach the goal seem a normal response to a problematic situation. Marxist theories view criminal behavior as a normal and unavoidable response to oppression. Cultural transmission theories similarly ask: What is abnormal about basing our behavior on beliefs that we have been taught? The normal response to a set of internalized beliefs favoring law violation is—law violation.

The sociological theories are to be credited as well with turning our attention away from the individual as a "bad apple" and focusing on such important social facts as economic deprivation and American society's remarkable heterogeneity. Whether or not strictly causal, these factors are undoubtedly implicated in crime.

However, despite their saving virtues, sociological theories of crime causation hold only a slight edge over other approaches. Most sociological theories have overstressed the notion of subculture and given too much attention to juvenile delinquency, especially gang delinquency. Moreover, as we noted in Chapter 3, the theories have concentrated almost totally on male criminal behavior. In addition, they have tended to focus on lower-class crime, generally ignoring the offenses of other classes. We currently have no systematic causal theory of adult criminal behavior, whether that behavior is lower class or upper class, male or female.

The fact that we still parrot crime theories developed in the 1950s and modified little since points to a stagnation in the causal analysis of crime. Part of the problem is frustration at our inability to develop sufficient tests of our theories. Part also is due to a lack of public receptiveness to many of the policy implications of sociological theories (discussed below). However valid the reasons for the stagnation, the sad fact remains that sociologists have recently been ignoring questions that will not go away.

Causal Analysis and Anticrime Policy

A sound anticrime policy must lean on at least tacit assumptions about crime. Empey (1977:6–7) has noted:

> Any time a [juvenile-justice] program is set up, or any time one technique is chosen over another, someone has an idea in the

back of his or her mind that it will make a difference—that it is somehow preferable to other programs and techniques. That person, in other words, does have a theory—however ill stated—as to what leads to delinquency and how it can best be dealt with.

Most certainly, different assumptions about the source of criminal behavior may lead to very different anticrime policies. Some theories target individuals for change; others focus on structural changes in society. Some direct attention toward treatment and rehabilitation of offenders; others emphasize preventing crime by eliminating the sources of crime. Still others encourage neither treatment of offenders nor elimination of crime sources but call instead for punishment of offenders to deter them from future crimes.

It is important to remember that anticrime policies rest on more than simply knowledge about causes of crime. There are ethical and legal limits to consider. A plan to study from the time of birth all XYY chromosomal pattern babies born in a given city could be expected to be quashed because, though it might lead to invaluable knowledge, the project could also seriously influence, in a negative way, the children's lives by branding them as "different" or even as "potential criminals."

Policy issues are also political and economic issues. Legislators may base support for a policy program on its potential influence on voter behavior. None wishes to be "soft" on crime, and "overspending" on crime is also not popular with voters. Yet, policy implementation costs money; some programs call for billions of dollars and receive only millions. Relatively speaking, millions are too little and, if the program fails, it is difficult to determine if it was faulty or if it simply was not given a chance.

The American public seems to prefer theories of crime causation which stress the individual abnormality of criminals: If criminals are not born flawed, then they have been damaged by family or bad companions. Not only are such theories more "sensible" to most people, they are also somewhat easier to live with, for they do not implicate the *average citizen* in either the cause or the cure for crime. Thus, anticrime policies constructed along this line of thought are less costly and can be accomplished without disrupting the public: Basically what is required is the identification of the bad apples and their subsequent custody, whether to punish them or treat them. If treated, the treatment program may require some form of behavior modification—a few prisons, for instance, now conduct volunteer treatment programs for child molesters which include the use of electric shocks to modify sexual desires. If the source of offenders' problems can be traced to something in their environment (a problem family, for example), then treatment may be extended there, too.

Today sociological crime theories—especially those with a structural approach—are less popular with the public, for they implicate *all* of society in both the cause and cure of crime. Structural changes (such as redistribution of wealth and restructuring education) would be both costly and disruptive and the governmental programs based on such theories would likely encounter political turmoil. At the same time, structural changes are also most prone to failure, the result of a combination of problems with the theories, general public distrust of them, and lack of financial support for their implementation.

Problems with Attempted Structural Change: The MFY Program

The sociological structural approach to the solution of social problems reached its height during Lyndon Johnson's Great Society era of the 1960s. Poverty and blocked socioeconomic opportunities were viewed as being the causes of most problems. The strategy to combat these ills aimed not at changing individuals but at making large-scale changes in the opportunity structure of American society.

An important example of attempted structural change was the Mobilization for Youth (MFY) program, begun in New York City in the early 1960s (Helfgot, 1974; Mobilization for Youth, 1964). Alarmed by an increase in juvenile delinquency and convinced that lack of opportunity lay behind delinquency, several welfare, civic, and religious groups developed an action program and gained financial support from the city and federal governments and the Ford Foundation. Unlike traditional social-reform projects that sought to alter delinquents so that they responded more conventionally to their environment (however conducive to crime) or that were primarily charity oriented, MFY mustered together several social services designed to incorporate the poor in systematic structural change—that is, in essence, to fight "the system," to politically effect needed changes that would create opportunities for the poor. Among its concerns were education, employment, legal services, community development, and family and group services. Once the barriers to opportunities for the poor were removed, social problems such as crime and delinquency were expected to diminish.

Was MFY successful? Few would argue it was. However, there is considerable disagreement as to why it failed. Liberals claim the program was but a drop in the bucket and could not be expected to alter the plight of the poor to any significant degree. Conservatives argue the project represented yet another avenue by which the "welfare element" could exploit the society; that is, rather than take the project seriously the poor allegedly sought only what immediate profit could be gained from it. Radical leftists assert that MFY was a cosmetic Band-Aid designed to co-opt the oppressed into thinking reform rather than revolution. If any of these analyses are correct, it is clear that MFY could not possibly succeed in combating crime.

But the most persuasive analysis of MFY's failure suggests that political and social pressures forced constant goal and organizational changes in the project and generally rendered it powerless. Helfgot (1974) argues that the political implications of any governmentally sponsored structural-change program render it doomed the moment it becomes effectual, that is, the moment it threatens status quo power relationships. He argues that as soon as the poor began to organize and demand participation in the MFY program, they were placated by MFY's hiring of professional middle-class minority workers. The poor themselves participated very little in MFY. Further, since MFY was so dependent on government and private foundation grants, it could hardly be expected to exist for long if it attacked the power structure that the funding agencies represented. In fact, Helfgot argues, increasing financial insecurity slowly forced MFY away from its structural-change goals to more traditional social reform aimed at changing individuals through such means as vocational training. In short, it became just "another program."

The MFY example illustrates a major point concerning the relationship of causal theory (especially structural theory) to anticrime policy. The ultimate test of a causal theory is the *implementation* of the social intervention it suggests. Yet, the intervention strategy is so tied to social and political concerns that it is most often doomed to failure. The result is twofold: (1) no impact on the social structure and consequently on the crime situation, and (2) neither confirmation nor negation of the causal theory.

Summary

In this chapter we reviewed criminological attempts to answer the well-worn but still unanswered question: What causes crime? The search for the causes of crime has, at different times, centered on the biological, psychological, and social aspects of the criminal. Although it would seem we have developed a progressively sophisticated understanding of criminal behavior, if we review these theories we see that we have minimal knowledge about the causes of crime.

In fact, causal analysis seems to have progressed little in over fifteen years. The frustrations encountered in trying to answer a question of such magnitude—together with the social, political, economic, and ethical problems of forming and testing causal theories—have caused many criminologists to shift their attention to other types of questions, some of which are explored in the coming chapters.

Regarding the average citizen's concerns about crime and personal safety, this chapter has tried to illuminate the complexity of the causes of crime and demonstrate that complex problems do not have simple answers. Criminal behavior is not caused *simply* by biological or psychological disorders. Nor is it *simply* the result of such factors as urban overcrowding or poverty or bad companions or lax parents. "Better education" by itself will certainly not eliminate crime, and eliminating poverty, though it will undoubtedly rid us of many related problems that encourage crime, will not ensure which problems or how much crime.

The complexity of the problem should make us suspect of recent government anticrime policies: more jobs for youths will not necessarily bring down the crime rate. Equally, we should suspect simple, conservative anticrime proposals: incarcerating "habitual criminals" will not necessarily lead to a sharp drop in crime rates. Complex problems rarely have such simple answers.

References

Bordua, D.
    1961   "Delinquent subcultures: sociological interpretations of gang delinquency." The Annals of the American Academy of Political and Social Science 338:120–36.

Chilton, R. J.
    1964   "Continuity in delinquency area research: a comparison of studies for Baltimore, Detroit, and Indianapolis." American Sociological Review 29:71–83.

Cloward, R. A., and L. E. Ohlin
    1960   Delinquency and Opportunity. New York: The Free Press.

Cohen, A.
    1955   Delinquent Boys: The Culture of the Gang. New York: The Free Press.

Cressey, D. R.
    1953   Other People's Money. New York: The Free Press.

Dominick, J. R.
    1973   "Crime and enforcement on prime-time television." Public Opinion Quarterly 37:241–50.

Empey, L. T.
    1977   A Model for Evaluation of Programs in Juvenile Justice. Washington, D.C.: U.S. Government Printing Office.

Ennis, P. H.
    1967   Criminal Victimization in the United States: A Report of a National Survey. Field Survey II: President's Commission on Law Enforcement and Administration of Justice. Washington, D.C.: U.S. Government Printing Office.

Eron, L. D., L. R. H. Mann, M. Lefkowitz, and L. O. Walder
    1972   "Does television cause aggression?" American Psychologist 27:253–63.

Farrell, R. A., and J. F. Nelson
    1976   "A causal model of secondary deviance: the case of homosexuality." Sociological Quarterly 17:109–20.

Fox, R. G.
    1971   "The XYY offender: a modern myth?" Journal of Criminal Law, Criminology and Police Science 62:59–73.

Galtung, J.
   1967   Theory and Methods of Social Research. New York: Columbia University Press.

Gibbons, D. C.
   1977   Society, Crime and Criminal Careers. 3rd edition. Englewood Cliffs, N.J.: Prentice-Hall.

Glueck, S., and E. Glueck
   1950   Unraveling Juvenile Delinquency. New York: Commonwealth Fund.
   1956   Physique and Delinquency. New York: Harper.

Helfgot, J.
   1974   "Professional reform organizations and the symbolic representation of the poor." American Sociological Review 39:475–91.

Henry, A. F., and J. F. Short, Jr.
   1954   Suicide and Homicide. Glencoe, Ill.: The Free Press.

Hirschi, T.
   1969   Causes of Delinquency. Berkeley: University of California Press.

Hirschi, T., and M. J. Hindelang
   1977   "Intelligence and delinquency: a revisionist review." American Sociological Review 42:571–87.
   1978   "Reply to Ronald L. Simons." American Sociological Review 43:610–13.

Hooton, E. A.
   1939   Crime and the Man. Cambridge, Mass.: Harvard University Press.

Jensen, G. F.
   1972   "Parents, peers, and delinquent action: a test of the differential association perspective." American Journal of Sociology 78:562–75.

Kassebaum, G., D. A. Ward, and D. M. Wilner
   1971   Prison Treatment and Parole Survival. New York: Wiley.

Light, I.
   1977   "The ethnic vice industry, 1880–1944." American Sociological Review 42:464–79.

Lombrozo, C.
   1911   Criminal Man. New York: Putnam's.

Merton, R. K.
   1957   Social Theory and Social Structure. Revised and enlarged edition. New York: The Free Press.

Miller, W. B.
   1958   "Lower class culture as a generating milieu of gang delinquency." Journal of Social Issues 14:5–19.

Mobilization for Youth
   1964   Action on the Lower East Side, Program Report: July 1962–January 1964. New York: Mobilization for Youth.

Nettler, G.
   1974   Explaining Crime. New York: McGraw-Hill.

Nye, F. I.
   1958   Family Relationships and Delinquent Behavior. New York: Wiley.

Orcutt, J. D.
   1970   "Self-concept and insulation against delinquency: some critical notes." Sociological Quarterly 11:381–90.

Quinney, R.
   1975   Critique of Legal Order. Boston: Little, Brown.
   1977   Class, State, and Crime. New York: David McKay.

Reckless, W. C.
   1967   The Crime Problem, 4th ed. New York: Appleton-Century-Crofts.
Robinson, W. S.
   1950   "Ecological correlations and the behavior of individuals." American Sociological Review 15:353–57.
Rosen, L.
   1970   "The 'broken home' and male delinquency." Pp. 489–95 in M. E. Wolfgang, L. Savitz, and N. Johnston (eds.), Sociology of Crime and Delinquency. 2d ed. New York: Wiley.
Schur, E.
   1969   Our Criminal Society. Englewood Cliffs, N.J.: Prentice-Hall.
Shah, S., and L. Roth
   1974   "Biological and psychophysiological factors in criminality." Pp. 101–73 in D. Glaser (ed.), Handbook of Criminology. Chicago: Rand McNally.
Sheldon, W. H.
   1942   Varieties of Temperament. New York: Harper.
Sheldon, W. H., S. S. Stevens, and W. B. Tucker
   1940   Varieties of Human Physique. New York: Harper.
Sheldon, W. H., E. M. Harth, and E. McDermott
   1949   Varieties of Delinquent Youth. New York: Harper.
Simons, R. L.
   1978   "The meaning of the IQ-delinquency relationship." American Sociological Review 43:268–70.
Surgeon General's Scientific Advisory Committee on Television and Social Control
   1972a   Television and Social Behavior: Volume 1—Media Content and Control. Washington, D.C.: U.S. Government Printing Office.
   1972b   Television and Social Behavior: Volume 3—Television and Adolescent Aggressiveness. Washington, D.C.: U.S. Government Printing Office.
   1972c   Television and Social Behavior: Volume 4—Television in Day-to-Day Life: Patterns of Use. Washington, D.C.: U.S. Government Printing Office.
Sutherland, E. H., and D. R. Cressey
   1974   Criminology. 9th ed. Philadelphia: Lippincott.
Sykes, J. M., and D. Matza
   1957   "Techniques of neutralization: a theory of delinquency." American Sociological Review 22:664–70.
Tangri, S. S., and M. Schwartz
   1967   "Delinquency research and the self-concept variable." Journal of Criminal Law, Criminology and Police Science 58:182–90.
Tarde, G.
   1912   Penal Philosophy. Boston: Little, Brown.
Taylor, I., P. Walton, and J. Young
   1973   The New Criminology. New York: Harper.
Toby, J.
   1957   "The differential impact of family disorganization." American Sociological Review 22:505–12.
Vaughn, Ted R.
   1967   "Governmental intervention in social research: political and ethical dimensions in the Wichita jury recording." Pp. 50–77 in Gideon Sjoberg (ed.), Ethics, Politics, and Social Research. Cambridge, Mass.: Schenkman.

Vold, G.
    1958   Theoretical Criminology. New York: Oxford University Press.
Waldo, G. P., and S. Dinitz
    1967   "Personality attributes of the criminal: an analysis of research studies, 1950–65." Journal of Research in Crime and Delinquency 4:185–201.

Suggested Readings

Readers interested in further discussion of causal analysis of crime should first read the original works which were summarized in this chapter or, at least, a collection of pieces of these works. R. A. Farrell and V. L. Swigert have edited a well-rounded anthology, *Social Deviance* (Philadelphia: Lippincott, 1975), as have S. H. Traub and C. B. Little, *Theories of Deviance* (Itasca, Ill.: Peacock, 1975).

A look at some of the theory and research inspired by major criminological theories is also helpful. For example, R. L. Burgess and R. L. Akers provide us with a clearer understanding of differential association theory through their efforts to refine it. See their article, "Differential Association—Reinforcement Theory of Criminal Behavior," *Social Problems*, Fall 1968: 128–47.

Causal theories are best understood when their theoretical assumptions are clearly stated and placed within a historical context. Two books do this very well: Travis Hirschi, *Causes of Delinquency* (Berkeley: University of California Press, 1969) and D. C. Gibbons and J. F. Jones, *The Study of Deviance* (Englewood Cliffs, N.J.: Prentice-Hall, 1975). N. J. Davis offers a particularly critical analysis of sociological theories of deviance in *Sociological Constructions of Deviance* (Dubuque, Iowa: Brown, 1975). An equally critical Marxist analysis of the same theories is found in I. Taylor, P. Walton, and J. Young, *The New Criminology* (New York: Harper, 1973).

5
Victims

The American system of justice is often accused of ignoring the victims of crime—a criticism that can also be directed at criminologists, who have traditionally concentrated their research on the relationship between society and individual as it affects criminal behavior. A few voices in the wilderness have argued that criminologists must also direct attention to the role of the victim in the criminal act. Hans von Hentig (1948) first stirred interest in this theme when he suggested that we cannot have crimes unless we have victims; that many victims are actively involved in their victimizations (as in con games); and that some victims, through personality factors, actually invite or even encourage criminal acts.

Despite a critical receptivity to von Hentig's speculations and an occasionally provocative study of victim-precipitated crime (Wolfgang, 1958; Amir, 1971), criminologists have only recently begun systematically to devote attention to patterns of crime victimization. "Victimology," the study of victims—not only of crime but of accidents as well—is fast gaining acceptance as a social science subfield. This chapter explores two victimology themes—patterns of victimization and victim-offender relationships—and then examines the theoretical and policy implications of these themes.

Patterns of Victimization

In American society, criminal victimizations do not occur randomly. Surveys of victims during the past several years consistently demonstrate that some groups and categories of people represent higher-risk victim populations. The variables thus far examined in victimization research are basic demographic characteristics: sex, age, race, income, marital status, and residence. Any patterns discovered in these investigations undoubtedly mask more complex relationships involving other variables. The following discussion of victim characteristics is based on data collected for a U.S. Department of Justice (1976) national survey of 1973 crime victims.

118   Part Two / Criminals and Victims

Figure 5–1
Victimization rates by sex

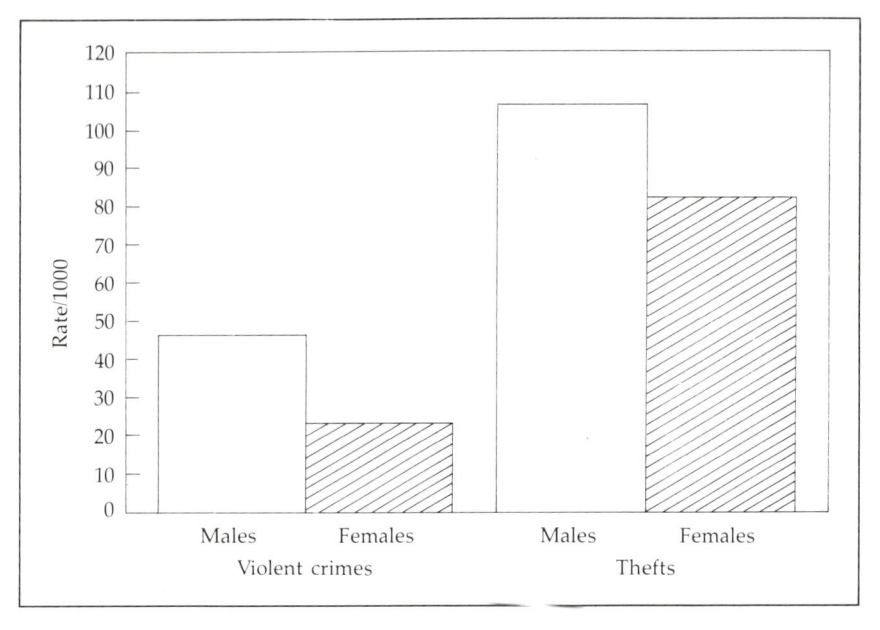

Source: U.S. Department of Justice, *Criminal Victimization in the United States—1973* (Washington, D.C.: U.S. Government Printing Office, 1976), p. 68.

Sex

Except in the crime of rape, males are more often than females the victims of most offenses. As Figure 5–1 indicates, males suffer twice the rate of crimes of violence as females do: 46 per 1,000 males versus 23 per 1,000 females. Males are also more likely to be victims of theft: 106 per 1,000 as opposed to 82 per 1,000 for females.

Age

Figure 5–2 indicates that crimes of violence are committed most often against persons sixteen to nineteen years of age (68 per 1,000). For theft, people twelve to fifteen years of age are more likely to be victims (176 per 1,000). For both violent and theft offenses, the rates decline steadily with age after age twenty. Age-victimization patterns are similar for both sexes, though age seems to have no impact on robbery victimizations of females.

Why higher victimization rates among young people? One possible

Figure 5–2
Victimization rates by age

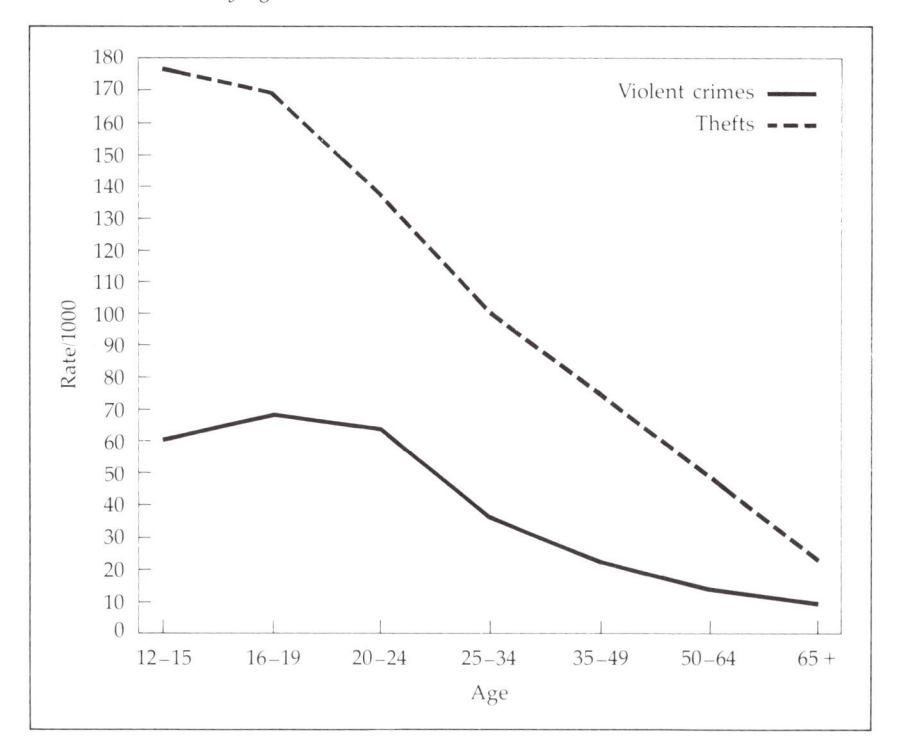

[Figure 5-2: Line graph showing victimization rates per 1000 by age group (12-15, 16-19, 20-24, 25-34, 35-49, 50-64, 65+) for Violent crimes (solid line) and Thefts (dashed line). Both decline with age.]

Source: U.S. Department of Justice, *Criminal Victimization in the United States—1973* (Washington, D.C.: U.S. Government Printing Office, 1976), p. 69.

explanation is that younger victims are more likely to be in more frequent contact with a high-offense rate group: youth. Also, given physical differences between age groups in the teen years, younger teenagers are more vulnerable to coercive acts by older youth (Skogan, 1976:138).

Race

Figure 5–3 shows victimization rates according to race. Blacks are victimized much more by violent crime (47 per 1,000) than whites are (32 per 1,000)—that is, they are more likely to be robbed, assaulted, or raped. (They are also more likely to be victims of homicide, according to the FBI *Uniform Crime Reports.*) Black males are more apt to be victimized by violence (59 per 1,000) than their white counterparts are (45 per 1,000), and black females exceed (37 per 1,000) white females (21 per 1,000) in violent victimizations.

120   Part Two / Criminals and Victims

Figure 5-3
Victimization rates by race

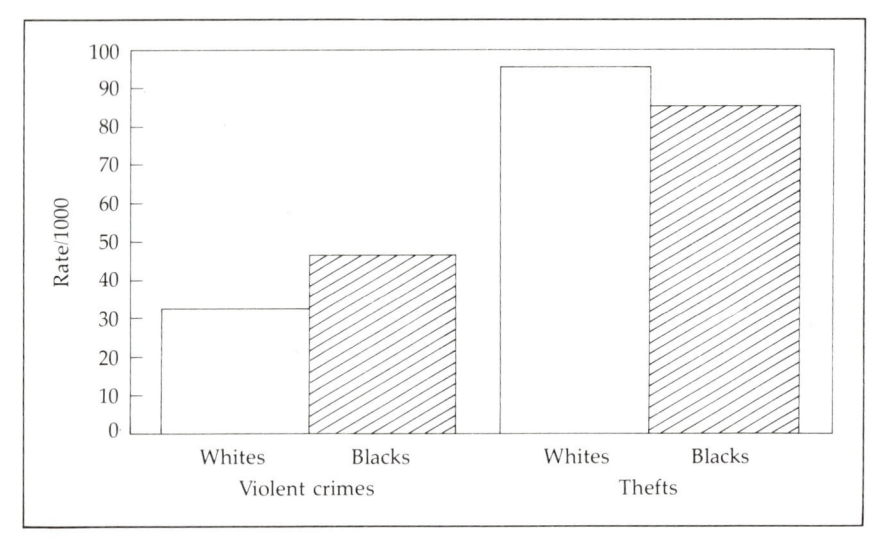

Source: U.S. Department of Justice, *Criminal Victimization in the United States—1973* (Washington, D.C.: U.S. Government Printing Office, 1976), p. 70.

But whites are more often victimized by theft (95 per 1,000) than blacks are (85 per 1,000). This is to be expected, since the white population has a higher income level and greater wealth, yet, given white-black economic differences, it is surprising that the theft victimization rate is not more disparate. The rate for blacks is greater than expected probably because blacks are more vulnerable to theft owing to the fact they often live in poorer neighborhoods and have poorer home security. Thus, though the potential "take" from blacks is less, it is often nonetheless more easily taken. This notion is supported by the finding that the homes of blacks are burglarized more often than those of whites: 135 per 1,000 for blacks versus 88 per 1,000 for whites.

Income

As Figure 5-4 indicates, lower economic groups tend to have higher rates of victimization for violent crimes than upper economic groups do. But for theft offenses the opposite is true: the higher the income, the higher the victimization rate. In general, these patterns hold for both whites and blacks.

We can only speculate as to why violent-crime victimization patterns differ so, but whether prompted by gain or frustration, violent crime seems to be a lower-class phenomenon. The victimization findings further the view that most violent crime is intracommunity, intra-

Figure 5–4
Victimization rates by income

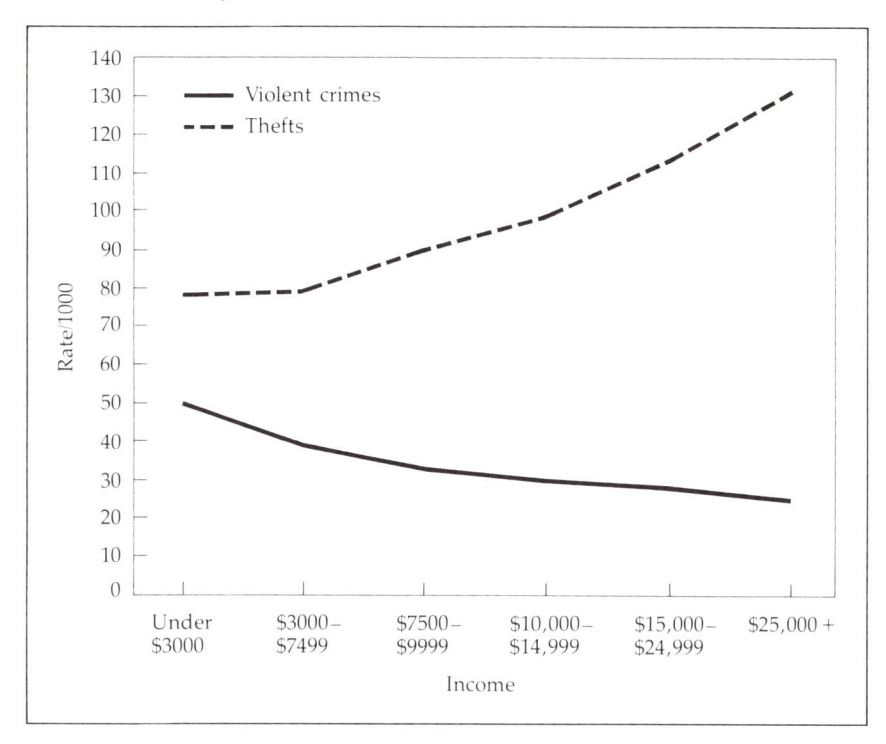

[Figure: Line graph showing victimization rates per 1000 by income bracket. Violent crimes (solid line) decrease from ~50 at "Under $3000" to ~25 at "$25,000+". Thefts (dashed line) increase from ~78 at "Under $3000" to ~130 at "$25,000+". Income brackets: Under $3000, $3000–$7499, $7500–$9999, $10,000–$14,999, $15,000–$24,999, $25,000+.]

Source: U.S. Department of Justice, *Criminal Victimization in the United States—1973* (Washington, D.C.: U.S. Government Printing Office, 1976), p. 73.

racial, intrasubcultural, and intrafamilial. The fact that theft victimizations correlate with income is not surprising, for upper-income persons obviously have more to steal. Still, it is noteworthy that lower-income homes are burglarized more often than are upper-income homes (which are usually better protected).

Marital Status

As Figure 5–5 suggests, for both violent and theft offenses, those who have never married or are separated or divorced have much higher rates than married or widowed persons do. Although males generally have higher rates than females do, the overall victimization patterns according to marital status are relatively the same for both sexes. The key to explaining marital-status differences in victimization rates undoubtedly rests with a link between marital status and age. The "never married" category contains the greatest number of younger victims, followed by those "separated or divorced," "married," and

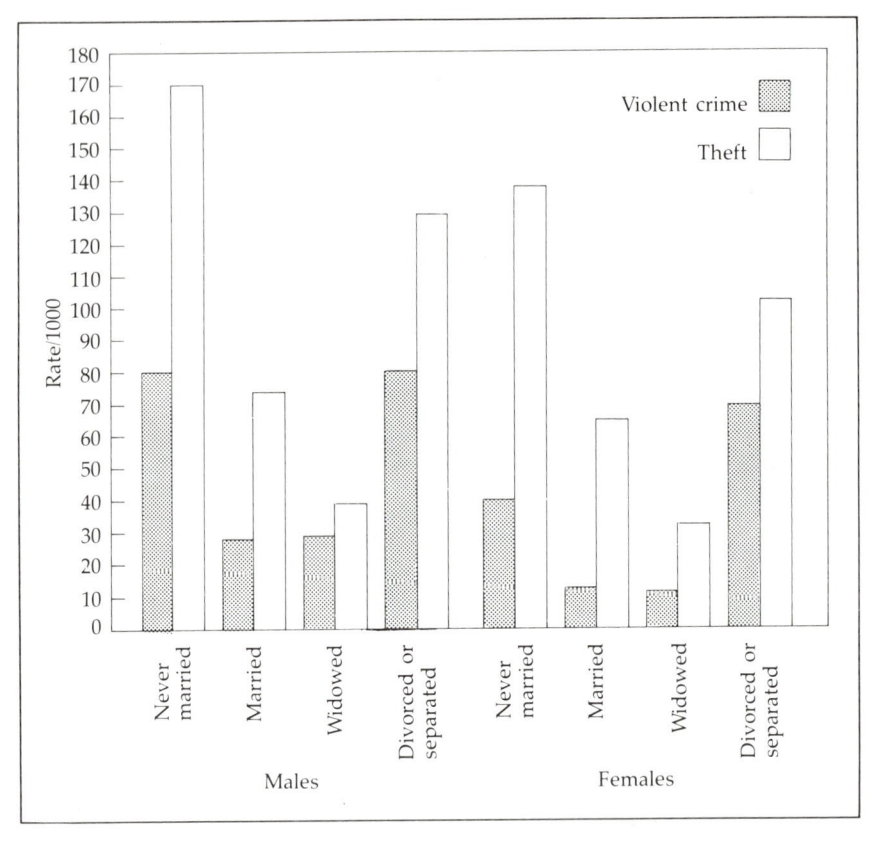

Figure 5–5
Victimization rates by marital status and sex

[Bar chart showing victimization rates per 1000 by marital status (Never married, Married, Widowed, Divorced or separated) for Males and Females, with bars for Violent crime and Theft]

Source: U.S. Department of Justice, *Criminal Victimization in the United States—1973* (Washington, D.C.: U.S. Government Printing Office, 1976), p. 73.

"widowed," respectively. Thus, we suggest that it is not marital status per se that influences victimization rates but factors related to marital status, such as age and life-style.

Residency

Figure 5–6 indicates that nonmetropolitan areas have lower victimization rates than metropolitan areas do. Within metropolitan areas, central city and noncentral city settings differ somewhat in violent-offense victimization rates but show almost no differences in rates for theft. The size of the metropolitan area does not seem to determine victimization rates; rates neither rise nor fall consistently as the metropolitan areas increase in size.

Figure 5-6
Victimization rates by area of residence

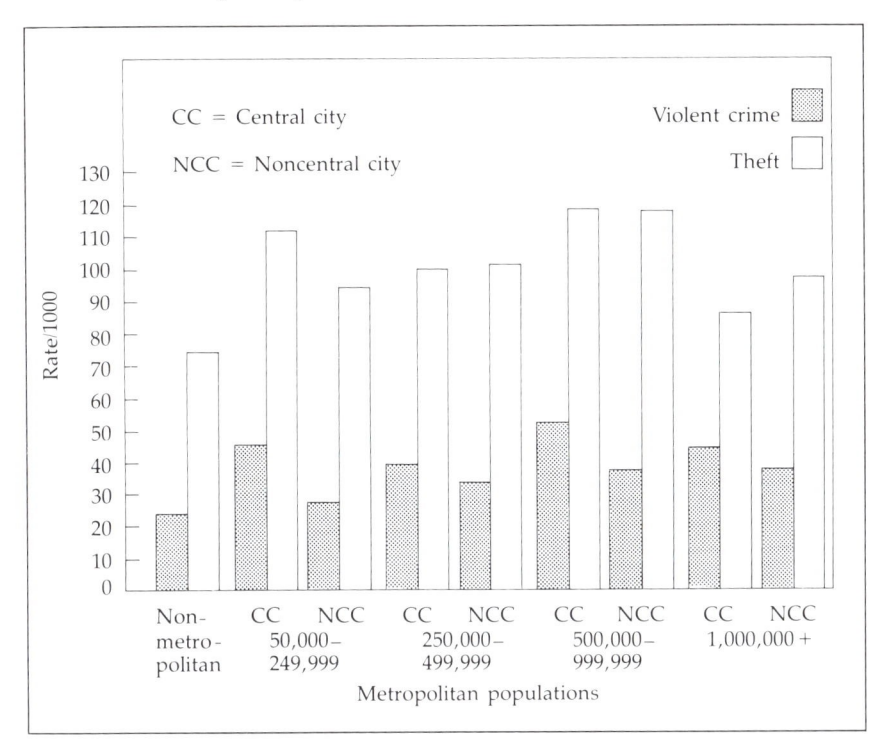

[Bar chart showing victimization rates per 1,000 by area of residence. CC = Central city; NCC = Noncentral city. Categories on x-axis: Nonmetropolitan; CC/NCC 50,000–249,999; CC/NCC 250,000–499,999; CC/NCC 500,000–999,999; CC/NCC 1,000,000+. Bars show Violent crime and Theft rates across Metropolitan populations.]

Source: U.S. Department of Justice, *Criminal Victimization in the United States—1973* (Washington, D.C.: U.S. Government Printing Office, 1976), p. 80.

In sum, victimization surveys have found that some segments of society represent greater target populations for crime than other segments. The single most likely victim of index offenses is the young black male—the member of the population segment that also, as we noted in Chapter 3, is more likely to commit such offenses. The higher crime and victimization rates for this group testify to the consequences of socioeconomic inequality.

The victimization patterns described above, basic though they may be, should aid in crime-prevention strategies. Higher burglary rates for the poor, for example, should prompt some thought concerning preventive patrols. Equally important, however, the victimization patterns should cause the average citizen to give serious consideration to his or her own chances of victimization. As we noted in previous chapters, an increasing public fear of crime has prompted changes in people's personal habits and resulted in increased pressure being brought to bear on government agencies. However, the average citizen must recognize that victimizations are not random occurrences and that, for many, such changes in personal habits are needless.

Victim-Offender Relationships

Von Hentig's (1948) thesis that crime victims bring about their victimizations and Wolfgang's (1957) report that at least 20 percent of homicides are "victim precipitated" (see Chapter 2) have slowly focused criminological attention on the relationship of victim to offender. An examination of crimes reported in the newspapers of any major city reveals that many are committed by persons known by the victims. Here are two examples from the New Orleans Times-Picayune:

> A 15-year-old girl was raped Friday night while babysitting. Police arrested [a 19-year-old] after the girl reportedly identified him as the attacker. According to police reports, the girl invited the man, who was a friend, to visit her while she babysat. [After] she asked him to leave, he forced her into a bedroom and allegedly committed the rape (1978a).
>
> The young men were playing pool in the back room of a First Street bar . . . when 19-year-old Willie Moran criticized a shot his half-brother, 25-year-old Vernon Pittman, had just made.
> "When I want advice from boys, I call 'em by name," sneered Pittman. . . .
> That stung Moran. "Don't call me boy," he retorted. . . . The two exchanged words. Everyone who talks about it now calls it a minor incident, no big thing. No one thought it was serious until the young Moran pulled out a small, chrome, .32 caliber snub nose revolver.
> "Put that away before you hurt someone," said Pittman.
> "You don't think I'll shoot you, do you?" asked Moran, who then fired once, hitting his half-brother in the stomach . . . (1978b).

The 1975 FBI *Uniform Crime Reports* indicates that 30 percent of the nation's homicides were committed by persons who knew the victim well or were related to the victim. Another 38 percent involved "other arguments," many of which presumably occurred between acquaintances. A recent survey by the National Institute of Law Enforcement and Criminal Justice (1977:20) of 238 law enforcement agencies reports that approximately 40 percent of reported rapes occur between acquaintances, friends, or relatives. A U.S. Department of Justice national victimization survey (1973:22) reports that one-third of violent offenses involved nonstrangers. Of these, assault is most likely to occur between nonstrangers (41 percent); rape (26 percent) and robbery (15 percent) by nonstrangers occur less often. Findings such as these clearly point to a need for an examination of victim-offender relationships for various types of crime. They also suggest that we should revise our stereotype of the criminal, that it is not always the stranger we should fear.

Victim-Precipitated Crimes

"Victim precipitation" has become a popular term in discussions of victim-offender relationships. Wolfgang (1957) seems to be the first to have used the term when he argued that as many as 20 percent of homicides result from violence initiated by the person who is the eventual victim of the altercation. That is, it is the eventual victim who strikes the first blow.

Amir (1971) further popularized the victim-precipitation theme through his study of forcible rape. Using police records, Amir analyzed 646 rapes that occurred in Philadelphia in 1958 and 1960. He found that in 58 percent of the rapes, the victim had at least some knowledge of the rapist's identity. In 47 percent of the cases, the rapist was at least an acquaintance of the victim. Spurred by these findings, he examined the role of the victim in the Philadelphia rape cases. In Amir's (1971:259) opinion, some rapes represent the victim's

> ... acting out, initiating the interaction between her and the offender, and by her behavior she generates the potentiality for criminal behavior of the offender or triggers this potentiality, if it existed before in him. Her behavior transforms him into a doer by directing his criminal intentions which not only lead to offense but also may shape its form.

Included within Amir's possibilities of victim-precipitated rape is the woman who supposedly gives sexual cues—wittingly or unwittingly—and somehow leads an offender to believe she desires sexual relations with him. Amir (1971:266) is unclear about what constitutes such cues but does note that they might include "indecency in language and gestures, or . . . what could be taken as an invitation to sexual relations." By Amir's estimate, 19 percent of the Philadelphia rapes were victim precipitated.

Criticism of the Idea of Victim Precipitation

The concept of victim precipitation, especially Amir's use of it, has drawn criticism. Not the least of the problems with the concept is that it has been overemphasized in subsequent summaries of Amir's work. The result is that victim-precipitated rape has come to be pictured as the norm rather than as the exception, and this misinterpretation has been used to bolster sexist views of rape. Beyond this, the term implies a passive offender, one who would not have committed his crime were it not for the victim's provocation, and an active victim, one who *intended* the offense to occur. "Proof" of this claim is often noted in the fact that some women do not physically resist the rapist. Such "evidence" takes little note of the fact the victim may be paralyzed with fear or certain that resistance will only increase her injuries (Weis and Borges, 1976:241).

The active victim–passive offender view of victimization has stressed the offender's interpretation of the victim's actions. Amir (1971:261) writes:

> The [precipitative] behavior can be of an outright and overt seduction, or covert and suggestive. Whether it is really so is not as important as the offender's interpretation of her actions within the then current situation. Because *even if erroneous*, it leads to action. . . . [The] offender may see the victim's behavior as being contrary to the expectation about appropriate female behavior as well as conflicting with the whole image of a woman's propriety. [Emphasis added.]

Whether or not the offender's definition of the situation is erroneous is more important than Amir would have us believe. If the offender's definition is correct, then the victim-precipitation concept is viable, and we should devote study as to why some females give such sexual cues. If the offender is misinterpreting the situation, however, then our research should be directed more toward his interpretative processes and less toward the victim's actions. It is certainly not unusual for rapists to claim that the victim's behavior was precipitative (Landau, 1973). Yet only one study has made any attempt to assess the accuracy of that claim, and it underscores the hazards in relying on the offender's definition of the situation as the criterion for determining the degree of victim precipitation. The research (Gebhard et al., 1965: 177–206) examined the sexual case histories of 146 persons convicted of sexual aggression against adult females. The investigators found that it is not unusual for such offenders to claim that the female encouraged the rape even though official records indicate that she required "five stitches taken in her lip" after the attack. Further, the rapists are often surprised at their arrests, claiming that the victims wanted it "since they did not fight the attacker or protest his actions." In other words, victim precipitation is defined rather liberally by offenders.

A final criticism of the victim-precipitation concept is offered by Franklin and Franklin (1976). They argue that causation and facilitation are often confused. That is, not every key left in an ignition results in a car theft. Nor can we speak of victim-precipitated (as opposed to facilitated) car theft if the thief was actively looking for a car to steal—the keys in the ignition did not cause the theft. Beyond this, the authors argue that at no time has victim precipitation been proven independent of the victimization itself. One cannot use the outcome of an act as an explanation of that act. Some other measure of victim precipitation must be devised.

In sum, we see that the victim-precipitation concept has numerous problems. It is logically flawed in the sense that it implies that a victim's provocation is necessary and sufficient for an offense to occur. It treats the offender as overly passive in the victimization situation. It suffers from measurement problems. And it carries questionable moral and legal implications (who is the guilty party?). Somehow, we must find an analytical framework that salvages the positive contribution of the victim-precipitation concept (that is, the demonstration of the fact that not all offenses reflect an active offender victimizing a passive victim) while avoiding its flaws.

Victim-Offender Interaction

In an effort to avoid the pitfalls of the victim-precipitation concept, we suggest that offenses be understood in terms of the extent that they involve interaction between victims and offenders and the extent of activity or passivity of both parties. In so doing, we need not become involved in problematic issues of cause and unconscious intent on the part of the victim. Instead, we may develop a continuum of various victim-offender patterns of interaction and describe their implications for anticrime policy.

With the exception of some victimless crimes, every crime involves at least two parties, an offender and a victim. We must assume that a crime is the product of the interaction of two social-action systems, the offender's and the victim's. As the continuum in Figure 5–7 indicates, the activity and passivity of either of these parties may vary greatly and produce very different types of offenses. A victim may be passive and, simply by fate, become the target of an offender (situation A in Figure 5–7). The shopper whose purse is snatched and the man who is robbed while leaving his office building are victims of this type. The activity level of the victim increases when, for example, keys are left in the automobile or one walks through New York's Central Park at two in the morning (situation B). An assault by one person upon another when both are ready to come to blows represents yet another increase in victim activity, this time roughly equal to that of the offender (situation C). Some crimes involve victims who are more active than the offender—for instance, a homicide in which the victim strikes the first blow (situation D). Finally, there is the rare case of the active victim and the passive offender (situation E). The best example available is the crime of passion occurring when, for instance, an individual discovers his or her spouse in bed with another and impulsively assaults either or both of the lovers.

The continuum illustrated in Figure 5–7 may eliminate some of the problems with the traditional victim-precipitation concept. Although it leaves open the possibility of offenses intended or caused by the victim, it does not assume either intention or causation in cases deviating from situation A. To point to a victim's more than passive role in an offense neither suggests that the victim desired or caused it nor absolves the offender of guilt. Thus, while we may argue that the person

Figure 5-7
Victim-offender interaction situations

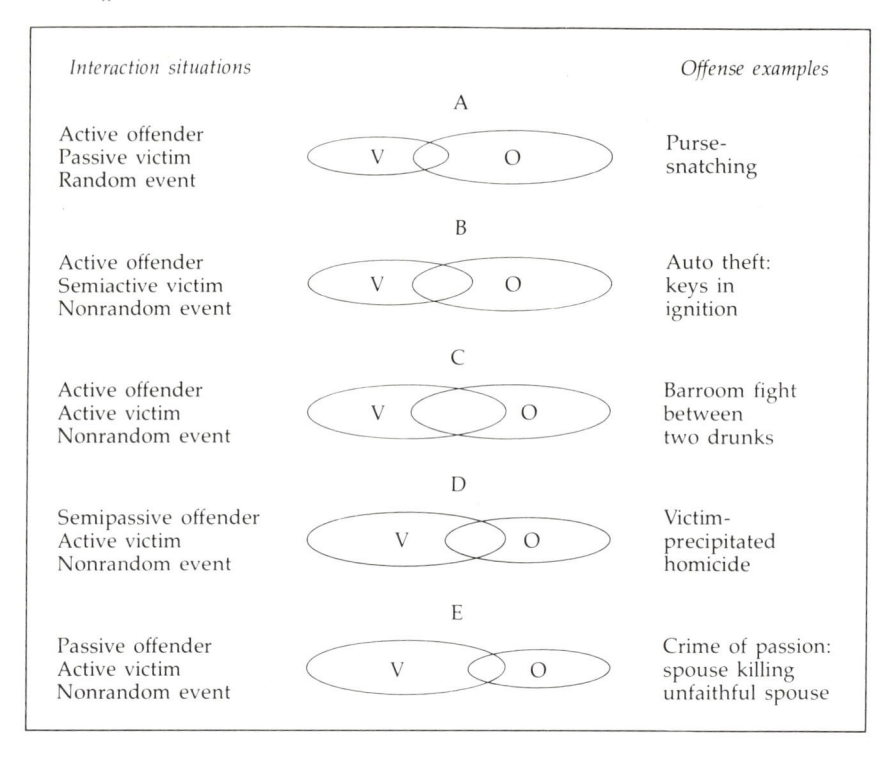

Interaction situations		Offense examples
Active offender Passive victim Random event	A V O	Purse- snatching
Active offender Semiactive victim Nonrandom event	B V O	Auto theft: keys in ignition
Active offender Active victim Nonrandom event	C V O	Barroom fight between two drunks
Semipassive offender Active victim Nonrandom event	D V O	Victim- precipitated homicide
Passive offender Active victim Nonrandom event	E V O	Crime of passion: spouse killing unfaithful spouse

who enters Central Park at night more actively facilitates a mugging than one who enters the park during the day, we do not argue that either wishes to be mugged. Nor is the mugger any less a criminal at night than during the day.

Immediate Environment

To complicate the notion of victim-offender interaction somewhat, we must also recognize that a third element in an offense situation also helps form its outcome—namely, the immediate social environment. The environment in which the interaction occurs is probably as important as the predispositions and actions of the interactants in determining whether or not a crime results. In fact, it undoubtedly partly shapes the extent to which the victim takes an active or a passive role in the offense. The immediate social environment includes all aspects of the arena in which the interaction occurs: physical characteristics (a room, outdoors, and so on) and other persons and the degree to which they participate in the event. For example, the result of a marital dispute may be violence or simple yelling, depending on where the disagreement occurs, how many other people are present, and whether or not those present encourage, discourage, or ignore the dispute.

Theoretical and Policy Implications

Taking a victim-offender interaction approach to the study of crime carries implications for a number of policy areas.

Crime Prevention

Greater knowledge of victim-offender relationships for specific forms of crime would greatly aid in crime-prevention strategies. What is especially needed is a description of various crimes in terms of degree of victim-offender interaction. Homicide and robbery represent contrasting examples. We noted in Chapter 2 that between 66 and 75 percent of homicides occur between relatives or acquaintances. It appears that most of these cases would fall within situations C, D, and E of Figure 5-7. The police are relatively powerless to prevent such murders. Thus, it would be foolish to allocate police resources as if the majority of murders were street crimes, falling within situations A and B of Figure 5-7 and theoretically preventable by police patrols. However, our discussion of robbery in Chapter 3 suggests that most robberies occur between strangers. Thus, we would expect them to fall within situations A and B of Figure 5-7 and therefore to be more preventable. Depending upon which situation—A or B—best reflects robberies, increased police patrols and decoy work (responding to situation A) or increased public education about potential robbery situations (responding to situation B) might effect a change in robbery rates.

Correction of Offenders

Current knowledge of victim-offender interactions indicates that there are degrees of predatoriness among offenders. Corrections programs traditionally design their rehabilitation programs around the classification of offenders by type of offense for which they have been convicted. Perhaps their success rates could be improved if prisoners were also classified according to patterns of interaction with victims in their offenses, if such patterns can be found. Offenders who habitually commit crimes falling within situations A and B of Figure 5-7 are clearly more asocial and predatory than those committing crimes of the situation C, D, or E variety and would require evaluation and treatment aimed at making the offender more responsive to social norms and the rights of others. Offenders who are continually involved in offense situations of types C, D, and E seem to be displaying an inability to sustain interactions with others within conventional bounds. Evaluation and treatment of these persons would be directed toward making the individual better able to interact with others.

Compensation of the Victim

Many believe that the victim is the forgotten person in legal and criminological interest in crimes. As noted in Chapter 1, criminal law treats offenses as acts against the state, not against its individual members. Violations are punished by and on behalf of the state, not the victim.[1] Similarly, governmental programs and criminological research have concentrated on treatment of the offender. Little attention has been devoted to the negative consequences of crimes for victims and to methods of combating these consequences.

One recent political response to the plight of the victim is consideration by state legislatures of victim-compensation programs (see Geis: 1976). These programs provide some form of monetary compensation from public funds to crime victims. At present, fewer than twenty states have such programs, though more are expected to develop them if the U.S. Congress approves federal subsidies for state compensation programs.

States with victim-compensation programs vary somewhat in underlying philosophies regarding aid to victims. Many seem to justify aid by claiming that the government is responsible for protecting citizens from criminals. When crimes occur, the government has failed its responsibility and should compensate victimized citizens. Others point to the welfare principle held by most states: people in need through no fault of their own should be helped by the government. Finally, some argue that, at the present time, potential criminal victimization should be considered as much a fact of everyday life as health and employment problems and natural disasters. If federal and state governments can administer various insurance and compensation programs for the latter ills, they can widen the scope of the programs to offset losses from crime (expenses resulting from injury or death, loss of earning power, losses by dependents, and pain and suffering).

States with victim-compensation programs also vary in organization and administration of the programs. Some favor an autonomous quasi-judicial body to handle claims, others favor expansion of current court systems to deal with claims, and others argue for assignment of

---

[1] There are exceptions to this general rule. Occasionally a court sentence will require some form of restitution to the victim of a crime. Embezzlers are often required to make at least partial repayment of the money they misappropriated, for example.

compensation programs to extant organizations such as the state welfare department. Whatever their differences in administration techniques, most of the programs offer compensation only to victims of violent crime that is not family-related. Most set a limit on the amount that can be awarded to a victim. In some jurisdictions, the victim must be able to show financial need before receiving state money. Finally, most consider the degree to which a crime was "victim precipitated" in arriving at a just compensation.

Critics of victim-compensation programs claim that they will encourage more crime by discouraging citizens' fear of crime's consequences and subsequent precautions to avoid victimization. It is also argued that compensation programs will eliminate feelings of guilt by criminals, who will feel free to steal or injure knowing that the losses or injuries will be "insured." Finally, some critics argue that victim-compensation programs represent a demoralizing statement as to the hopelessness of crime prevention, encouraging society to "live with crime" and perhaps encouraging exaggerated claims of injury to gain compensation funds.

In rebuttal, proponents of victim-compensation programs argue that it is unlikely that many people will purposely place themselves in danger of serious physical harm for a limited monetary reward that they would have to convince the state they deserve. Nor is it likely that criminals will make the possibility of state compensation of their victims a major factor in decisions about whether to commit a crime. Exaggerated injury claims could be offset by effective management of compensation programs. Finally, proponents argue that if society becomes demoralized by the crime problem, victim-compensation programs will not be the primary cause of the demoralization.

Clearly, then, we see a shifting social concern for the victim, which in turn fosters a similar criminological concern, for victim-compensation programs require research into victim-offender relationships. At the most obvious level, the research results can help form the basis for criteria concerning victim precipitation used in awarding compensation. At a more general level, knowledge about victim-offender relationships can aid policymakers in making decisions concerning the types of victim-compensation programs necessary for various states and communities.

In sum, recent interest in victimization patterns and victim-offender relationships has raised a number of research problems that will occupy criminologists for some time. Most basic among these problems is the assessment of the victimological implications of various forms of crime. While we know much about some offenses (such as homicide), we know very little about others (such as arson). We conclude this chapter with an example that illustrates that most offenses have at least *some* victimological implications, even commercial and corporate crimes.

An Example: Victims of Commercial and Corporate Crime

Gilbert Geis (1973) has enumerated some of the victimization patterns and implications of two forms of white-collar crime, commercial and corporate crime—crimes related to the furtherance of business interests. He notes that this crime category includes such offenses as "antitrust violations, false weighing and measuring by retailers, commercial espionage, and deceptive advertising" (1973:90).

Victimization Patterns

According to Geis, patterns of victimization in commercial and corporate crime are more difficult to discern than are patterns for other offenses. Occasionally, we can point to a specific victim, as in the theft of trade secrets by a competitor or the overcharging of a customer by a mechanic. More often than not, however, it is the general consumer who is victimized, through unnecessary price increases for goods and services (the result of such offenses as corporate price fixing) or lost government revenue (the result of corporate tax evasion). Commercial and corporate victimization is not a matter of businessmen searching out a weak prey, though an unorganized and unaware public is weak. Instead, victims will be any persons whose losses will help resolve an offender's financial difficulties. Thus, the strong (other businesses) and weak (the poor, the elderly) are both likely targets.

Victim Involvement

There is little evidence of victim precipitation or active victim involvement in commercial and corporate crimes. For many types of such offenses—for example, overpricing merchandise—victimizations are randomly distributed and victims enter into the offense passively. For other types—for instance, physician malpractice or overcharging—certain classes of people are more vulnerable: the uneducated, the poor, the elderly. Again, however, their involvement in the offense is highly passive.

Anticrime Policy

Victimization patterns for commercial and corporate offenses are linked to policies to combat them or, more precisely, to a lack of such policies. Elimination of such crimes is hindered by the lack of a complaining victim. Specific victims are often too embarrassed to complain. The more general victim, the public, is either unaware of the offenses or not disturbed by them. The lack of public indignation is due to the relatively small losses suffered by individual members of society, the fact that many of these acts have only recently been criminalized and therefore lack traditional moral weight, and the fact that perpetrators are powerful enough to control the mass media to the extent that public ire is not provoked. Geis's discussion makes it abundantly clear that commercial and corporate crimes will continue until victimization patterns are deciphered and impressed upon the public.

Summary

In this chapter, we introduced the victim into the "crime problem," with important implications for the average citizen's crime fears and for various types of anticrime policy. The discussion suggests that victimization is not a random occurrence. Some classes of persons are more likely targets of crime than are others. The extent to which individuals must fear and take precautions against victimization therefore varies. It would seem appropriate that the average citizen attempt to calculate his or her apparent chances of being a victim before devising personal anticrime strategies.

Governmental anticrime policies should also be grounded in knowledge about societal victimization patterns. Resources are easily wasted if the patterns are ignored. Further, this chapter's discussion of victim involvement in various types of crime indicates the need for research into victim-offender interaction patterns for most forms of crime. Such research holds great promise for crime-prevention strategies, treatment of offenders, and compensation of victims.

References

Amir, Menachim
    1971   Patterns in Forcible Rape. Chicago: University of Chicago Press.
Franklin, C., and A. Franklin
    1976   "Victimology revisited." Criminology 14:125–36.
Gebhard, P. H., J. H. Gagnon, W. B. Pomeroy, and C. V. Christenson
    1965   Sex Offenders: An Analysis of Types. New York: Harper.
Geis, G.
    1973   "Victimization patterns in white-collar crime." Pp. 89–105 in I. Drapkin and E. Viano (eds.), Victimology: A New Focus, Volume V. Lexington, Mass.: Lexington.
    1976   "Crime victims and victim compensation programs." Pp. 237–59 in W. F. McDonald (ed.), Criminal Justice and the Victim. Beverly Hills, Calif.: Sage.
Landau, S. F.
    1973   "The offender's perception of the victim." Pp. 137–54 in I. Drapkin and E. Viano (eds.), Victimology: A New Focus, Volume I. Lexington, Mass.: Lexington.

National Institute of Law Enforcement and Criminal Justice
    1977   Forcible Rape: A National Survey of the Response by Police. Washington, D.C.: U.S. Government Printing Office.

New Orleans Times-Picayune
    1978a   "Police reports." January 9, sec. 1:6.
    1978b   "Teen is convicted of killing brother." January 12, sec. 1:9.

Skogan, W. G.
    1976   "The victims of crime: some national survey findings." Pp. 131–48 in A. L. Guenther (ed.), Criminal Behavior and Social Systems, 2d ed. Chicago: Rand McNally.

U.S. Department of Justice
    1976   Criminal Victimization in the United States—1973. Washington, D.C.: U.S. Government Printing Office.

von Hentig, Hans
    1948   The Criminal and His Victim: Studies in the Sociobiology of Crime. New Haven, Conn.: Yale University Press.

Weis, K., and S. S. Borges
    1976   "Rape as a crime without victims and offenders? A methodological critique." Pp. 230–54 in E. Viano (ed.), Victims and Society. Washington, D.C.: Visage.

Wolfgang, M.
    1957   "Victim-precipitated criminal homicide." Journal of Criminal Law, Criminology and Police Science 48:1–11.
    1958   Patterns in Criminal Homicide. Philadelphia: University of Pennsylvania Press.

Suggested Readings

As Chapter 5 has indicated, victimization is a relatively unexplored aspect of crime. The Department of Justice victimization surveys cited in this and other chapters provide the majority of our data concerning victims and crime situations. I. Drapkin and E. Viano have collected a large number of papers on various aspects of victimology. They appear in five volumes under the general title, *Victimology: A New Focus* (Lexington, Mass.: Lexington, 1973). Viano has also edited another volume of victimology papers, *Victims and Society* (Washington, D.C.: Visage, 1976).

    As interest in victimology grows, more books and articles should appear. Recently, for example, D. F. Luckenbill has analyzed criminal homicides to determine to what extent they are the product of interaction between offender and victim. See his article, "Criminal Homicide as a Situated Transaction," *Social Problems*, December 1977:176–86.

Part Three

Creating Crime and Criminals

People tend to view American society and its criminal justice system as *reacting* to a crime problem. In many ways, this is correct. ☐ Yet it is also correct to say that society and various criminal justice agencies *create* crime problems. They do so by choosing to outlaw certain types of behaviors and determining when, how, and against whom to enforce laws. Thus, our crime situation is not simply an occurrence; it is, at least partially, a product of organizational activity. ☐ Chapters 6, 7, and 8 pursue this theme.

6

Criminal Labels

So far in this book, we have been concerned with more traditional criminological questions: How much crime? Who commits crimes? Why are they committed? Who is victimized? As we hinted in previous chapters, however, recently many criminologists have shown interest in other questions, one of the more important being: Why do we call certain acts and certain people "Criminal?"

At first glance, this question seems to have a simple answer. We call acts "crime" when they pose a threat to society. We label people "criminal" when we catch them committing these acts. Definitions of people and acts as criminal are not so neatly explained, however. A number of assumptions may be called into question. Can we speak of society as if all members are affected similarly by crime? Can we easily say what constitutes a threat for society or groups within it? Is breaking the law the only criterion for gaining criminal status? Will it assure this status?

In this chapter, we will explore criminal status as a definitional problem through discussions of interest groups, labeling, and crime. We suggest that the worth or quality of acts and persons is primarily a matter of the meanings we give them. The *interest-group conflict perspective* examines such meanings as they relate to the economic, status, and power interests of various groups in society. Who or what is called criminal at a given time reflects the socioeconomic power relationships of that time. The *labeling perspective* investigates the processes by which individuals are selected and defined as criminals and the effects of this label on them.

Both of these perspectives are important to public perceptions of the crime problem and its potential solutions, for they foster a healthy skepticism about crime and its control. As we shall see, they tend to make people more cautious when confronted with proclamations about the "threat of crime" and proposals to outlaw certain acts. As noted in the introduction to this book, this critical approach helps form a framework for asking questions first and acting later. Hence, potentially disastrous "knee-jerk" responses to crime are more easily avoided.

The Interest-Group Conflict Perspective

At base, the interest-group conflict perspective argues that no act or individual is intrinsically moral or criminal, immoral or noncriminal. If a criminal label is attached to an act or a person, there is an underlying reason; such definitions serve some interests within society. If these labels are tied to interests, then they are subject to change as interests change. Thus, every definition of an act as immoral, deviant, or criminal (or as acceptable) must be viewed as tentative, always subject to redefinition.

Prime examples of the definition-redefinition process are seen in our perpetually changing attitudes, laws, and law-enforcement patterns concerning "vices." Several states have recently decriminalized certain sexual acts between consenting adults. At one time, possession of marijuana was legal in this country; currently it is not, though recent public opinion suggests that it may again become legal. Abortion, once illegal, has been given new legal definitions. Gambling, once illegal in Atlantic City, New Jersey, has recently been legalized. Prostitution is legal in certain areas of Nevada but outlawed in all other states. Being the customer of a prostitute is likewise legal in some states but not in others. For all of these acts, we may wonder which definition reflects their "true" quality or nature: evil (illegal) or good (legal). In practice, we must treat current meanings as "truth," for they are the meanings that count in a court of law. From a conflict perspective, however, we soon realize that nothing is inherently sacred or sacrilegious; all definitions are subject to change.

Some may argue that the emphasis of the conflict perspective on the relativity of moral and criminal definitions is easily demonstrated with respect to "vices," about which there is little societal consensus, but may not apply so easily to acts that seem uniformly defined by most people over time. For example, cannot murder be called intrinsically wrong if nearly everyone considers it wrong and has done so for a very long time?

The conflict theorist will likely counter that universal acceptance of a criminal definition, even for a long time, may be mere coincidence and certainly need not be permanent. Radical structural changes such as those created by a severe famine or cultural changes like those fomented in Germany by the Nazis during the 1930s could cause changes in the value placed on human life (see, for example, Hughes, 1962). Further, the conflict theorist might argue that definitions of homicide are currently being negotiated. Continual legislative and courtroom debates over the criminal status of abortion and euthanasia are, at base, debates about the limits of acceptable life-taking versus criminal homicide. The same holds true for the fight over capital punishment. Finally, history suggests that a revolutionary political assassin's status as hero or murderer depends on the success of the revolution, not on the act itself.

Functions of Crime

If definitions of morality and legality are relative, we must ask: Relative to what? As a general rule, definitions of criminal acts reflect the interests of various members of society—sometimes all, sometimes the majority, and sometimes a powerful minority. Emile Durkheim provided some classic statements about the functions of crime for a society:

> Crime is a factor in public health, an integral part of all healthy societies (Durkheim, 1958:67).

> Crime brings together upright consciences and concentrates them. We have only to notice what happens, particularly in a small town, when some moral scandal has just been committed. They stop each other on the street, they visit each other, they seek to come together to talk of the event and to wax indignant in common. From all the similar impressions which are exchanged, for all the temper that gets itself expressed, there emerges a unique temper, more or less determinate according to the circumstances, which is everybody's without being anybody's in particular. That is the public temper (Durkheim, 1933:102).

Both Durkheim and, later, G. H. Mead (1918) were pointing up a paradox about crime. While it has obvious dysfunctions for a community—cost, injury, disruption—it may also be functional in some important ways. Crime and other forms of deviance tend to remind members of a community about the interests and values they share. Community bonds are strengthened in the common outrage and indignation inspired by a deviant act. Further, deviance reassures individual members of a community of their own moral normality and forthrightness.

Some authors caution us not to emphasize the functions of deviance alone. While noting the unifying functions of punishment, Mead (1918:91) also points out that punitive reactions to deviance lead to repressive societal conditions that stifle the creativity that deviance often represents. Repressive hostility will also prevent societal self-examination and subsequent attempts at improvement. Finally, Coser (1956:87–95) notes that if solidarity is weak in the first place, deviance and reactions to it can divide a community into factions.

The "functions of deviance" theme continues to be explored, however. Some students of Durkheim suggest that a society actually encourages, or at least allows, a certain amount of deviance for its functional aspects. Obviously, the balance between functional and dysfunctional amounts of deviance is delicate. Too much would destroy a society, yet too little would mean the loss of societal unification derived from deviance. This unification function is so imperative that Durkheim (1958:67) once noted that if all present forms of criminal activity were suddenly eliminated, a society would immediately create new forms. Even in a society of saints, he wrote, "faults which appear venial to the layman will create the same scandal that the ordinary offense does in ordinary consciousness."

Kai Erikson's (1966) study of deviance in the early Puritan colonies has furthered Durkheim's work. He discovered three "crime waves" during the first sixty years of settlement in Massachusetts: the Antinomian controversy (a challenge to the community's religious establishment), the arrival of the Quakers from Pennsylvania, and the Salem witches hysteria. All precipitated considerable turmoil. Erikson notes, however, that these crime waves were matters of shifts of public attention from one form of trouble to another. In fact, despite the crime waves, crime rates remained relatively stable over the six decades. In Erikson's mind, this suggests a deviance "quota"—that is, the encouragement or allowance of a sufficiently functional amount of deviance.

Erikson's study of the three Puritan crime waves also caused him to extend Durkheim's notion of the unification functions of deviance. He argues that crime in the colonies served certain boundary definition and maintenance functions. Deviance and reactions to it helped set the boundaries of acceptable behavior and provide a sense of stability and direction for a fledgling society. As time passes, these boundaries tend to become somewhat vague and new possibilities of societal growth arise. Deviance again causes the society to refocus on its character and mission, to reemphasize the common beliefs and interests of its members. Deviance thus serves to maintain the social and moral boundaries of societies.

Crime in the Larger Society

It is important to realize that Erikson's research was concerned with a small, highly homogeneous society. In general, the "functions of deviance" thesis applies to smaller societies far better than to larger, heterogeneous ones. In discussing crime in the larger society, we must heed Robert Merton's (1957:79–82) warning: "Functional for whom?" As a society grows and becomes more differentiated, it tends to form clusters, smaller subcultures or groups that differ from each other in world view, social status, and economic interests. Generally, these groups compete for various scarce economic and status rewards in society. Crime and deviance *within* these smaller segments of society may serve the same unification and boundary maintenance functions as crime in smaller societies such as the Puritan colonies. More importantly, however, definitions of and reactions to crime and deviance in the larger society are integrally tied to competition and conflict *among* the smaller segments or interest groups.

This society is composed partly of groups aware of and organized in various degrees to maintain and enhance their interests and partly of groups unaware of their interests and, therefore, unorganized (see Figure 6–1). Although the organized groups vary in their power to benefit themselves, none is so well organized that it enjoys total freedom in maintaining its interests. Power relationships and, therefore, the positions of interest groups in the power structure are continually subject to threat of change as groups increase or decrease in awareness and organizational might. New groups are constantly becoming conscious of and organizing around their interests and posing threats to the traditional power structure. The women's movement is a recent clear case in point.

There are three basic means of maintaining and enhancing interests in the larger society: force, compromise, and dominance of social institutions. Force is the least desirable, for it calls attention directly to interest preservation and basically dares others to summon enough counterforce to alter the power structure. Compromise is preferred, since all groups involved somehow benefit. Compromises and concessions bear witness to the absence of absolute power in the hands of any one interest group. All powerful groups require the support of other powerful groups above and below them in the power hierarchy. Further, no group can afford to incur the wrath of the unorganized. Failure to keep this group placated may result in discontent that breeds awareness of interest and organized threats to the status quo.

Compromises and concessions, though preferable to force, still carry liabilities. They point up the weaknesses of certain groups and encourage others to further organize to exploit those weaknesses.

Figure 6–1
Interest-group awareness and organization: examples

Awareness of interests	Organization around interests		
	High	*Moderate*	*Low*
High	Major U.S. corporations	NAACP	Homosexuals
Moderate	Unknown*	California migrant farm workers	Women
Low	Unknown*	Unknown*	Urban poor

*Since awareness generally precedes organization, it is difficult to conceive of degrees of organization higher than degrees of awareness.

Hence, the strongest mechanism for gaining or holding power is dominance of social institutions. Control of such institutions as the law, religion, education, government, economics, and science means control of the world views of members of society, especially regarding questions of interests and power. With respect to the problem of crime and criminals, control of legal institutions means that more powerful groups gain legal support for their interests by outlawing behaviors and attitudes that threaten them or by focusing attention away from their own legal wrongdoings. Control of other institutions, such as religion and education, is used to promote the interests of the more powerful by shaping the opinions of the less powerful concerning the legitimacy of the economic, political, and legal status quo.

Groups in power will have laws passed when they perceive their power position as threatened. Groups trying to gain power will attempt to influence legislation to benefit them. As Richard Quinney (1970:15) writes, laws that outlaw particular behaviors and make others mandatory are passed by legislators who have gained office through the backing of various interest groups. A group's ability to have its interests translated into public policy is, in fact, a primary indicator of power. No law exists in a vacuum; every law represents some group's interests. At times, a law may reflect the interests of nearly everyone—for example, laws against murder. At other times, laws protect the interests of more powerful segments—for example, tax laws.

Law enforcement also reflects group interests. Some laws receive more attention from the criminal justice system than do other laws. As we noted in chapter 2, more concern is given to larceny and burglary, for example, than to embezzlement and employee theft, though the latter crimes are more costly to the American public. The creation of laws necessitates the creation of law enforcers. Once formed, law-enforcement agencies themselves become interest groups whose existence may be threatened by other groups' attempts to decriminalize the behaviors they police. Hence, law-enforcement lobbies and public-relations divisions attempt to sway legislative and public opinion to preserve or strengthen laws against such activities as drug use, prostitution, homosexuality, and gambling.

Howard Becker (1973:135–46) provides an illustration of law-enforcement pressure groups in his discussion of the passage of the Marijuana Tax Act. Prior to 1937, the American public and governmental agencies charged with policing drug use showed little concern about marijuana. In the mid-1930s, the Treasury Department's Bureau of Narcotics began pressing for marijuana legislation. Its crusade included cooperation with state agencies in drafting antimarijuana laws and use of the mass media to sway public opinion against the drug.

Becker notes that numerous articles condemning marijuana suddenly appeared in popular journals and magazines of the time. Many contained atrocity stories about the effects of the drug. Most appealed to the same sentiment that had earlier caused the prohibition of alcohol and opiates: anything that causes the loss of self-control and is used purely for pleasure is evil.

In the spring of 1937, the Treasury Department approached Congress with proof of the popular sentiment that it had, in fact, created. In the summer of the same year, the Congress passed the Marijuana Tax Act, which allowed the Federal Bureau of Narcotics, under the auspices of revenue laws, to join with state agencies in arresting and prosecuting marijuana traffickers. In Becker's view, the fact that marijuana is presently outlawed in this country is the direct result of the work of an interest group, the Bureau of Narcotics, seeking to perpetuate its existence by creating its own "business."

In sum, the acts and people we call criminal at any given time reflect the work of various interest groups within society's current power structure. When these definitions become problematic, as is currently the case with abortion and mercy killing, we may assume a certain amount of instability in the power structure. Some groups are losing power; others are gaining it.

Some important points must be noted here. First, we must not assume that those groups in power are ever fully aware of their own interests or of their manipulation of institutions for their own ends. The institutional arrangement that legitimizes the power status quo shapes the world view of the more powerful as well as that of the less powerful. Thus, there are times when institutional changes would enhance the interests of the more powerful, but such changes are not pursued because they violate "moral principles" learned through such institutional structures as religion. Second, we must not assume that all group conflict involves economic interests. As we shall see in an example below, some conflict reflects moral, ideological, and status interests. Although a case can be made that all conflict is *indirectly* related to the economic structure, issues such as abortion and pornography clearly reflect conflicts that are not directly economic in nature. To illustrate both the economic and the noneconomic content of interest-group conflict, we offer two examples in the area of law: the development of vagrancy statutes and the passage of prohibition laws.

Example 1: Vagrancy Laws

Few people would look beyond the moral indignation that tramps arouse in a society dedicated to work and prosperity for the inspiration behind vagrancy laws. Yet a historical look at these laws indicates that they have had very little to do with morality or work ethics. Rather, as William Chambliss (1964) argues in an analysis of vagrancy statutes in Anglo-American law, the laws have generally been designed and used to protect special economic interests and to control "undesirables."

Chambliss notes that the first known law related to vagrancy was a 1274 statute in England that forbade religious houses from giving food or shelter to travelers. So many persons, rich and poor, had taken advantage of these houses that they faced financial ruin. The new law was designed to give them economic relief.

The first specific vagrancy laws in England were passed around 1350. These statutes made it a crime to give alms to anyone who was unemployed but healthy. Further, they made unemployment among the healthy illegal if work at the standard wage of the time was available. Finally, they prohibited movement from one county to another to find work for higher wages. These laws represented attempts by rural landowners to maintain cheap labor in the face of drastic labor reductions caused by the Black Death, a plague that struck England in 1348. The unemployment statutes effectively prohibited workers from economically "blackmailing" the landowners. The ordinance making it criminal to move in search of work was designed to prevent laborers from fleeing to rapidly industrializing larger towns, which offered higher wages.

England eventually recovered its economic footing, and revisions of the vagrancy laws did not appear again until 1530. New laws called for whippings, maimings, and imprisonment for beggars, transients, and people engaging in "unlawful games" (for example, peddlers and con men). Chambliss points out that these changes coincided with increased threats to England's movement toward international commercialism. Foreign merchants were becoming hesitant to enter the country because they were constantly being robbed on English roads. In an attempt to better control the "criminal classes" that undoubtedly included the robbers, the government passed harsher vagrancy laws.

The control pattern established by the 1530 laws continued into modern-day England and into the United States, until the U.S. Supreme Court recently struck down vagrancy laws. Vagrancy statutes have been used to control members of undesirable groups—the lower classes, racial and ethnic minorities, student radicals—and were used extensively in the Great Depression and dust-bowl era to prevent migrants from taking jobs or joining the welfare rolls of towns throughout the country.

In sum, Chambliss's examination of the history of vagrancy laws indicates that morality and law do not exist in a vacuum. At no time have the vagrancy laws been directed at vagrancy alone. Instead, they have been written and enforced to protect special interests. The analysis of the vagrancy laws should prompt us to take little for granted when faced with any legislative attempt to "control crime."

Example 2: Prohibition Laws

We noted earlier that not all interest-group conflicts are economic in nature. Nowhere is this made clearer than in Joseph Gusfield's *Symbolic Crusade* (1963), a historical analysis of the temperance movement in America. In addition to arguing persuasively that the fight over the prohibition of alcoholic beverages was primarily a cultural and status conflict, Gusfield suggests that contested behaviors often reflect deeper-rooted, less distinct issues.

According to Gusfield, nineteenth-century America was controlled primarily by rural, white, middle-class Protestants. The dominant cultural views of the era stressed moderation and hard work. Nondrinking was characteristic of higher-status groups, drinking a sign of lower status. The dominant position of the more powerful, higher-status groups was challenged in the late nineteenth and early twentieth centuries by the influx of new cultural values and life-styles accompanying massive European immigration into this country. America's newcomers—lower-class, predominantly Catholic, urban dwellers—placed different values on work and leisure, including drinking behavior. Alcoholic-beverage consumption played an important role in their leisure activities.

The focus of life in America began to shift. The traditional status position of rural, Protestant America began to erode. These general shifts were undoubtedly relatively imperceptible. Inevitably, some more tangible issue would rise to the surface and force a conflict symbolic of the deeper status and cultural problems. Gusfield argues that prohibition became this symbolic issue. A primary method of maintaining a group's status position is the translation of the group's views into public law. Enforced or not, a law represents a symbolic stamp of approval for the group it favors. Thus, the Prohibition laws of 1919, banning the importation, manufacture, and sale of alcoholic beverages, represented a symbolic victory for traditional higher-status Americans. Life in America seemed destined to remain as it had been for these people. The dream faded with the repeal of the Eighteenth Amendment in 1933, a symbolic defeat for the traditional higher-status groups. The end of Prohibition signaled the coming of major political and cultural changes in America.

Gusfield's analysis of the symbolic content of an interest group–initiated law might also be applied to more recent legal debates over such issues as pornography, abortion, liberalized homosexual laws, and gun control. The legislation and enforcement of drug laws in the 1960s may have symbolized an attack on "New Left," "unpatriotic," anticapitalist, antiwar college youth by "middle America" seeking to preserve traditional values. These examples suggest that we always look beyond contested behaviors in the larger, more complex society for the underlying issues they mask.

The Labeling Perspective

In the mid-1960s the interests of some students of crime and deviance began to shift. Frustrated with the inability of causal analysis to produce significant answers to traditional criminological questions, their concern with these questions began to fade. The discovery, through self-reported deviance studies, that most people violate the law but few are treated as criminals suggested a new line of inquiry. Rather than ask why people commit crimes, some criminologists began to ask why and how people come to be called criminals. This approach developed into the *labeling perspective*, the study of the process by which an individual is defined as criminal by society and the effects of the definition on the individual's self-concept and behavior.

Initiated by Edwin Lemert (1951) and Howard S. Becker (1973), the labeling perspective quickly found favor with many criminologists. It continued a long-standing theoretical strain in sociology that stressed the negotiability of meanings given to people, objects, and acts and argued that social meanings emerge from the interaction of actors and reactors—no act has a predetermined meaning. Studies of various forms of deviance supported this view. The official diagnosis of an individual as mentally ill, for example, often appeared less a matter of the individual's disruptive actions and attitudes than a matter of his or her inability to successfully communicate with a mental-health diagnostician. Finally, the labeling perspective found social and political support during a period in our history when previously accepted values and ideas were being questioned. Causal analysis was rejected by many simply because it was *traditional*. The labeling perspective was accepted by many simply because it appeared *innovative* and *critical*. It refused to take for granted that criminal labels were simply the result of criminal acts.

Although the labeling perspective has never fostered a systematic set of theoretical propositions, it does rest on some identifiable assumptions:

1. Before individuals can be labeled criminal, their behavior must be observed or thought to be observed by society.
2. Societal observation must be followed by societal reaction. Individuals cannot be labeled criminal unless society reacts to their alleged offenses—that is, an act is void of social meaning until society attempts to give it a meaning.
3. Society's attempt to label people criminal may succeed or fail. The attempt alone will not guarantee the successful imposition of a label.
4. The outcome of the negotiation of a label between society and individuals involves more than qualities of alleged criminal acts. Characteristics (such as race, sex, economic situation) of the alleged offenders and the social and political

climate in which the negotiation occurs will also influence the outcome.
5. The eventual effects of labels for individuals are also negotiable, dependent on individuals' reactions to their labels, society's perception of those reactions, and society's willingness to negotiate.

The Process of Being Labeled Deviant

Figure 6–2 depicts the steps leading to the imposition of a deviant label on an individual. The process begins with the perception by society (or community or group) that an individual appears to have violated a societal norm. The violation—whether real or assumed—is referred to by labeling theorists as *primary deviation*. It is the stimulus that begins the labeling process. It provides something to which society can react. Norm violations that are not observed by society are meaningless

Figure 6–2
Stages in the labeling process

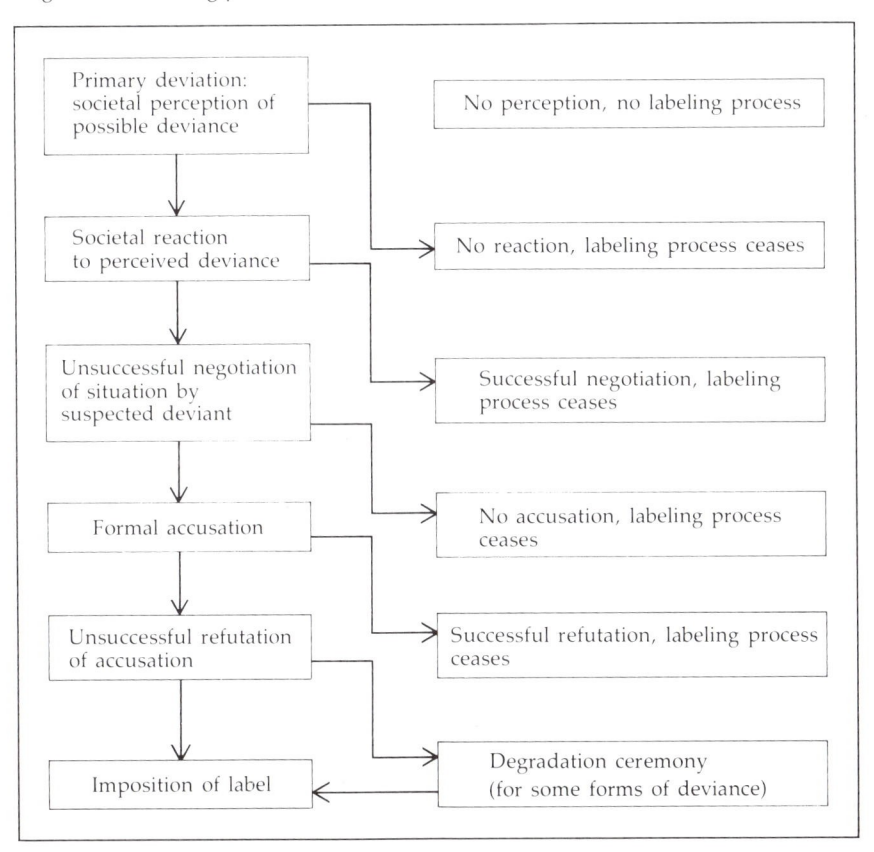

```
Primary deviation:
societal perception of  ─────►  No perception, no labeling process
possible deviance
        │
        ▼
Societal reaction
to perceived deviance   ─────►  No reaction, labeling process ceases
        │
        ▼
Unsuccessful negotiation
of situation by         ─────►  Successful negotiation, labeling
suspected deviant                process ceases
        │
        ▼
Formal accusation       ─────►  No accusation, labeling process
                                 ceases
        │
        ▼
Unsuccessful refutation ─────►  Successful refutation, labeling process
of accusation                    ceases
        │
        ▼
Imposition of label     ◄─────  Degradation ceremony
                                 (for some forms of deviance)
```

in terms of the eventual creation of a population of labeled deviants. Labeling theorists are not interested in the causes of primary deviation. They are concerned instead with what prompts societal reaction to it and the results that follow the reaction.

Perception or observation of primary deviation does not automatically lead to the imposition of a label. The average member of society often observes possible norm violations—some very serious—and does nothing by way of initiating a societal reaction. The decision to react, in the sense that the member of society makes verbal or nonverbal inquiries about the perceived deviance, highlights the fact that the deviant label is negotiable. For in making the decision to move toward reaction, the member of society takes into account various aspects of the situation and potential deviant. The potential deviant can influence the outcome of the decision-making process through his or her basic presentation of self. That is, age, sex, race, apparent socioeconomic status, dress, demeanor—all are factors with which the potential deviant influences the potential reactor. The potential reactor's biography and general attitudes about deviants, as well as the immediate environment in which the encounter occurs, will also influence the outcome.

Research by Steffensmeier and Terry (1973) illustrates the interactional quality of the early stages of the labeling process. They designed an experiment to determine whether the sex and appearance (hippie or straight) of an apparent shoplifter influence a customer's willingness to report the thief to store personnel. To find the answer, the researchers "staged" a number of shoplifting incidents in a store. An actor would very obviously steal an item of merchandise in front of a customer. He would then move out of hearing distance but within sight of the customer. A second actor played the role of a store employee and, as the shoplifter moved away, would enter the area in which the customer stood and arrange merchandise on the shelves. This would provide the customer with the opportunity to report the incident. If no report occurred, the store employee left and another actor-employee would approach the customer and ask if he or she had observed a shoplifting incident. Steffensmeier and Terry varied the sex and appearance of the shoplifter—male hippie, male straight, female hippie, female straight. They found that the sex of the shoplifter did not influence reporting, but the thief's appearance did. Customers were more likely to report hippies than straights. In other words, extralegal considerations such as dress enter into the negotiation process, which may eventually lead to a deviant label.

The negotiation process may continue to another level of interaction and negotiation. The decision to react—either personally or by referral to the rest of the society—does not ensure the imposition of a label. Rather, it demands an account from the potential deviant.

This account or explanation of the situation, together with social-environmental facts and various characteristics of the potential deviant, will determine whether or not the labeling process stops or continues.

Some examples will clarify matters. Assume that one man observes another cutting a chain that secures a bicycle to a pole. The observer, convinced that he sees a possible case of deviance, asks the chain cutter whether or not he is stealing the bicycle. Thus begins a negotiation process that will ultimately determine the direction of the labeling process. The interaction will be influenced by such environmental factors as whether or not the observer and potential deviant are alone or in a crowded area. Perceived social characteristics of both parties will also be influential—for example, the black observer of the white potential deviant will probably react differently from the white observer of the black potential deviant. Beyond this, the observer may demand an account of the apparent deviation. The potential deviant may either stand mute or provide an explanation of the situation. Either posture represents a response to the demand and will influence the observer's decision to react.

Not all accounts are sufficient to persuade the observer not to further the labeling process. Some accounts are socially more acceptable than others. That is, most acceptable accounts are merely extensions of societal beliefs that make certain forms of deviance acceptable, if not right (Mills, 1940; Matza, 1964). Delinquents may find a partially sympathetic ear, for example, when they account for beating a person by noting that the victim was some form of "second-class citizen," such as a homosexual (Hartung, 1965). Scott and Lyman (1968) argue that an account will be deemed illegitimate when the event it seeks to explain is more serious than the account allows. For example, a contractor can excuse a slight plumbing malfunction in a new house by pleading oversight. However, oversight is not a legitimate excuse for installing an entirely defective plumbing system in the house. Accounts are labeled unreasonable, Scott and Lyman further argue, when they exceed social expectations of normal behavior. To argue that one has shoplifted food because he or she is starving is to offer a far more reasonable account than if one claims he or she is driven by "inner voices." In sum, the labeling process will cease or continue depending on the social acceptability of the potential deviant's response to an observer's inquiries.

If the potential deviant—for example, the man cutting the bicycle chain—is unsuccessful in accounting for his actions, the observer will generally bring the matter to the attention of the rest of the community or society. Again negotiation occurs, centering on the seriousness of the alleged deviance of the potential deviant and the acceptability of his account. If the potential deviant again fails in his negotiation, he is subjected to the imposition of a deviant label—that is, he is no longer considered a potential deviant but is, in fact, considered a deviant.

Depending on the form of deviance in question, the social-political climate in which the labeling occurs, and various characteristics of the deviant, a status degradation process may also occur (see Garfinkel, 1956). That is, the label of deviant may be extended beyond reference to the fact that the labeled individual violated a norm and instead convey the meaning that the individual is *inherently* deviant. In fact, the society may engage in building a deviant biography for the individual; that is, try to make sense of the individual's present deviant act by reinterpreting past events. Thus, the surprising discovery that a friend thought heterosexual is, instead, homosexual will be followed by attempts to go back and review past interactions with the person for missed clues as to his or her sexual deviance (Kitsuse, 1962). Hence, we hear statements such as, "Now that I think about it, he always was kind of weird." Or, "She was always kind of quiet, kept to herself; I just never thought about it much until now." Or, "Thinking back, he never did talk much about girls."

The status degradation and deviant biography processes reflect society's attempts to remain secure in its definitions about deviants. If deviants are viewed as a special category of persons—whether evil or sick or both—protection from deviants becomes a matter of identifying and avoiding them or treating or incapacitating them. If, however, deviants are unpredictable—anyone may suddenly deviate—we lose our sense of security and feel unable to protect ourselves.

The Effects of Labeling

Whether totally or partially labeled, the stigmatized individual is now interacted with in terms of that label. The label is, in the words of Everett Hughes (1945), the individual's "master status," the primary attribute by which society identifies and refers to the deviant. For the nondeviant, the master status is based on such characteristics as age, sex, race, and occupation. For the deviant, the master status is based on the fact that the individual is or was deviant. Thus, we hear persons referred to as ex-convicts, mental patients, former alcoholics, and drug users, with only secondary reference to their other qualities.

Figure 6–3 depicts various consequences of a label for an individual. The figure also points out that the effects of a label are not predetermined but, like the label itself, emerge from an interaction with nondeviants and, sometimes, with other deviants. Although students of deviance have to this point not studied and identified the various combinations of variables in the interaction process, so that we can predict the effects of labeling, we do know that the variables include the seriousness of the deviance that led to the label, socioeconomic-status characteristics of the deviant, the social-political climate of the time, the posture adopted by the deviant regarding the label, and the extent of positive reinforcement from a deviant subculture.

Figure 6-3
Effects of labeling

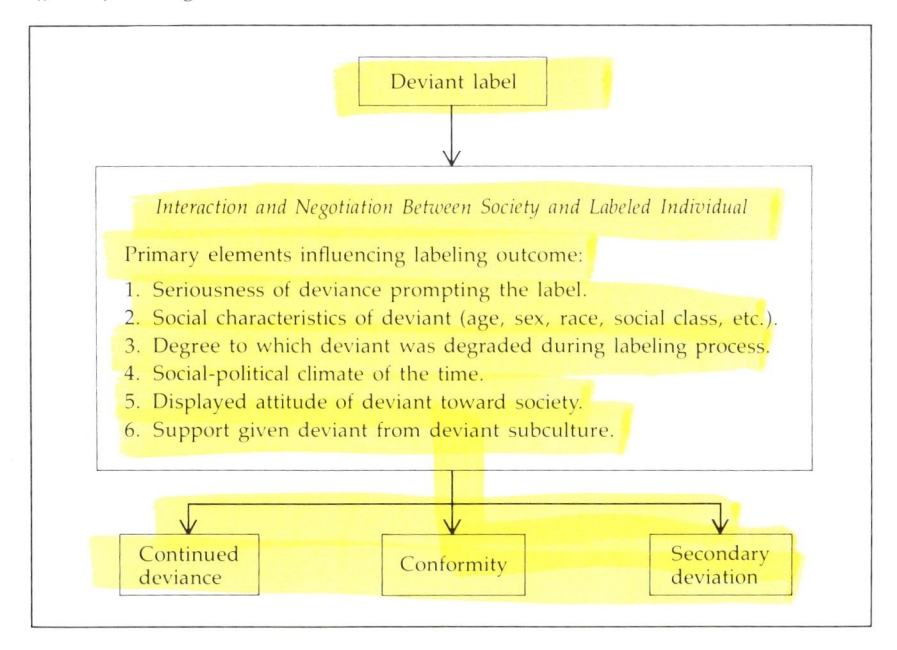

```
                    ┌──────────────────┐
                    │  Deviant label   │
                    └──────────────────┘
                              │
                              ▼
┌────────────────────────────────────────────────────────────────┐
│  Interaction and Negotiation Between Society and Labeled Individual │
│                                                                │
│  Primary elements influencing labeling outcome:                │
│  1. Seriousness of deviance prompting the label.               │
│  2. Social characteristics of deviant (age, sex, race, social class, etc.). │
│  3. Degree to which deviant was degraded during labeling process. │
│  4. Social-political climate of the time.                      │
│  5. Displayed attitude of deviant toward society.              │
│  6. Support given deviant from deviant subculture.             │
└────────────────────────────────────────────────────────────────┘
          │                    │                    │
          ▼                    ▼                    ▼
    ┌──────────┐         ┌──────────┐         ┌──────────┐
    │ Continued│         │Conformity│         │Secondary │
    │ deviance │         │          │         │deviation │
    └──────────┘         └──────────┘         └──────────┘
```

The seriousness of deviance and the socioeconomic status characteristics of the deviants—what they did and who they are—are fairly obvious determinants of the effects of labeling. Whether or not people were fully degraded as deviant will affect the extent of society's willingness to interact with them and perhaps "give them another chance." The social-political climate with regard to deviance is also important; for example, the consequences of being labeled a sex offender will vary depending on whether or not society is currently upset about this form of deviance. The posture of deviants with respect to their labels is also of consequence; for example, we can expect society to react somewhat differently to the deviant who acts repentant than to one who acts defiant. In addition, the acceptability of any accounts deviants may offer are important. Finally, the effects of a label will be influenced by the extent to which the deviant is able to find support from others. Occasionally a deviant subculture (discussed further below) will act as a buffer for a labeled individual and thus remove some of the sting of societal rejection.

The variables above determine the consequences of being labeled. Again, as with the imposition of the label in the first place, the consequences of a label are determined by a two-party negotiation between society and the deviant. As Figure 6-3 indicates, there are three possible consequences of labeling: conformity, continued deviance, and secondary deviance. The latter two can occur simultaneously.

Conformity or Deviance. Labeling can have positive effects in terms of converting deviants to conforming behavior. This is often the consequence of a family's imposition of the label of alcoholic or mentally ill on one of its members (Jackson, 1954). The label of alcoholic by the family may force the individual to accept the fact that he or she is deviant and to attempt to conform. If the social-political climate is acceptable—that is, the family is willing to readmit the alcoholic—the deviant may join Alcoholics Anonymous and cease drinking. Sometimes the seriousness of the deviance that occasioned the label causes a form of societal reaction that makes conformity the only possible outcome. Ostracism or imprisonment, for instance, means that an individual will no longer violate social norms.

Labeling can also have minimal effects on the deviant's behavior. If the seriousness of the deviance is minor or if the deviant refuses to accept society's label, it is possible he or she will simply continue the form of deviance that occasioned the label. Professional thieves, for example, are known to "do their time" in prison and return to theft immediately upon release (Letkemann, 1973). Or an alcoholic may accept society's definition of him or her as deviant and make no effort to reform, or may refuse to accept the label and continue drinking.

Secondary Deviance. The possible consequence of labeling that has gained the most attention is *secondary deviation*. According to Lemert (1951:76), "when a person begins to employ his deviant behavior or a role based upon it as a means of defense, attack, or adjustment to the overt and covert problems created by [his label], his deviation is secondary." Lemert thus argues that the label of deviant may force an individual into forms of deviance that would not have occurred had it not been for the labeling or into greater commitment to the deviance that occasioned the label than would otherwise have occurred.

The oft-told story of the problems of ex-convicts relates a classic example of secondary deviation. Having paid their debt to society and returned to the outside world, former prisoners soon discover that the label "ex-con" has many negative consequences. Unable to obtain work or legitimately secure money, they soon commit new crimes or drift into the company of other criminals and subsequently increase their own commitment to crime (see Irwin, 1970).

Labeling theorists have probably overemphasized secondary deviation in their writings. The result has often been a mistaken interpretation of the labeling perspective. Some have criticized labeling theory for apparently claiming that labeling *necessarily* causes secondary deviation (see Schur, 1971:7–36). The picture of deviants thus presented is that of individuals passively minding their own business until seized by society, labeled deviant, and forced to commit deviant acts. One need only review self-reported criminality studies to realize that much deviance occurs without societal reaction. The concept of "primary deviation" also suggests that not all rule violation is secondary. It must be stressed that labeling theory is not causal theory. Secondary deviation is but *one possible* outcome of labeling. Whether or not it occurs depends on the interaction of the variables depicted in Figure 6–3.

Deviant Subcultures. Labeling theorists' discussions of secondary deviation have often led to discussion of *deviant subcultures*. According to Becker (1973:81–82):

> Where people who engage in deviant activities have the opportunity to interact with one another they are likely to develop a culture built around the problems rising out of differences between their definition of what they do and the definition held by other members of the society. They develop perspectives on themselves and their deviant activities and on their relations with other members of the society. . . . Since these cultures operate within, and in distinction to, the culture of the larger society, they are often called subcultures.

In essence, Becker is referring to a mini-culture, a culture within a culture. Subcultures share the general values, traditions, and behaviors of the greater culture but also have values, traditions, and behaviors that are shared only within the subculture and that set it apart from the greater culture. Thus, we are able to speak of Italian-Americans, Mexican-Americans, and black Americans as subcultures.

We also can sometimes talk about deviant subcultures, groups set off from the majority of the society by the fact that they violate, or are thought to violate, certain norms honored by the majority. Further, they are committed to the norm violations in question and offer moral support to members of the subculture. In addition to being characterized by norm violations, subcultures are identifiable by their vocabularies and jargon. Members develop "languages" with which they can communicate with each other but that cannot be understood by outsiders. The average person could not easily communicate and interact with a group of jazz musicians, for example. As Becker (1973:100) notes about these musicians:

> The process of self-segregation is evident in certain symbolic expressions, particularly in the use of an occupational slang which readily identifies the man who can use it properly as someone who is not square and as quickly reveals as an outsider the person who uses it incorrectly or not at all. . . . Such words enable musicians to discuss problems and activities for which ordinary language provides no adequate terminology.

While we can point to some delinquent gangs (Short, 1968) and professional criminals (Letkemann, 1973) as deviant subcultures, two of the better examples are drug and homosexual subcultures (see Bell, 1976:175–209; 265–307). The subculture of drug addicts has its own language ("horse," "dealer," and so on), its own rules, and its own status symbols. The subculture teaches new members the skills necessary to carry on addiction without problems. In a sense, addict subcultures serve as information centers. They pass on knowledge about the quantity, quality, and availability of drugs. They also keep members informed about police activities and the availability of outlets for stolen goods to procure money for drugs. Highly important, the subculture provides positive support to the addict: rationales for addiction, comfort in the face of negative societal definitions, a shelter against isolation.

Like the drug subculture, the homosexual subculture represents a shared life-style, values, and a language that sets it somewhat apart from the larger culture. Although homosexuals differ in socioeconomic backgrounds, their interaction patterns have led to a subculture that cuts across these lines. The gay subculture provides a sense of identity for the homosexual and reinforces positive self-conceptions. Techniques for meeting other gays and for coping with the police and the public are transmitted through subcultural channels. For homosexuals who have "come out" (publicly admitted their homosexuality), the subculture may serve as the focal point around which friendships and leisure activities are planned. For those who have not "come out," it offers the opportunity for interaction with other homosexuals on an immediate, short-run basis. In recent years, the subculture has brought gays together politically in opposition to legislative attempts to constrain their movement in society.

According to the labeling perspective, the deviant subculture may be involved in the labeling process in a number of ways. First, an individual's drift into or decision to enter such a subculture may mark the primary deviation to which society reacts. Second, involvement in subcultural deviance may also cushion the society's reaction, thereby influencing the eventual outcome of the labeling process. Finally, and most important with respect to secondary deviation, labeling may place limits on an individual's social options, resulting either in isolation or drift into a deviant subculture. As the discussions above suggested, the deviant subculture provides support for the labeled deviant. It also induces the person into further commitment to the deviance. In this sense, labeling may cause secondary deviation—a greater involvement in and commitment to deviance than would be expected were it not for the label.

In sum, the labeling process is extremely open ended. The imposition of the label involves interaction between the actor and the labelers.

The effects of the labeling process are also governed by the interaction of the labeled deviant and the labelers. Labeling may produce conformity or deviance. Two examples illustrate this point.

Example 1: Labeling the Shoplifter

Amateur shoplifting appears to be one form of deviance that can be halted by actual or threatened labeling of the offender as criminal. The source of this change lies in the effect of labeling on the pilferer's self-conception. Cameron (1964) conducted a study of a sample of persons caught shoplifting in a Chicago department store between 1943 and 1950 and a sample of women charged in Chicago courts with shoplifting between 1948 and 1950. Cameron argues that pilferers—amateur shoplifters—differ from other thieves in that they do not view themselves as thieves or criminals. The typical pilferer is an adult woman from a modest-income family. Her budget is fixed to allow her to meet the family's basic food and clothing needs. There is little room for luxury purchases without cutting into the budget. Thus, the woman steals items for her own use and convinces herself that the theft is less wrong than to steal from the family money.

The arrest of the shoplifter by a store detective forces a confrontation with reality. Cameron notes that it is often difficult for the detective to convince the pilferer that he or she has actually been arrested. Interrogation of suspects is deliberately conducted in a manner calculated to shake their view that their actions are noncriminal. Thus, the shoplifters are treated as criminals—questioned, searched, made to explain the contents of packages and purses, informed that they will be tried in court. Store employees may be brought in to view the arrestees, as in a police lineup. This treatment leads to the shoplifters' recognition of their criminality.

Because the possibility of exposure to their families is viewed by shoplifters as a disgrace, this threat alone will generally deter future thefts. Cameron's data indicate that, even if they are not prosecuted, arrested shoplifters will usually not shoplift from department stores again. Cameron thus considers amateur shoplifters patently "reformable." The labeling (through arrest) of their actions as criminal eliminates that form of activity from the realm of acceptable behavior for them. Shoplifting cannot be reconciled with a positive self-image. In this sense, labeling produces conforming behavior.

Example 2: Labeling the Drug Addict

While labeling may produce conventional behavior among amateur shoplifters, the labeling process as it relates to other forms of deviance may propel labeled persons further toward nonconformity. Ray (1961) provides an illustration of this syndrome in his discussion of heroin addicts and their unsuccessful attempts to kick their habits.

Ray notes that addicts can be cured from the psychological dependence on opiates, that they continually and repeatedly seek cures, and, despite this, continually revert back to heroin. The key to both attempted cure and relapse seems to lie in the way others treat addicts. Addicts' attempted abstinence is generally prompted by identity and self-concept problems stemming from others' negative definitions of them. The success of their attempted cure depends greatly on the extent to which they can resume conventional interaction and relationships with nonaddicts. Their attempted cure also has publicly labeled them as addicts, and they must reverse the label and gain a feeling of acceptance.

Relapse occurs when ex-addicts are not able to feel a part of nonaddict society. They develop a view of self as socially different from nonaddicts. Sometimes this image is fostered by pressures brought to bear by addict acquaintances. Often it is caused by the inability of nonaddicts to see beyond the individual's label. Ray notes that nonaddicts can demonstrate degree of acceptance of the ex-addict by indicating how committed they feel ex-addicts are to nonaddict values, by referring to their former identities as addicts, and by "talking behind their backs" about their concern that they are not really cured.

Thus, the label causes social stress for ex-addicts, and they seek comfortable situations and persons with whom they can relate. This initiates a drift back to heroin. Relapse undoubtedly widens the gap between the addict and the nonaddict world, makes further attempts at abstinence more difficult, and, in this sense, propels addicts toward greater commitment to the drug subculture—a case of secondary deviation.

Summary

Chapter 6 has described an approach to the study of crime and criminals that highlights criminal labels. Unlike traditional criminological orientations, the interest-group conflict perspective and the labeling perspective do not take for granted definitions of acts and persons as criminal. Rather they view such definitions as tentative and negotiable. Criminal laws are reflections of the socioeconomic power structure in a social system. Changing laws and enforcement patterns indicate tension within the system. The labeling of an individual as criminal reflects both the structure of power in the society and the failure of the individual to successfully negotiate a conventional label following charges of primary deviation.

As noted in the introduction to this chapter, the conflict and labeling perspectives are important to public perceptions of crime and, generally, to policy recommendations concerning it. The ideas discussed above should prompt some questions about efforts to outlaw various activities and about the control of institutions that give us our picture of the "crime problem." Our knowledge of the labeling process should also lead to questions about the characteristics of the people we have come to call criminals and classes of people we suspect of criminal behavior. In this vein, Chapter 6 also serves as a general introduction to the coming chapters on the criminal-justice system. Specifically, we will examine that system as an organization that produces officially labeled criminals.

References

Becker, Howard S.
    1973   Outsiders, 2d ed. New York: The Free Press.
Bell, Robert
    1976   Social Deviance. Rev. ed. Homewood, Ill.: The Dorsey Press.
Cameron, M. O.
    1964   The Booster and the Snitch. New York: The Free Press.
Chambliss, William
    1964   "A sociological analysis of the law of vagrancy." Social Problems 12:67–77.
Coser, Lewis
    1956   The Functions of Social Conflict. Glencoe, Ill.: The Free Press.
Durkheim, E.
    1933   The Division of Labor in Society. Trans. by G. Simpson. New York: The Free Press.
    1958   The Rules of Sociological Method. Trans. by S. A. Solovay and J. H. Mueller. Glencoe, Ill.: The Free Press.
Erikson, Kai
    1966   Wayward Puritans. New York: Wiley.
Garfinkel, H.
    1956   "Conditions of successful degradation ceremonies." American Journal of Sociology 61:420–24.
Gusfield, Joseph
    1963   Symbolic Crusade. Urbana, Ill.: University of Illinois Press.
Hartung, F. E.
    1965   "A vocabulary of motives for law violators." Pp. 454–73 in D. Cressey and D. Ward (eds.), Delinquency, Crime, and Social Process. New York: Harper.
Hughes, Everett C.
    1945   "Dilemmas and contradictions of status." American Journal of Sociology 50:353–59.
    1962   "Good people and dirty work." Social Problems 10:3–11.
Irwin, J.
    1970   The Felon. Englewood Cliffs, N.J.: Prentice-Hall.
Jackson, J. K.
    1954   "The adjustment of the family to the crisis of alcoholism." Quarterly Journal of Studies on Alcohol 15:564–86.

Kitsuse, J. I.
    1962   "Societal reactions to deviant behavior: problems of theory and method." Social Problems 9:247–56.

Lemert, Edwin
    1951   Social Pathology. New York: McGraw-Hill.

Letkemann, Peter
    1973   Crime as Work. Englewood Cliffs, N.J.: Prentice-Hall.

Matza, D.
    1964   Delinquency and Drift. New York: Wiley.

Mead, G. H.
    1918   "The psychology of punitive justice." American Journal of Sociology 23:577–602.

Merton, R. K.
    1957   Social Theory and Social Structure. Glencoe, Ill.: The Free Press.

Mills, C. Wright
    1940   "Situated actions and vocabularies of motive." American Sociological Review 5:904–13.

Quinney, Richard
    1970   The Social Reality of Crime. Boston: Little, Brown.

Ray, M. B.
    1961   "Abstinence cycles and heroin addicts." Social Problems 9:132–40.

Schur, Edwin M.
    1971   Labeling Deviant Behavior. New York: Harper.

Scott, M. B., and S. M. Lyman
    1968   "Accounts." American Sociological Review 33:46–62.

Short, J. F., Jr. (ed.)
    1968   Gang Delinquency and Delinquent Subcultures. New York: Harper.

Steffensmeier, D. J., and R. M. Terry
    1973   "Deviance and respectability: an observational study of reaction to shoplifting." Social Forces 51:417–26.

Suggested Readings

A number of readings provide an understanding of legislation as a product of interest-group conflict. Quinney's *Social Reality of Crime*, Chambliss's "A Sociological Analysis of the Law of Vagrancy," and Gusfield's *Symbolic Crusade* are all cited in the Chapter 6 notes.

    The following readings are also particularly helpful: E. H. Sutherland, "The Diffusion of Sexual Psychopath Laws," *American Journal of Sociology*, September 1950, pp. 142–48; Jerome Hall, *Theft, Law and Society* (Indianapolis, Ind.: Bobbs-Merrill, 1952); Pamela A. Roby, "Politics and Criminal Law: Revision of the New York State Penal Law on Prostitution," *Social Problems*, Summer 1969, pp. 83–109; W. J. Chambliss, "The State, the Law, and the Definition of Behavior as Criminal or Delinquent," in *Handbook of Criminology*, ed. D. Glaser (Chicago: Rand McNally, 1974), pp. 7–43.

    All of these materials provide examples that illustrate that the creation and enforcement of laws are not simply reflections of how "the public" feels about certain behaviors. Rather, they are indicators of shifting power positions among major interest groups.

Among the books that can provide the reader with a more thorough grasp of the labeling perspective are Howard Becker's *Outsiders*, 2d. ed. (New York: The Free Press, 1973) and Edwin Schur's *Labeling Deviant Behavior* (New York: Harper & Row, 1971). A more critical discussion of the labeling perspective can be found in N. J. Davis' *Sociological Constructions of Deviance* (Dubuque, Iowa: Wm. C. Brown, 1975), pp. 164–91.

7

The Criminal Justice System and Its Products

When a society creates rules, it also creates the need for rule enforcers (Becker, 1973:155). In smaller societies, legislators and law enforcers may be the same persons. In larger societies, legal systems generally are more complex, and legislative, enforcement, and judicial duties become more distinct. Larger societies usually have highly developed criminal justice systems for preventing crime, apprehending suspects, determining legal innocence or guilt in criminal cases, and punishing or treating persons found guilty of crimes.

In this chapter we will analyze two elements of our criminal justice system: the police and the courts. Analysis of the corrections system is reserved for Chapter 8. The present discussion differs from most others on the subject in that it treats the criminal justice system as an organization that has two products: official crime rates and officially labeled criminals. In a very real sense, the ultimate product of the activity of the American criminal justice system is a *picture* of crime in this society. This picture is transmitted to the public and forms the basis of crime fears and demands for "law and order." As we shall see, whether or not this picture of crime and criminals reflects reality is open to question.

Criminal Justice Agencies

The criminal justice system in the United States is a collection of interrelated, semiautonomous bureaucracies. Figure 7–1 displays the various stages through which persons are processed in the criminal-justice system and indicates the primary agencies that comprise the system: law enforcement, prosecution, courts, and corrections. Law enforcement involves a diverse number of agencies such as local police and sheriff's departments and state and federal police organizations (for example, state and federal narcotics bureaus). Prosecutorial agencies, whether state or federal, investigate cases, make decisions about charges against criminal suspects, present cases to grand juries, negotiate pleas, and try cases in criminal courts. The courts supervise the treatment of accused persons, decide bail arrangements and trial dates, conduct trials, and sentence offenders. Finally, the corrections system is composed of prisons and probation and parole agencies that serve various custody, rehabilitation, and punishment functions.

Figure 7–1 does, however, present a somewhat deceptive picture of the interrelationships among the various criminal justice agencies. It suggests a far more organized and compatible system than actually exists. Ideally, a case would proceed through the criminal justice system in the following manner:

1. Police observe a possible offense or answer a complaint and initiate an investigation.
2. If the investigation indicates that a crime has occurred, the suspected offender is located and arrested.
3. The suspect is informed of his or her rights, taken to police headquarters, and booked; that is, the arrest is entered into police records. The suspect is also taken before a magistrate so that the arrest is duly noted.
4. The process now moves into the prosecutorial stages. The district attorney investigates the case and determines whether it warrants prosecution. If it is decided that charges are deserved, after a hearing before a magistrate concerning the merits of the evidence and the legality of the manner in which it was obtained, the D.A. will take the case to the grand jury and seek an indictment.
5. The grand jury, a representative group of citizens, hears the evidence presented by the prosecutor. If it agrees with the prosecutor, the grand jury returns a true bill or indictment, formally declaring that the suspect should be tried. If the grand jury does not indict, the prosecutor may still file an "information," the rough equivalent of an indictment.
6. The indicted suspect appears before a judge for arraignment. The formal charges are read and the suspect enters a plea: if guilty, the suspect is held for sentencing; if not guilty, he or she is given a choice of having the trial before either a judge or a jury.
7. A trial is held and the judge or jury reaches a verdict based on the evidence presented by the prosecutor and criticized by the defense attorney. If found guilty, the convicted criminal is held for sentencing.
8. In some cases, specific penalties are legally prescribed for an offense. In other cases, a judge has discretion in sentencing. Usually, the judge relies on a presentence report from probation officers in determining the sentence. Following sentencing, the criminal is turned over to the corrections department.

Figure 7-1
Overview of the criminal justice system

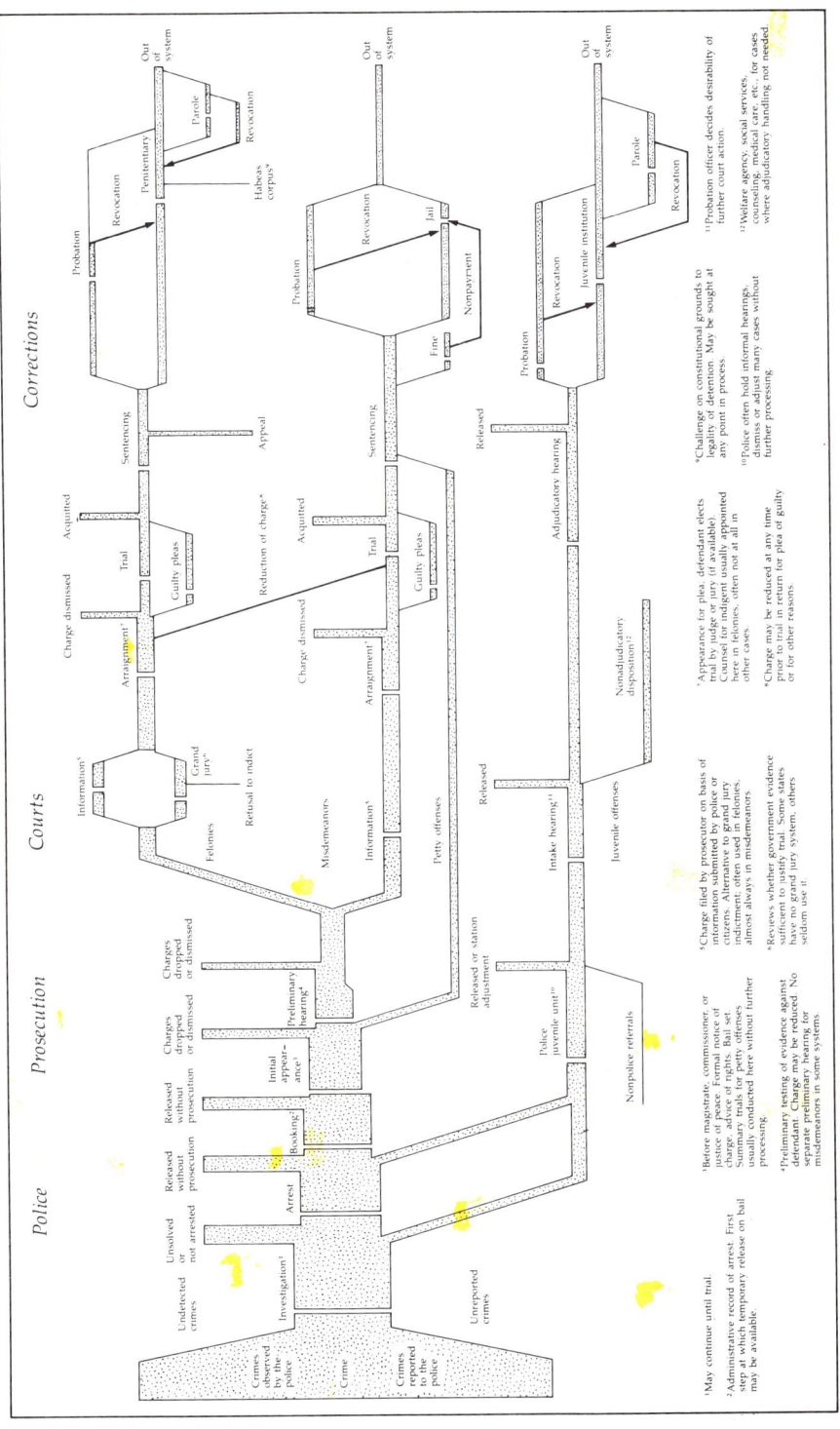

Source: President's Commission on Law Enforcement and Administration of Justice, *The Challenge of Crime in a Free Society* (Washington, D.C.: U.S. Government Printing Office, 1967), pp. 8–9.

In reality, the process by which the citizen-suspect moves through the criminal justice system is not as smooth and systematic as the above description implies. Nor is the interdependence and cooperation among criminal justice bureaucracies as strong as this description suggests. While the process is indeed governed by rules and formulas, criminal justice agencies possess considerable discretion and can circumvent the rules. The suspect-defendant can also do much to thwart the smooth operation of the system. For example, a capable defense attorney can, in many cases, delay a trial long enough for the prosecution's chief witnesses to move away, die, or become less cooperative.

Criminal justice agencies are themselves often at odds. Police departments often complain that district attorneys do not prosecute the cases brought to them. D.A.s counter that the police do not provide them with sound evidence or that judges are too restrictive in allowing evidence to be presented. Judges argue that police and prosecutors constantly present them with weak cases, try cases incompetently, or violate procedural rights in forming a case. Judges are criticized for turning too many felons back onto the streets. They, in turn, argue that they cannot in good conscience place individuals in such inhuman settings as overcrowded and understaffed prisons. In granting too many probations, the judge incurs the probation department's wrath. In sentencing too many persons to prison, the judge is criticized by prison officials.

In sum, the workings of the criminal justice system cannot be fully understood through a chart such as that presented in Figure 7–1. The system is not fully subject to a hierarchical chain of command. Interagency cooperation is often less the result of commitment to criminal justice goals than of the fact that each agency has the power (through the media) to discredit and embarrass the other agencies.

Peripheral Agencies

Discussions of the criminal justice system often overlook two of its peripheral yet important segments: the legislature and the citizenry. The legislature clearly influences the criminal justice system by passing laws and controlling criminal justice budgets. By enacting or rescinding laws, the legislature can increase or decrease the work load of other criminal justice agencies and can complicate or simplify the nature of that work load. The legislature can also greatly control the amounts and types of criminal justice activity by controlling the purse strings of funds for police and corrections programs. In general, the legislature's primary effect on the criminal justice system involves the structuring of its activities around the interests of the major power groups in this society (see Chapter 6).

Citizens influence the criminal justice system in at least three ways. First, as Chapter 1 suggested, the public applies pressure on the legislatures and on criminal justice agencies. Since most upper-level positions in the criminal justice system are political in nature, decisions made by persons in these positions can be swayed by public opinion. The passage of laws, the deployment of police patrols, decisions to plea bargain, sentencing of convicted criminals, and granting of parole are all examples of criminal justice decisions and acts that do not occur in a vacuum. Rather, they occur within a general social and political climate. To understand this point, we need only view the cutbacks in prison work furloughs when a prisoner on furlough is caught committing a crime. Similarly, we note the flurry of political-crime investigations following the Watergate scandal.

Citizen crime-reporting practices represent the second form of impact the citizenry has on the criminal justice system. As Chapter 2 notes, a rise or fall in crime rates may be caused by an actual increase or decrease in crime *or* may simply reflect a change in citizen willingness to report crimes observed or committed against them.

A number of factors govern willingness to "get involved" in reporting crimes. As Chapters 2 and 3 indicated, witnesses or victims may be concerned about the inconvenience or economic hardship that involvement may entail (for example, loss of work time owing to having to appear as a witness) or about harrassment or reprisal for involvement. Or the witness may even be a criminal who cannot afford police attention.

A National Opinion Research Center (NORC) study (Ennis: 1967) asked crime victims why they did not report their victimizations to the police. Two percent cited fear of punishment and 9 percent cited potential inconvenience or confusion as to what to do. More importantly, 34 percent felt the crime was not a police matter, and 55 percent felt that the police would be ineffective in dealing with the offense.

While the NORC findings clearly point to a need for better relations between police and public, it is doubtful that the reasons offered by the NORC sample fully account for nonreporting. The study did not consider various situational factors—sex, age, and demeanor of the parties involved; the presence of witnesses; and the victim's previous history of victimization—which could influence a citizen's decision to initiate the labeling process (see Chapter 6). Further, the NORC study asked victims, in a sense, to provide reasons for avoiding their civic duty. The reasons given may have had little to do with what occurred at the time of the offense but may instead represent attempted "accounts" (again see Chapter 6) offered to an inquirer.

The third area in which the citizenry becomes involved in the criminal justice process is in the personal decision as to whether or not to be a prosecution witness. Prosecutors often complain that they cannot bring an alleged offender to trial because witnesses refuse to cooperate with the police or district attorney. A major study (National Institute of Law Enforcement and Criminal Justice, 1976) of 1973 felony and misdemeanor cases in Washington, D.C., attempted to identify the reasons for noncooperation by victims and witnesses. Twenty-four possible explanatory factors were examined. Surprisingly, demographic factors (for example, age, sex, income, education), attitudes toward the criminal justice system, and fears of reprisal were found to be *unrelated* to cooperation.

The study found three factors that were implicated in prosecutors' labeling of witnesses as uncooperative. First, if prosecutors had a large number of witnesses in a particular case, they would be less likely to pursue a witness they thought uncooperative and would more readily label the witness so. Second, if the relationship between the offender and the witness was close, witnesses would not cooperate or prosecutors would assume they would not and would label them uncooperative. Third, communication breakdowns between the police or prosecutor and the potential witness would cause many witnesses to be labeled uncooperative when, in fact, they were willing to cooperate. That is, potential witnesses were not contacted or given adequate information about their role as witnesses. The last factor was deemed most important by the researchers. It suggested that the blame for noncooperation lies not with the public but with the criminal justice system.

The Criminal Justice Filter

One approach to understanding the criminal justice system as a production organization is to view it as a giant filtering system. As Figure 7–2 indicates, the number of persons arrested in 1974 represents only one-fifth of the number of major crimes reported to the police. Only about 16 percent of those arrested are held for prosecution. Forty percent of those held for prosecution are eventually found or plead guilty and about 60 percent of that group is sent to prison.

What governs these reductions? The largest gap, occurring between crimes reported and arrests, reflects the expertise of and decisions made by police. The percentage of persons charged, found guilty, and sentenced reflects decisions made by prosecutors, jurors, and judges. The key to understanding the filtering effect of the criminal justice system is understanding the *discretion* inherent in the system— the ability to choose one option from among more than one in dealing with a situation or case. For example, police officers have discretionary powers in dealing with family disputes, and may try to calm the situation by talking or resolve it by making an arrest. District attorneys have

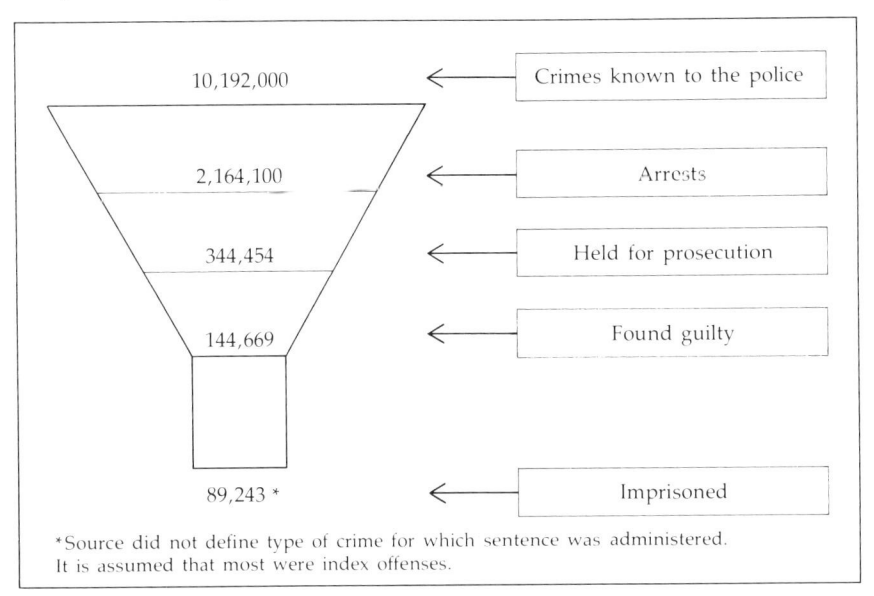

Figure 7–2
The criminal justice filter, 1974. These figures are for FBI-index offenses only and for state jurisdictions only.

```
10,192,000      ←——— Crimes known to the police

 2,164,100      ←——— Arrests

   344,454      ←——— Held for prosecution

   144,669      ←——— Found guilty

    89,243 *   ←——— Imprisoned
```
*Source did not define type of crime for which sentence was administered. It is assumed that most were index offenses.

Source: M. J. Hindelang et al., *Sourcebook of Criminal Justice Statistics—1976* (Washington, D.C.: U.S. Government Printing Office, 1977), pp. 443, 524, 587, 698.

discretion in negotiating pleas. Judges exercise discretion in sentencing offenders.

Process Versus Production

If we ignore the notion of discretion in the criminal justice system, we come to view the system primarily as a passive processing organization or simply as a number of steps through which a person passes on his or her way to receiving justice. However, if we take discretion into account, the criminal justice system may be viewed a *production* organization. That is, it is a system that provides two products: official crime rates and officially labeled criminals.

Figure 7–3 aids in clarifying the production aspects of the criminal-justice system. The figure displays three elements:

1. a pool of potential candidates for labeling as official criminals (A);
2. the criminal justice system (B);
3. a population of officially labeled criminals (C).

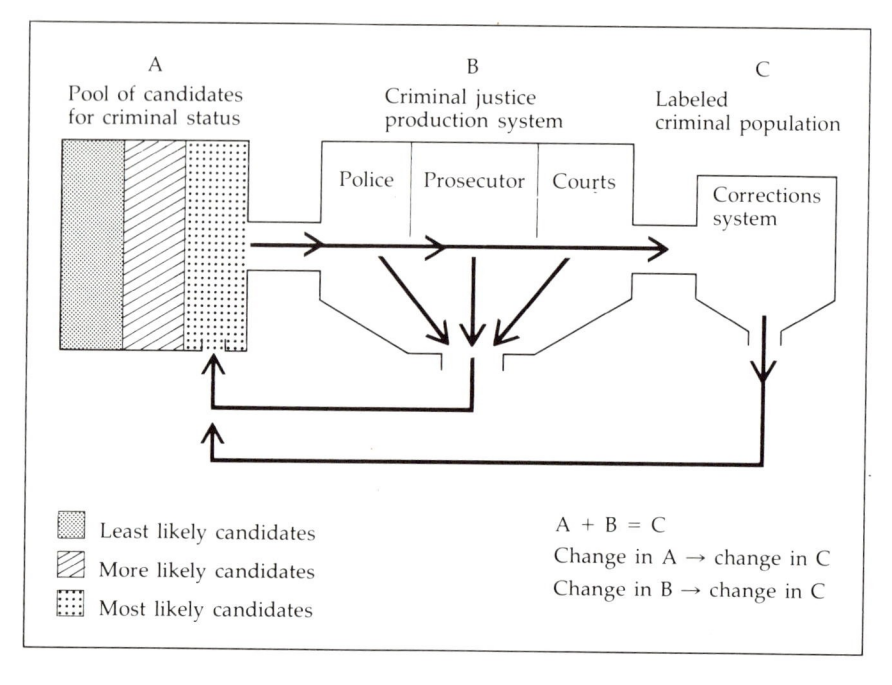

Figure 7–3
The criminal justice production system.

```
A                          B                         C
Pool of candidates      Criminal justice           Labeled
for criminal status     production system          criminal population

                        Police | Prosecutor | Courts
                                                     Corrections
                                                     system
```

▨ Least likely candidates
▥ More likely candidates
▦ Most likely candidates

A + B = C
Change in A → change in C
Change in B → change in C

At any given time, the size and composition of the labeled criminal population (C) is a function of the interaction of activities from within the pool of candidates for labeling (A) and decisions made within the criminal justice system (B) (Johnson et al., 1977).

In theory, every member of society is eligible for selection from the pool of potential labeled criminals by virtue of real or suspected criminal actions. In reality, however, selection from the pool of candidates is not random. Some persons are more likely than others to be drawn into the criminal justice system process by virtue of differential involvement in crime (see Chapter 3) and social-status characteristics that insulate some persons from criminal justice labeling activities (see Chapter 6).

As Figure 7–3 demonstrates, selection from the pool of candidates for criminal status does not guarantee that status. From among the persons selected from the pool, the criminal justice system filters out or produces a select few for eventual inclusion in the official criminal population. The filtering or production process is, in large part, a matter of criminal justice discretion. Officially labeled criminals are produced through decisions made by police, prosecutors, and courts.

Figure 7–3 also indicates that if the size and composition of the officially labeled criminal population (C) is a function of candidate characteristics and actions (A) and criminal justice decisions (B), then changes in the size and composition of C are functions of changes in either or both A and B. The following sections discuss the effects of changes in either A or B.

Changes in the Criminal-Candidate Pool

One reason for a change in the size or composition of the official criminal population may be a change in the characteristics or behaviors of segments of the pool of candidates for criminal status (that is, a change in A may be reflected in C). If the pool were altered through immigration, for example, or if a major change in society's power structure occurred, we could expect a change in the type of person selected by the criminal justice system. Changes in the number of persons committing crimes within the pool could also influence the eventual size and composition of the official criminal population, provided that the criminal justice system could detect and handle the increased criminal activity. Thus, an increase or decrease in a community's marijuana supply could alter the usage patterns of marijuana smokers and therefore the number of smokers caught and processed for violating the law. Similarly, an influx of prostitutes into a community could result in an increase in the number of prostitutes in the community's official criminal population.

Changes in the Criminal Justice System

The criminal justice system is a production organization that can alter the size and composition of its product (labeled criminals) regardless of changes in the pool of candidates for official labeling (that is, a change in B may be reflected in C). For instance, a police department's decision to deploy patrols in one part of a city rather than in another may eventually result in different numbers and types of persons labeled criminal. A city's better business association may intermittently pressure the police department and the district attorney to rid commercial areas of prostitutes and drug dealers. The resultant crackdowns on these violators will be reflected in the characteristics of the labeled criminal population: it will contain more prostitutes and drug dealers. When pressures are eased, the criminal population will contain fewer of these offenders.

Further, within the criminal justice system, a change in district attorneys may alter plea-bargaining procedures and so influence the number and kinds of cases sent to trial. Public pressure may influence district attorneys to file more severe charges than customary. Judges may become more reluctant to grant bail to alleged offenders or may become more liberal or more conservative concerning questions of due process. More defense lawyers may opt for trial before a judge rather than a jury. Such changes will ultimately be reflected in the size and composition of the officially labeled criminal population.

The remainder of this chapter will concentrate on the determinants of criminal justice system decisions as they influence the official criminal population. That is, the characteristics and behaviors of those in the pool of potential labeled criminals will be held constant, and all changes in population of those with criminal status (C) will be treated as functions of criminal justice system discretion (B). In order, we shall examine the police, the courts, and the corrections system.

The Police

In many ways, policing remains as it was in 1829 in London when Sir Robert Peel initiated the first centralized police patrols as we now know them. The only major changes in policing since Peel's day have occurred with the development of the automobile and two-way radio communications. Motor vehicles provide greater mobility for police officers and increase the size of the areas they can patrol. The radio puts the patrolling officer in better touch with headquarters and allows for faster response time in emergency situations.

Together these two technological innovations have made foot patrols a rarity. On the negative side, they have also served to divorce the police from the public. Police officers are generally not regarded as members of the communities they serve (Rubinstein, 1973: 3–25). Despite this alienation, much of police work today involves providing services—escorting ambulances, investigating accidents, answering suicide calls, searching for lost children, and so on (Cumming et al., 1965)—and regulating traffic. In line with the interests of this chapter, however, we wish to concentrate on three primary products of police organization: crime rates, arrest rates, and clearance rates. These three elements are of prime importance in public conceptions of crime and the success of the criminal justice system in fighting it.

Crime Rates

Crime rate refers to the number of crimes committed per a given number of people within a designated population (for example, number of crimes per 100,000 U.S. citizens). Officially, crime rates are computed on the basis of offenses discovered by the police and substantiated complaints made by citizens. People often treat these rates as approximations of the amount of crime in this society, but they may or may not be correct. Practically speaking, official crime-rate figures are nothing more than creations or products of the police. As Chapter

2 noted, much crime does not come to the attention of the police. Police and citizen activity regarding crime will greatly determine the number of crimes recorded. Yet Black (1970) argues that we cannot trust official crime statistics as indicators of crimes encountered by or reported to the police. The police do not officially record all crimes they hear of or discover.

Black analyzed data on 554 cases of police encounters with citizen complainants in crime situations in which the suspect was not present. He was interested in what influenced the responding officers to make an official report of the incident. Among the factors shaping the police officer's decision was the legal seriousness of the offense. Police wrote reports in 72 percent of the felonies and 53 percent of the misdemeanors. The complainant's preference also influenced the officer's actions. Even in some felony cases—for example, assault by a friend—the citizen has cooled down by the time the police arrive, and he or she may no longer wish to file a complaint but only to see an informal warning given the offending person. In 84 percent of the felony cases and 64 percent of the misdemeanor cases, the police complied with the complainant's request.

When the citizen requests official action, two additional factors enter into the police officer's decision: (1) the relational distance between the complainant and the suspect and (2) the complainant's deference to the police officer. Police more readily comply with requests for official action when the complainant and the offender are strangers; less readily when they are friends, neighbors, or acquaintances; and least readily when the offense involves members of the same family. Further, the complainant's behavior toward the police officer determines the officer's willingness to file a report. The less civil or more antagonistic the complainant, the less likely the officer is to file a report.

Finally, while Black found no evidence of racial discrimination in filing reports, he did find that white-collar complainants received greater compliance from police in felony cases than did blue-collar complainants.

It is noteworthy that Black's results concern only the immediate situational determinants of official crime-reporting decisions. Officers in the field may also be influenced by organizational directives and by personal biases. It is not uncommon for police departments to order, formally or informally, their officers to "lay off" certain offenses. Thus, citizen complaints about marijuana use may not result in official reports because the police department feels these reports will inflate the city's drug-violation statistics. Similarly, a department may direct officers not to file official crime reports in assault cases involving spouses. These cases increase the assault rate but rarely result in official indictments, thus making the criminal justice system appear inefficient. In somewhat similar fashion, police may file reports that downgrade the offense in question—for example, from robbery to theft. Seidman and Couzens (1974) discovered this practice occurring in a situation in which police commanders' jobs rested on a promised decrease in serious crime in their districts.

Personal biases of investigating officers also influence their decisions in the field. Attitudes about the types of persons believed to be involved in crimes may affect reports. In years past, for example, fistfights between whites were recorded as crimes (assaults) while fights between blacks were simply treated as normal behavior. Today the extent to which an officer will report marijuana offenses may be linked to the extent to which he himself (or she) smokes marijuana.

In sum, since government and public perception of crime are in large part based on official crime reports, it is fair to say that these perceptions are the products of police activity and decisions. Whether or not the rates and perceptions reflect the reality of the crime situation depends on the types of decisions the police are making. Also important, police decisions to report crimes influence arrest rates, since much arrest activity is based on follow-ups of initial crime reports.

Arrest Rates

A second product of police discretion and activity is the arrest rate—that is, the number of arrests per 100,000 population in the area serviced by a police department. Arrest statistics are often used to evaluate police department effectiveness and to learn the characteristics of persons committing crimes (see Chapter 3). The extent to which the statistics are useful for either purpose depends on the extent to which police departments and individual officers employ discretion in arrest situations. Available research suggests that arrest discretion is extremely prevalent.

Like crime rates, arrest rates do not simply occur; they are manufactured. Although existing laws do not specifically allow for nonenforcement, police departments and their employees have considerable latitude in making arrests. For both parties, the latitude is the result of relatively high levels of autonomy. Although somewhat responsive to political and social pressures and occasionally monitored by civilian review boards, police departments by and large police themselves (Wilson, 1968:227–77). Similarly, though answerable to superior officers, individual police officers are relatively unsupervised in the field.

The following factors seem to influence police departments in their arrest policies:

Orientation of the Department Toward Policing. J. Q. Wilson (1968:140–226) suggests that styles of policing are tied to the types of communities being served. Some communities perceive themselves to be plagued by crime. The police department may respond in legalistic fashion, using little discretion and making an arrest in every possible arrest situation. Other communities demand order and are given a watchman-style department, one that exercises a considerable amount of discretion in an effort to achieve order without involving citizens in legal problems. Finally, a service-style department often occurs in communities without a serious crime problem and provides such services as emergency medical care.

Political Pressures. Police departments are political organizations that, while avoiding day-to-day interference, must also avoid serious conflicts with the more powerful leaders of a community who choose the police chief and control the police budget. These leaders may influence arrest policies. District attorneys and judges, by virtue of their ability to embarrass a police department in the news media, also affect arrest policies. Recent attempts to implement police-community relations programs testify both to the increasing political power of lower socioeconomic groups and to the need to cultivate the cooperation of these groups in enforcing the law.[1]

Technical Sophistication. Clearly, arrest rates will be influenced by the technical expertise of police departments. The training of officers and the equipment employed in police work vary by department. Arrest rates vary in some degree with the differences in technical sophistication.

Perceived Need for Nonarrest. At times, investigations into criminal activity seem to dictate a nonarrest policy. An attempt to break an organized crime syndicate or a narcotics ring might be hindered, for example, by arrests at lower levels. Hence, it is common for police departments to trade an arrest for information about upper-level criminals. This practice, of course, never allows the effects of full enforcement of the law to be determined (Goldstein, 1960).

Procedural Law. The criminal justice system must operate under rules of due process. That is, there are procedural rules that define *how* the police and other criminal justice agencies may investigate and arrest a citizen (see Chapter 1). Police may not search a home without a warrant, for example. Police officers currently treat procedural laws as technical hindrances and generally attempt to circumvent them when possible. Skolnick (1975) argues that police work (including the number and types of arrests made) would change if police orientation to procedural law were changed.

---

[1] For a critical review of the police-community relations concept, see Manning (1975).

As noted above, individual police officers lead a relatively autonomous existence in the field. They are subject to a number of pressures that influence their decisions on the job, such as the following:

Organizational Pressures. Much of police field work is structured by the department in the sense that directives are given, arrest records are monitored, and superiors' wishes are made known. Promotions are based on evaluations of the officer's performance in the field. Considerable emphasis is placed on the "good pinch," the arrest that results in charges filed by the district attorney. Rubinstein (1973:26–68) argues that a police officer's immediate superior, the sergeant, exerts the major influence on this work in the sense that the superior evaluates the officer's performance in the territory to which he or she is assigned.

Personal Biases. In addition to the normal prejudices every individual harbors, the police officer gradually develops stereotypes of criminals and crime situations. Although these images sometimes facilitate police work, they also sometimes form the basis of discriminatory arrests and police brutality. Based on a study of police encounters with juveniles, Piliavin and Briar (1964) suggest that the major determinants of police decisions to arrest a youth for a minor crime are the youth's appearance and demeanor. To the extent that the youth was disrespectful and looked like a "tough guy," the police were likely to arrest him. Studies of police brutality indicate that police are most likely to abuse segments of the population thought to be "problems" by the majority (Chevigny, 1969).

Seriousness of the Crime Investigated. Clearly, there are some offenses that the police officer cannot ignore. In general, arrest discretion occurs more frequently regarding lesser offenses and vice crimes.

Situational Factors. As with the police officer's decision to file an official report for a crime incident, immediate situational factors affect decisions to arrest. These include the physical setting in which the police-citizen interaction occurs, the number of witnesses present and their involvement in the interaction, and the presence of a complainant.

Procedural Laws. Apart from departmental policies regarding due process in arrests, the individual officer also develops attitudes toward procedural law. Officers vary in the extent to which they are willing to circumvent (and to lie about circumventing) the rules. The question of entrapment in prostitution arrests provides an example.

Arrests cannot be made unless the prostitute first quotes a price for prostitution services; if the police officer cites the price first, subsequent arrest of the prostitute constitutes entrapment. Entrapment in this situation cannot be controlled since there are generally no witnesses involved. Whether or not the officer is willing to entrap will, in part, determine whether an arrest occurs (Skolnick, 1975:91–111).

Corruption. Nonenforcement of laws may occur because police accept payoffs to "look the other way." Corruption represents more than a few "bad apples" on a police force. Most graft is related to vice crimes, and most police officers receive some form of encouragement to accept payoffs. A number of factors provide the encouragement: lack of community consensus regarding the morality of the vices, relative community apathy regarding enforcement of vice laws, a demand for vice services, lack of control over the police department by honest powerful citizens, low visibility of police graft, greater monetary rewards for graft than for its avoidance, lack of sanctioning from the police hierarchy, explicit encouragement by fellow officers, the occasional usefulness of graft to gain order within a given police territory, and constant offers of payoffs from every form of business (Rubinstein, 1973:373–434; Gardiner, 1970:93–104).

In sum, we again note that arrest rates are a product of police activity and discretion, some of which is departmentally encouraged. As such, arrest rates may or may not constitute a representative sample of arrests that could be made by police. Regardless, arrest statistics are used to make evaluative and policy decisions. Departmental efficiency is judged partially by arrest records. Individual officers are also evaluated in large part on arrest performance. Finally, decisions about anticrime strategies are often based on arrest trends and characteristics of arrestees. As De Fleur (1975) has demonstrated in reviewing Chicago's drug arrest trends over a twenty-nine-year period, apparent changes in populations using drugs, areas of drug use, and amounts of drug use over time actually reflected police decisions about when, where, and against whom drug laws were enforced.

Clearance Rates

The major criterion of effectiveness by the police department and a standard measure of performance by detectives is the clearance rate—that is, the percentage of known crimes that the police feel they have solved. Like crime and arrest rates, clearance rates are products of police activity and discretion, not simply measures of these elements. That is, police clear crimes through decisions about whom to arrest and, in clearing crimes apart from arrest, about the validity of the information used to classify a crime as "solved" (Skolnick, 1975: 164–81).

Clearance statistics are highly problematic. The ordinary citizen often assumes that they represent actual arrests. In fact, crimes are often labeled "cleared" when detectives feel they can attribute them to identified individuals either through confessions or on the basis of method of operation. Thus, the police become convinced by similarities in a number of crimes that one person committed them. Upon the person's arrest, those crimes may be labeled "cleared" whether or not the suspect admits to them. We should also not assume that all offenses cleared by arrest result in criminal prosecution. District attorneys often refuse to press charges either because of weak evidence or of procedural rights violations. Nonetheless, the crimes are classified as "solved" or "cleared" in police files.

Pressures on police departments to increase clearance rates undoubtedly result in some rather liberal classifications of crimes as "cleared." Since the FBI publishes monthly clearance statistics for major cities, poor clearance rates are seen by police departments as negative indicators of their performance. The resultant pressure placed on individual investigators to produce higher clearance rates often results in compromises of justice. Police officers bargain with suspects, promising no arrest in return for information leading to clearances or a single charge in return for confessions regarding a number of crimes. In some respects, the multiple-offense arrestee has an advantage over the single-offense arrestee, for the former has more bargaining power with respect to information leading to clearances.

In sum, it is difficult to know exactly what a police department's clearance rate represents. It may or may not mean that a department is energetically fighting crime. It may or may not signify a high number of arrests. It may or may not reflect a high level of convictions for offenders. However, it *does* represent a set of decisions made by police investigators in a political context. For this reason, we must view clearance statistics with great skepticism.

The discussion above about clearance rates, arrest rates, and crime rates, gives us a sense of what it means to say the criminal justice system is a production rather than a processing organization. The organization *creates* a product; it does not simply stamp and process an already existing product. Changes in the structure, goals, or methods of police agencies will likely be reflected in their end-products: officially defined crimes and officially designated persons to be moved into the court system. The following description (Sheley and Hanlon, 1978) of the consequences of a police decision actively to seek certain arrests graphically illustrates this point.

An Example: Factoryville's Antiheroin Campaign

In 1974, an older northern industrial city called Factoryville (a pseudonym) was embarrassed by a state official's accusation that the city was the heroin distribution center for a multistate region. The claim received extensive news coverage and caused considerable political and public pressure on the police to rid Factoryville of heroin traffickers. The police responded with an antiheroin campaign designed to increase the number of heroin arrests in the city. To this end, narcotics unit personnel were doubled, overtime hours were greatly increased, and investigation funds were more than doubled. The campaign was to last six months.

In light of this chapter's oft-stated hypothesis that policy changes in the criminal justice system will alter the characteristics of a community's official criminal population, we might expect Factoryville's official criminal rolls to swell with heroin traffickers. Yet, at first glance, the hypothesis seems unsupported. Heroin arrests increased only 9 percent during the campaign. The publicity surrounding the campaign apparently disrupted normal heroin patterns in the city, driving distributors and users further underground.

A second look at changes in Factoryville's official criminal population during the six-month campaign suggests that the campaign was not without impact. The number of arrests for possession of stolen goods and illegal weapons rose as police increased drug raids and subsequently encountered other offenses. Prostitution arrests declined as plainclothes undercover officers were transferred from the sex offenses unit to the narcotics unit. Arrests for disturbing the peace rose as uniformed officers employed that charge to arrest prostitutes. However, the greatest effect of the antiheroin campaign was a drastic increase—228 percent—in arrests for possession of marijuana. Though not actively seeking such arrests, the police encountered more marijuana violations through increased "street work," more frequent drug raids, and drug tips from the public in response to the antiheroin publicity.

In sum, though there were no apparent changes in the size and composition of Factoryville's marijuana-user population, the police antiheroin policy produced a "marijuana problem" for the city. It also greatly altered the characteristics of its arrest population—the same population from which the prosecutor selected persons for potential labeling as the community's official criminals.

The Courts

Although police arrest decisions create a population from which officially labeled criminals will be drawn, the court system performs the actual selection and labeling of official criminals. Despite popular notions, the courts do not simply weigh evidence and determine guilt or innocence. Rather, like the police, they produce a product—labeled criminals—through a series of decisions. Were the structure of this decision-making process altered, the product would also be changed; we would see different numbers or types of persons granted criminal status.

Orientation of the Courts

Ideally, American courts employ an adversary model in evaluating the merits of state-imposed criminal charges against a defendant. This model pits the prosecution against the defense and uses a judge or jury to determine the winner of the conflict. The prosecution and defense do not cooperate in any way. Instead, within legal limits, they do everything in their power to thwart each other's efforts.

Since the state is more powerful than the individual it prosecutes, the adversary model somewhat favors the defense in our system. Defendants need not be proven innocent of the charges against them; they need only show that the prosecution has not proven them guilty beyond a reasonable doubt. Procedural law also limits the manner in which the prosecution builds a case against defendants. Defendants have a right to counsel, and if they cannot afford counsel, one will be provided. There are time limits within which the prosecution must bring the case to trial. Illegally obtained evidence cannot be introduced against defendants. Defendants cannot be retried if acquitted of an offense. Ideally, then, defendants are considered not guilty until proven otherwise.

Many critics argue that the operation of our present court system deviates radically from the adversary ideal. They claim that we have developed a crime-control or cooperative model that downplays conflict between prosecution and defense. The crime-control model processes individuals assumed to be guilty by virtue of arrest and pretrial investigations (Packer, 1968; Blumberg, 1967). With guilt presumed, critics argue, the prosecution, defense, and judge cooperate to move cases through the courts as quickly as possible. Characteristic of this attempt at efficient processing are a reliance on negotiated pleas, avoidance of trials, conservative rulings on procedural rights, and the conduct of trials in a manner favoring the prosecution.

Clearly, the pure crime-control model is no more a reality than is the pure adversary model. Courts in America vary in the extent to which they lean toward either model. Their variation greatly shapes differences in communities' crime situations and the size and composition of their official criminal populations. Changes in orientation within court systems should bring changes within those criminal populations.

Greater reliance on the adversary approach should cause decreases in the numbers of official criminals. The numbers should increase as the cooperative approach gains favor. Different approaches will also change the composition of the criminal population. A move toward the cooperative model may, for example, result in the convictions of members of organized crime who have avoided conviction by using safeguards in the adversary model (see Chapter 1). In sum, then, criminal status is largely a function of the orientation of a court system.

Prosecution and Defense

Within the court system, the key figures in determining the outcome of a criminal case are the prosecuting and defense attorneys. We are presently interested in the factors that influence their decisions regarding criminal cases.

The office of prosecutor is, first and foremost, a political position. Whether elected or appointed, district attorneys must assure the public that the community is safe, that criminals are being tried and punished, and that justice is being dispensed. Prosecutors face a number of decisions in trying to maintain this image. They must first decide whether or not to bring charges against a suspect. If they do bring charges and they are accepted by a grand jury, prosecutors must choose between negotiating a plea (discussed below) and taking the case to trial. Going to trial also involves decisions about when the trial should take place and how best to present the state's case to a judge or jury.

Among the important factors governing these decisions are (1) the potential impact of the successful handling of the case on the prosecutor's reputation (Skolnick, 1967), (2) the quality of evidence in the case, (3) the cooperativeness of victims and witnesses, (4) the courtroom credibility of potential witnesses, (5) the cooperativeness of the defendant and defense attorney, (6) the potential usefulness of the defendant in a criminal justice system role (such as police informant), (7) community pressure to crack down on certain forms of crime, and (8) the need to placate other members of the criminal justice system (such as the police, who may complain to the news media that the prosecutor is refusing to prosecute the criminals they apprehend—see Cole, 1970). These decisions are typically made within an organizational framework marked by a large number of cases. If all cases went to trial, the court system would be so overwhelmed that it would cease to function.

Between 60 and 90 percent of convictions in major urban court systems result from negotiated pleas rather than trial verdicts. The negotiated plea or plea bargain generally involves concessions made by the prosecution in return for information from a defendant or a guilty plea. Most negotiated pleas involve reducing the charges (for example, from burglary to criminal trespassing), dropping some charges, or promising lighter sentences. Most court observers argue that plea bargaining has become second nature for the attorneys involved, that it occurs so often that pleas are decided in minutes—almost by recipe (Mather, 1974). The key factor in this process is the development of notions of "normal crimes," stereotypes of offenders, offense situations, and standard charge reductions developed through experience in the courts. So common are these stereotypes, Sudnow (1965) argues, that prosecutors and defense attorneys begin to "force" cases into them, ignoring individual qualities of a case; the result is a form of assembly-line justice.

Defense attorneys are also subject to a number of pressures that influence decisions regarding their clients. Public defenders feel primarily organizational pressures. They are given large numbers of cases to represent and are encouraged to process them as quickly as possible. Although they do not automatically assume that their clients are guilty, public defenders are likely to try to fit a client's case into their conception of a "normal crime" in order to process it more easily. The fact that public defenders are members of the "system," constantly interacting with prosecutors and judges and seeking to minimize tensions with these persons, encourages them to negotiate pleas for their clients.[2]

The private defense attorney is influenced primarily by the economic features of his practice. Those few attorneys who represent wealthier clients will likely take an adversary approach in building a defense—pushing the prosecution and using every legal loophole available to the interests of their clients. If this approach fails, the attorney will attempt to obtain the best deal possible for his client.

The practice of criminal law is generally not lucrative, however, for most persons charged with crimes are from the lower classes. Attorneys generally charge a flat fee for representation, and it is therefore to their advantage to minimize the amount of work on a given case and move on to another. To become involved in a trial is to lose money. Hence, the pressure to negotiate a plea of guilty for the client. This pressure is further increased by the need to maintain good working relations with other members of the court whose favor may be required in future cases (Blumberg, 1967).

In sum, the size and composition of a community's official criminal population is in large part shaped by the structure of the practice of criminal law. Changes in this element of the criminal justice system should be reflected in the population of those labeled criminal. For

---

[2] For opposing views of the public defender and plea bargaining, see Sudnow (1965) and Skolnick (1967).

example, U.S. Supreme Court decisions about boundaries of plea bargaining could significantly alter the number and types of cases that result in criminal charges and trials. Similarly, changes in the practice of divorce law may drive more lawyers to the practice of criminal law. The resultant competition for criminal cases will certainly affect the quality of representation a defense attorney provides a client.

The Trial as Image Management

As we previously noted, relatively few criminal cases are decided by trial. Those that are are in some ways special, because they are sensational, because the attorneys involved stand to profit from the trial, because the defendant is unusually stubborn (or foolish) in refusing to accept a negotiated plea, because the defense attorney is relatively certain of acquittal, or because the defendant has nothing to lose and everything to gain by trial (Mather, 1974).

Through courtroom enactments in the entertainment media, the public has formed an impression of the trial as a fact-finding endeavor. In reality, if "the truth will out" in the trial, it will probably do so accidentally, for the adversary-trial model does not actually emphasize facts. The prosecutor is already convinced of the defendant's guilt and will be intent on gaining a conviction. The defense is interested in discrediting the prosecutor's case. Both parties seek to make a favorable impression upon their audience—the judge and jury, which will reward the performance of one side or the other with the verdict it desires. If, in creating the desired impression, an attorney feels that the facts are useful, the facts will be pursued. Sometimes the impression is best managed when the facts are downplayed or ignored.

If a defense attorney feels the prosecutor's case is technically weak, generally the client will be advised to seek a trial before a judge. If, however, the attorney feels the prosecutor's case is technically strong, the client will be advised to choose trial before a jury—a group that is more impressionable. In selecting a jury prior to a trial, both the prosecution and the defense are allowed a number of free challenges by which they may exclude individuals from the jury. Beyond this, they may have an individual excluded on such grounds as racial prejudice or pretrial exposure to the case. In selecting jurors, both attorneys seek persons they feel will be susceptible to the image they wish to project. Generally, they do not seek the best "fact finders."

The attempt by attorneys to choose an impressionable jury is best highlighted by the recent use of scientific surveys and computer analysis in selecting jurors for highly publicized trials (for example, the trials of Angela Davis, John Mitchell and Maurice Stans, and Joan Little). Social scientists are hired to survey the population from which the jury will be chosen. From the survey data, the researchers attempt to find correlations between demographic characteristics and attitudes favoring the defense. From the findings, the researchers develop a profile of the juror most likely to acquit. The defense attorney uses the information in selecting jurors. To date, the method has been extremely successful (Tivnan, 1975). It also lays to rest any doubt that trials are more a matter of image building than fact-finding.

In the actual trial situation, attorneys choose their witnesses carefully. They are chosen not on the basis of the information they have but on the basis of the impression they will make on the jury. Jurors are known to give more attention to witnesses' confidence than to the content of their statements (Erlanger, 1970). Hence, lawyers carefully select the order of appearance of witnesses and the content and order of the questions asked of them. In addition to their concern with witnesses, attorneys are aware that jurors are also influenced by the dress and demeanor of defendants and attorneys. Strategies for image management are thus also planned around these factors.

Social-status characteristics of jurors also seem to influence their collective deliberations and decisions. High-status jurors are more likely to engage in jury deliberation; they are also more likely to be chosen jury foremen. Strodtbeck and Mann (1956) suggest that the more educated juror is more active in deliberations and female jurors are less active than male jurors. Whether or not deliberating jurors follow the judge's instructions and concern themselves with questions of evidence is debatable. While some researchers (Kalven and Zeisel, 1966:162) report that jurors are attentive to facts and instructions, many observers tend to agree with Frank's (1949:108–25) claim that juries create law by applying their own rules to their selective interpretation of the facts of the case.

In sum, the trial situation differs little from other elements of the criminal justice system. It is an organizational enterprise that produces a product: officially labeled criminals. As we have seen, the influences on the creation of that product extend beyond the facts of criminal cases and the quest for justice. In line with the theme of this chapter, we also realize that changes in the structure of the trial will alter the characteristics of its product.

Sentencing

A criminal conviction (whether through trial or plea) necessitates sentencing. Occasionally, the legislature specifies the exact sentence for an offense. Generally, however, judges have a number of options in determining a sentence. They may place an individual on probation for a specified time. They may suspend the sentence they impose. They may levy a fine in addition to or in lieu of imprisonment. They may send an offender to a prison, a jail, a work farm, or any number of community-based halfway-house programs.

In sentencing an individual to prison for most offenses, judges may impose a specific sentence within the minimum and maximum number of allowable years determined by the legislature. In some instances, they may structure the availability of parole opportunities. Most often, judges impose an indefinite sentence, assigning the minimum and maximum years to be served and leaving the actual number of years served to be determined by the state parole authority.

Judges vary in the severity of the sentences they impose. For the most part, these differences are linked to variations in world view and penal philosophy—the result of the judges' personal and professional backgrounds (Hogarth, 1971; Nagel, 1962). Sentences also partially reflect the ideals of the community in which a judge sits. Thus, we see "inconsistent" sentences: a judge in one community sentencing an offender to a few years in prison while a judge in another community imposes a more severe sentence on a similar offender. As Richard Quinney (1970:167) notes, this sentence disparity occurs even in federal judicial-circuit courts. In 1966, for example, a forgery conviction in the 1st Federal Judicial Circuit brought an average prison sentence of 13.7 months, but the same conviction in the 10th Circuit resulted in an average sentence of 36 months.

Although the public notices sentencing disparity, it generally does not realize that, in most large court systems today, judges rely on presentence reports and recommendations based on probation department investigations of convicted offenders. Carter and Wilkins (1967) report that the probation officer's recommendations for probation are honored by judges about 95 percent of the time. The courts follow the probation officer's recommendation for imprisonment in 80 to 85 percent of the cases.

Ideally, the presentence report should include a thorough investigation of the offender's background, criminal justice record, and special treatment needs. That is, a suggested sentence should be tailored to the individual offender. Yet it is doubtful that this occurs. The number of cases requiring presentence reports is generally too large to allow such individual attention. Further, as with other members of the court system, probation officers tend to develop notions of "normal cases," stereotypes to which they fit cases, generally ignoring their unique aspects.

The major concern regarding sentencing disparity is that it reflects systematic discrimination, especially against racial minorities. Although there is evidence that capital punishment has been imposed discriminatorily against the poor and racial minorities,[3] the question of discrimination in other types of sentencing remains unanswered. Some studies claim to have discovered racial discrimination in sentencing

---

[3] Established in Furman v. Georgia, 408 U.S. 238, 371 (1972).

(Bullock, 1961); others report no links between sentences and such extralegal factors as sex, age, and race when other factors such as seriousness of offense are held constant (Green, 1961). A recent examination of prison sentences received by 10,488 inmates in the southeastern United States also produced no evidence of socioeconomic status bias in sentencing (Chiricos and Waldo, 1975). Hagan's (1974) recent review of sentencing disparity studies suggests that at present the general consensus among those studying sentencing disparity appears to be that there is no sound evidence of discrimination and that existing evidence seems to point away from the possibility.

In conclusion, the court system reflects a matrix of legal philosophies, political orientation and pressures, bureaucratic tendencies, and personal interests. The ideal adversary model to which it aspires is largely absent. It is eroded by a tendency toward a cooperative, crime-control model that places efficient organizational processing of assumedly guilty persons above due process. As such, it structures the characteristics of our current population of official criminals. Changes in various aspects of the present system (for example, a renewed emphasis on due process or a change in plea bargaining formulas) can be expected to alter the size and characteristics of that population.

An Example: Bail Decisions and the Production of Official Criminals

Our discussion of the courts has argued that the court process represents a series of organizational decisions that produces a product: officially labeled criminals. One of the better examples of this production phenomenon lies in bail decisions. Bail refers to the practice whereby people arrested are allowed to go free pending trial after they (or a bondsman who receives a fee) have given the court a specified sum of money, to be forfeited if they fail to appear for trial. The bail concept strikes a compromise between two conflicting rights: (1) the right of the accused to be treated as innocent until proven guilty (that is, the right not to be incarcerated until proven guilty) and (2) the right of the state to expect that all who are charged with crimes will appear for trial.

Bail would appear primarily designed to benefit the accused. Ideally, the amount of bail is determined solely on the basis of the seriousness of the charge against the accused and the likelihood that he or she will abscond or commit another crime while awaiting trial. However, exorbitantly high bail is often used by the state to harass individuals who are difficult to bring to trial (such as members of organized crime) and to hold persons in jail in the hope that they will cooperate with the state (become police informers, for example) in return for freedom or other considerations. Further, high bail reflects attempts by judges and district attorneys to protect their reputations. If the district attorney does not request high bail and the judge does not set high bail, any bail jumping that occurs will be attributed to their "coddling" of criminals (Suffet, 1966). Finally, the bail process may be criticized as economically discriminatory: the wealthier citizen can buy a better brand of justice than can the poorer citizen (Foote, 1959).

Regarding this last point, bail decisions would appear at first glance to have little impact on the eventual outcome of a criminal case. These decisions cannot alter the facts that determine verdicts. In reality, however, the accused benefits greatly if he or she receives bail. The ability to make bail influences case outcomes in a number of ways (President's Commission on Law Enforcement, 1967:131):

1. It provides accused persons with the opportunity to work and raise money for their defense.
2. It affords defendants and their lawyers greater access to each other.
3. It allows defendants to participate to a greater degree in the preparation of their defense (for example, finding defense witnesses).
4. It avoids the possible self-fulfilling prophecy that may occur when a jury, seeing that the defendant is not free on bail and is therefore probably "dangerous," votes a verdict of guilty.
5. It discourages guilty pleas out of desperation; at times defendants who do not raise bail are encouraged to plead guilty in return for applying to their sentences the time already spent in jail awaiting trial.

Bail statistics seem to support the claim that ability to raise bail influences case dispositions. One early bail study (Foote, 1954) found that 58 percent of defendants out on bail were acquitted whereas only 18 percent of those held in jail were acquitted. Another study (Roberts and Palermo, 1958) reported a 31 percent rate of acquittal for defendants on bail as opposed to a 20 percent rate for those held in jail. A study of 1960 New York City bail decisions found higher acquittal rates for persons on bail in six of seven crime categories (Ares et al., 1963). The same study reported that those free pending trial received suspended sentences if found guilty more often than did those held in jail.

One study that added especially convincing evidence to these findings was the 1961 Manhattan Bail Project (Ares et al., 1963). In an attempt to discover a means of releasing defendants that did not necessitate raising bail money, members of the project staff interviewed defendants to determine (1) if they had lived at the same address for six months or more, (2) if they were currently employed, (3) if they had close relatives in New York City, (4) if they had no previous conviction record, and (5) if they had resided in New York for at least ten years. If at least one of these questions was answered affirmatively and the answer verified by the staff, the names of the defendants were placed in a pool for possible pretrial release without bail. After a more rigorous second screening by the staff, the remaining defendants were randomly assigned to either of two groups. One group received recommendations for pretrial release without bail. The other received no recommendations and was subjected to the traditional bail decision process.

Analysis of the results of the experiment indicated that 59 percent of those in the group released without bail received acquittal verdicts or had charges eventually dropped, whereas only 23 percent of those detained in jail received similar dispositions. Among those found guilty in the pretrial release group, most received suspended sentences. Ninety-six percent of those in the jailed group who were found guilty were sent to prison. Release without bail also seemed a superior method to release by bail. Only 14 percent of those who were eligible for the project release program but were not given recommendations eventually were released on bail. Fewer persons in the pretrial release group failed to appear for trial than persons who received bail.

In sum, court decisions are instrumental in shaping the size and composition of the official criminal population. This is evidenced by viewing the results of bail decisions. Changes in bail decisions—organizational changes—will alter the products of the court process, and different numbers and types of persons will be defined as criminal in this society.

Summary

In this chapter, we explored the criminal justice system not as a simple processing organization but as a production system. Criminal justice agencies are all linked to the creation of a population of persons with official criminal status. The police initiate the production by their selection of certain persons for arrest. Prosecutors further the production process by selecting persons to be charged from among those arrested. The court system completes the process by selecting from among those charged a number of persons to be labeled "guilty."

The key to the production of official criminals is discretion by members of the criminal justice system: police discretion to arrest, prosecution discretion to bring charges and negotiate pleas, and court discretion in determining guilt and in sentencing. As this chapter has emphasized time and again, the influences on use of discretion are often extralegal. That is, the size and composition of today's official criminal population are shaped by political and organizational factors. As these factors change, the size and composition of the criminal population is altered. In sum, criminal justice is not simply the processing of criminals or the sorting of the guilty from the innocent. Rather, it is the creation of a criminal population, which in turn shapes the public's view of crime and the types of people committing crimes.

References

Ares, C. E., A. Rankin, and H. Sturz
    1963   "The Manhattan bail project: an interim report on the use of pre-trial parole." New York University Law Review 38:76–86.

Becker, H. S.
    1973   Outsiders. New York: The Free Press.

Black, D. J.
    1970   "Production of crime rates." American Sociological Review 35:733–48.

Bullock, H. A.
    1961   "Significance of the racial factor in the length of prison sentences." Journal of Criminal Law, Criminology and Police Science 52:411–17.

Blumberg, A. S.
    1967   "The practice of law as a confidence game: organization cooptation of a profession." Law and Society Review 1:15–39.

Carter, R. M., and L. T. Wilkins
    1967   "Some factors in sentencing policy." Journal of Criminal Law, Criminology and Police Science 58:503–14.

Chevigny, P.
    1969   Police Power. New York: Vintage Books.

Chiricos, T. G., and G. P. Waldo
    1975   "Socioeconomic status and criminal sentencing: an empirical assessment of a conflict proposition." American Sociological Review 40:753–72.

Cole, G.
    1970   "The decision to prosecute." Law and Society Review 4:313–43.

Cumming, E., I. Cumming, and L. Edell
    1965   "Policeman as philosopher, guide, and friend." Social Problems 12:276–86.

De Fleur, L. B.
    1975   "Biasing influences on drug arrest records: implications for deviance research." American Sociological Review 40:88–103.

Ennis, P.
    1967   Criminal Victimization in the United States: A Report of a National Survey. Field Survey II: President's Commission on Law Enforcement and Administration of Justice. Washington, D.C.: U.S. Government Printing Office.

Erlanger, H. S.
    1970   "Jury research in America: its past and future." Law and Society Review 4:345–70.

Foote, C.
　1954　　"Compelling appearance in court: administration of bail in Philadelphia." University of Pennsylvania Law Review 102:1031–79.
　1959　　"The bail system and equal justice." Federal Probation 23:43–8.
Frank, J.
　1949　　Courts on Trial. Princeton, N.J.: Princeton University Press.
Gardiner, J.
　1970　　The Politics of Corruption: Organized Crime in an American City. New York: The Russell Sage Foundation.
Green, E.
　1960　　Judicial Attitudes in Sentencing. London: Macmillan.
Goldstein, J.
　1960　　"Police discretion not to invoke the criminal process: low-visibility decisions in the administration of justice." The Yale Law Review 69:543–94.
Hagan, J.
　1974　　"Extra-legal attributes and criminal sentencing: an assessment of a sociological viewpoint." Law and Society 82:357–83.
Hogarth, J.
　1971　　Sentencing as a Human Process. Toronto: University of Toronto Press.
Johnson, W. T., R. E. Petersen, and L. E. Wells
　1977　　"Arrest probabilities for marijuana users as indicators of selective law enforcement." American Journal of Sociology 83:681–99.
Kalven, H., and H. Zeisel
　1966　　The American Jury. Boston: Little, Brown.
Manning, P.
　1975　　"Survey review." Contemporary Sociology 4:481–87.
Mather, L. M.
　1974　　"Some determinants of the method of case disposition; decision-making by police defenders in Los Angeles." Law and Society Review 8:187–216.
Nagel, S.
　1962　　"Judicial backgrounds and criminal cases." Journal of Criminal Law, Criminology and Police Science 53:333–39.
National Institute of Law Enforcement and Criminal Justice, Law Enforcement Assistance Administration, U.S. Department of Justice
　1976　　Improving Witness Cooperation. Washington, D.C.: U.S. Government Printing Office.
Packer, H. L.
　1968　　The Limits of Criminal Sanction. Stanford, California: Stanford University Press.
Piliavin, I., and S. Briar
　1964　　"Police encounters with juveniles." American Journal of Sociology 70:206–14.
The President's Commission on Law Enforcement and Administration of Justice
　1967　　The Challenge of Crime in Free Society. Washington, D.C.: U.S. Government Printing Office.
Quinney, R.
　1970　　The Social Reality of Crime. Boston: Little, Brown.
Roberts, J. W., and J. S. Palermo
　1958　　"A study of administration of bail in New York." University of Pennsylvania Law Review 106:726–27.

Rubinstein, J.
    1973   City Police. New York: Random House.
Sheley, J., and J. Hanlon
    1978   "Unintended effects of police decisions to actively enforce laws: implications for analysis of crime trends." Contemporary Crises 2:265–75.
Seidman, D., and M. Couzens
    1974   "Getting the crime rate down: political pressure and crime reporting." Law and Society Review 8:457–93.
Skolnick, J.
    1967   "Social control in the adversary system." Journal of Conflict Resolution 11:52–70.
    1975   Justice Without Trial. 2d ed. New York: Wiley.
Strodtbeck, F. L., and R. D. Mann
    1956   "Sex role differentiation in jury deliberations." Sociometry 19:3–11.
Suffet, F.
    1966   "Bail setting: a study of courtroom interaction." Crime and Delinquency 12:318–31.
Sudnow, D.
    1965   "Normal crimes: sociological features of the penal code in a public defender office." Social Problems 12:255–76.
Tivnan, E.
    1975   "Jury by trial." The New York Times Magazine, November 16:30–31 and *passim*.
Wilson, J. Q.
    1968   Varieties of Police Behavior. Cambridge, Mass.: Harvard University Press.

Suggested Readings

Criminologists have conducted extensive research on the police, especially as interest in the conflict and labeling perspectives has risen. Two of the more recent—and the best—works on the police are *Justice Without Trial,* 2d ed. (New York: Wiley, 1975) by Jerome Skolnick and *City Police* (New York: Random House, 1973) by Jonathan Rubinstein. Both books resulted from extensive contact with police officers and both provide very balanced views of police work. A more detailed analysis of the factors influencing arrests can be found in W. R. LaFave's *Arrest: The Decision to Take a Suspect into Custody* (Boston: Little, Brown, 1965).

    One of the clearest looks at the operations of our courts comes in seminovel form. Arthur Rosett and D. R. Cressey have written a hypothetical account of a defendant's movement through the court system following an arrest for burglary. The book, *Justice by Consent* (Philadelphia: Lippincott, 1976), offers the reader without a technical, criminological orientation an understanding of the plea-bargaining process and where it fits in our court system. Howard James provides a similarly effective discussion of the courts in his *Crisis in the Courts,* rev. ed. (New York: McKay, 1977).

8

Corrections System

A criminal justice system that produces officially labeled criminals must develop a subsystem to deal with such persons. The products of our court system, convicted offenders, are subjected to various degrees of supervision, punishment, and treatment. Some receive suspended sentences and probation and must report regularly to a probation officer. Some are placed in minimum-security facilities and are sometimes allowed temporary leaves. Some are totally confined in maximum-security prisons. Depending on their records in prison, some offenders may be placed back into society before the completion of their prison sentences through supervised parole.

In this chapter we will examine the subsystem of the criminal justice system that supervises, punishes, and attempts to aid offenders—namely, the corrections system. We will present an overview of orientations toward punishment and correction of offenders and devote attention to the institutions and places where these activities occur: jails, prisons, and community corrections programs. Finally, we will discuss the failure of attempted rehabilitation of offenders and suggest the future direction of the corrections system.

What Is "Correction"?

"Correction" implies repair or alteration. Regarding criminals, correction theoretically refers to changing or correcting an individual's inclination toward or pattern of law violation. Though, as we shall see below, correction takes many forms—punishment, behavior modification, counseling, job assistance—all forms involve some degree of deprivation of liberty. Thus, we may define "correction" as *the deprivation of an individual's freedom in order to alter his or her behavior from criminal to conventional.*

Not everyone will agree that all correctional actions imply deprivation of freedom. Some will argue that deprivation of freedom constitutes punishment whereas modern correctional philosophy emphasizes treatment that aids the offender. Stated another way, can we really be punishing people if we are helping or curing them? The answer is yes. No matter what its form or its motive, the fact remains that corrections is activity in which offenders are *forced* to engage. They would not be undergoing correction had they not been caught committing a crime, and they would not choose correction if given the option of "no correction." As one report puts it (American Friends Service Committee, 1971:23–24):

> There is an easy test that can be applied to any purported abolition of punishment or imprisonment [in favor of "nonpunitive correction"]. Is the proposed alternative program voluntary? Can the subject take it or leave it? If he takes it, can he leave it any time he wants? If the answer to any of these questions is "no," then the wolf is still under the sheepskin.

Changing Corrections Orientations

The history of dealing with law violators in the United States reflects ongoing attempts to reconcile three primary objectives: (1) punishment of offenders, (2) rehabilitation of offenders, and (3) custody of offenders for society's protection. Though rehabilitation efforts have always characterized the prison system, punishment and custody orientations predominated until the 1950s. Prisons were, in fact, developed relatively recently as substitutes for "less humane" forms of punishment such as mutilation, beatings, or placement in such devices as stocks and pillories. Imprisonment of offenders also was seen as necessary for society's protection when other forms of punishment failed.

Punishment of offenders has generally been justified on the grounds that it is a deterrent to further criminal behavior by the offender, is a general deterrent to other members of society contemplating crimes, and is a source of revenge or justice. Emphasis on these different functions has shifted throughout the years, but the use of punishment, either by itself or combined with treatment techniques (such as vocational training), was a constant until fairly recently. The Auburn System (named after a New York penitentiary opened in 1817) served as the model for American prison systems for 150 years. It emphasized discipline designed to break a prisoner's criminal spirit and force him or her to conform. Prisoners worked and had meals together but were never allowed to speak or communicate with each other. The inmates were housed in individual cells within a fortresslike structure with many tiers—much like the design of maximum-security prisons today. Corporal punishment was used to enforce prison rules.[1]

---

[1] For a discussion of the development of American prisons, see D. Rothman (1971).

Strong humanitarian ideals, increasing confidence in the behavioral sciences' ability to predict and change individuals' behavior, and a growing frustration with the ability of the prison system to reform prisoners combined in the late 1940s and early 1950s to produce subtle changes in prisons. The punishment model, which viewed the offender as evil, began to give way to a medical or treatment model, which viewed the offender as sick or maladjusted and in need of rehabilitation.

The medical or treatment model gained prominence in the late 1950s and early 1960s. Penal institutions became "correctional facilities." A number of individual and group counseling and therapy programs were introduced into prisons. Guards were labeled "counselors." Educational and vocational training programs were expanded. Indeterminate sentences were widely used; that is, offenders were sentenced to prison for as long as it took to be judged "rehabilitated." It was in this atmosphere that punishment for reformation, revenge, justice, and general deterrence became deemphasized. "Corrections" came to represent attempts to remake, not to break, prisoners. The source of their illness (their criminality) would be diagnosed and treated.

For reasons we will discuss later in this chapter, most experts now consider the in-prison treatment model a failure. This failure and public fear of crime in the late 1960s and early 1970s have led to a renewed emphasis on the custody orientation to corrections. That is, the major function of the corrections system is seen as the protection of society from criminals. Questions of justice and rehabilitation have become secondary. What is left of the rehabilitation theme exists in the concept of community-based corrections. Community corrections programs attempt to submit the offender to noninstitutional treatment. Basically, any form of corrections that occurs outside of prison may be called community oriented. These alternatives to prison take the form of probation and parole, halfway-house residential treatment centers, and release and furlough programs, which are all described in this chapter. The programs seek to provide offenders with a full range of social services and, more importantly, to enlist the aid of the community in encouraging conventional values and behavior from the offenders. Because of community concern with safety, most community-based corrections efforts are directed toward lower-risk, lesser offenders. Thus, the value of the community-based corrections model lies not so much in the correction of lesser offenders as in removing them from the corrupting influences of the prison setting.

In sum, the corrections system has been and remains multi-oriented. At various times, it has operated within a punishment framework; at other times, a rehabilitation framework; and at other times, a custody framework. The constant shift in orientations signifies responses to a number of influential parties: the public that demands protection, the moralists who demand justice, the humanitarians who seek humane treatment of offenders, corrections "scientists" who are attempting to find "what works," and rehabilitation advocates who are convinced that offenders can be turned into conventional citizens. In the early 1960s, rehabilitation advocates prevailed. Today, the custody orientation predominates, though the treatment model exists in community-based corrections. Perhaps the best understanding of present-day corrections can be achieved through a description of current "places of correction." To this end, the bulk of this chapter is devoted to discussions of jails, prisons, and community-based corrections as they currently exist.

Jails

Jails are local detention and correctional facilities run by city or county administrators, often the sheriff's department. They are designed primarily as holding centers for persons awaiting trial, sentencing, or appeal decisions. However, jails are also utilized as short-term correctional institutions for "small-time" offenders who might be sentenced to serve a few months to a year in jail. Jails also serve as short-term holding facilities for community problem cases such as drunks, mentally ill persons, and individuals with drug problems.

According to a 1972 survey of local jails (U.S. Department of Justice, 1976a), we can expect to find about 142,000 persons confined in this country at any given time. Of this total, slightly more than half (about 78,000) have been convicted and are serving time or awaiting sentencing or appeals outcomes. Slightly less than half (about 63,000) have not been convicted of a crime (most are awaiting trial) or have an undetermined conviction status. The majority of jail inmates (94 percent) are males. Sixty-one percent are between the ages of eighteen and twenty-nine. Fifty-seven percent are white; 42 percent are black. Most inmates have not completed high school. The vast majority of inmates of both races earn less than $5,000 per year (based on income in the year preceding incarceration). Fifty-seven percent of the inmates of both races were unemployed at the time they were admitted to jail.

Because jails have been considered short-term or temporary holding facilities, they have generally been ignored by the public and by correctional reformers. Recently, however, jails have received severe criticism (see, for example, U.S. Department of Justice, 1975; Goldfarb, 1975). Locally controlled, they receive inadequate financial support. Most jails are overcrowded, poorly maintained facilities whose conditions endanger physical and mental health. Cells are small and cagelike. Sanitary equipment is poor or nonexistent. Adequate medical and recreational facilities are rare. Vocational and recreational programs are rarer still.

Unlike prisons, which generally maintain at least minimal standards for employment, local jails are extremely poorly staffed. Employees are few in number and generally untrained. Often they are sheriff's deputies who perform many other jobs besides jail duties. In some areas, assignment to jail duty is viewed as a punishment or demotion by deputies. The possibility of rehabilitative services is precluded by the lack of trained staff and by inadequate funds with which to hire professional rehabilitative personnel. Changes in staff qualifications and capabilities are unlikely, given community reluctance to allocate tax money toward jail improvements.

The major criticism leveled at local jails is that they do little screening and segregating of inmates. Thus, persons awaiting trial often share cells with convicts serving time. An individual serving a short sentence for drug possession may share a cell with a person charged with murder or rape. Young first offenders are thrown in with hardened criminals or mentally disturbed persons. With minimal supervision of prisoners, physical, sexual, and emotional assaults are common. It is no mere coincidence that jails are sometimes used by district attorneys to encourage defendants to plead guilty or somehow aid the state in return for a transfer to a state prison or community corrections program.

A number of reforms are currently being suggested or implemented in a few local jails, especially those in large, urban areas. More attention is being paid to staff qualifications; inmates are being segregated by detention status (that is, awaiting trial or serving time), by past record, and by current charge. Educational, recreational, and rehabilitation programs are being introduced. Many types of prisoners formerly kept in jails are now being assigned to community-based correctional facilities; for example, drug rehabilitation programs.

The key to the success of these reforms is financial backing. However, most reform programs are now sponsored by federal grants. If and when federal support ceases, local communities must assume support. Their historical reluctance to use community funds for local jails points to a bleak future for serious, long-term jail reform.

Prisons

Prisons are state or federally operated penal and correctional institutions. Three general types of prisons exist: maximum security, medium security, and minimum security. These classifications reflect both the criminal justice system's perceptions of the dangerousness of inmates and the extent to which security measures are used to confine inmates.

Maximum-security prisons most closely approximate the public's view of the prison (usually formed from movies). They generally resemble fortresses, with great walls separating prisoners from the outside world. Some guards patrol the walls of the prison while others keep watch within the various cell blocks. Dining, sanitary, recreation, work, and social activities are regimented and highly supervised. In essence, the prisoner is rarely unobserved.

Medium-security prisons generally resemble enclosed campuses. Dormitories replace cellblocks, and buildings are more clearly separated from each other. Recreational, vocational, and counseling facilities and programs exist in greater numbers. Still, prisoners are highly supervised and controlled. Guards man the perimeter of the institution, and prisoners are under relatively constant surveillance. The major difference between maximum- and medium-security prisons is that inmates in the latter institutions are considered more "reformable" and somewhat less dangerous.

Minimum-security prisons, more often called "correctional centers," differ greatly from maximum- and medium-security institutions. They are generally open, with few walls or fences and little perimeter supervision. Nearly all such facilities demand some form of work (for example, cutting lumber) from inmates. Some provide rehabilitation programs, but these are the exception since most prisoners in minimum-security facilities are not seen as needing rehabilitation. Most are small-time offenders or persons of social or political stature who have been caught in such crimes as embezzlement or accepting bribes. They are in prison not because they are considered dangerous but because they are seen as being in need of some form of just punishment. Since the Watergate scandal, which resulted in sentences in minimum-security prisons for several high-level political figures, the public has become more aware of minimum-security institutions.

There are about 45 federal and 350 state correctional facilities in the United States. Of the state prisons, about one-third are maximum-

Table 8–1
Distribution of State Prisoner Population, FBI-Index Offenses, and U.S. Population, By Region—1975

Region	Percentage of prisoner population	Percentage of FBI-index offenses	Percentage of U.S. population
Northeast	16	22	23
North Central	22	26	27
South	47	28	32
West	15	24	18
Total	100	100	100

Source: U.S. Department of Justice, Law Enforcement Assistance Administration, *Prisoners in State and Federal Institutions on December 31, 1975* (Washington, D.C.: U.S. Government Printing Office, 1977), p. 3, and 1975 F.B.I. *Uniform Crime Reports*, pp. 50–54.

security facilities, one-third medium-security, and one-third minimum-security.

Among the leading states in prison populations are Texas, California, New York, Florida, North Carolina, and Ohio (U.S. Department of Justice, 1977:3-4). Surprisingly, when the prison population is divided by region, the South accounts for nearly half of all prisoners, though it accounts for only 29 percent of the FBI-index crimes reported in the United States and contains only 32 percent of the country's population (see Table 8-1).

As of December 31, 1975, state and federal correctional facilities housed 242,750 inmates serving sentences of at least one year. Of this number, 90 percent were confined in state prisons (U.S. Department of Justice, 1977:1-2). As of this date, the number of prisoners in America was the largest in the nation's history. As Figure 8-1 illustrates, the number of inmates in prisons rose from 1925 to 1939, dropped steadily through the war years, and then began an upward climb until 1960. The early 1960s saw a steady decline in prison populations. However, with rising public concern about crime in the late 1960s and early 1970s, the trend was again reversed, and prison populations have now grown larger than ever.

Table 8-2 displays an increase of 46,658 prisoners between 1972 and 1975—a 24 percent rise. This growth has been so sudden that some prisons now face problems of overcrowding, a shortage of staff, and difficulty in maintaining adequate health conditions. So great has the problem become that some prisons have refused to accept, or have been ordered by the courts not to accept, more inmates. This in turn places burdens on other facilities such as local jails. Although the public wishes to see more criminals behind bars, it is not willing to increase financial support of correctional facilities.

As the data in Table 8-2 indicate, most prisoners are males. Males constitute about 96 percent of prison inmate populations, though the percentage of female prisoners has been increasing in recent years. According to a survey of inmates in state institutions in 1974 (U.S. Department of Justice, 1976b:24-25), prison populations were composed of 51 percent white inmates and 47 percent black. Two-thirds of the inmates were between the ages of twenty and thirty-four. Most had not completed high school, only 9 percent had attended college. Most inmates had been employed in the month prior to arrest, though the majority had earned less than $6,000 during the year prior to arrest. Most had held jobs such as truck driver, welder, service worker, or laborer.

The Inmate Social System

A major characteristic of total institutions such as prisons and mental hospitals is the development of an inmate culture, a set of rules, roles, and statuses that shape the lives of inmates (Goffman,

Figure 8–1
Number of sentenced prisoners in state and federal institutions at year end, 1925–75.

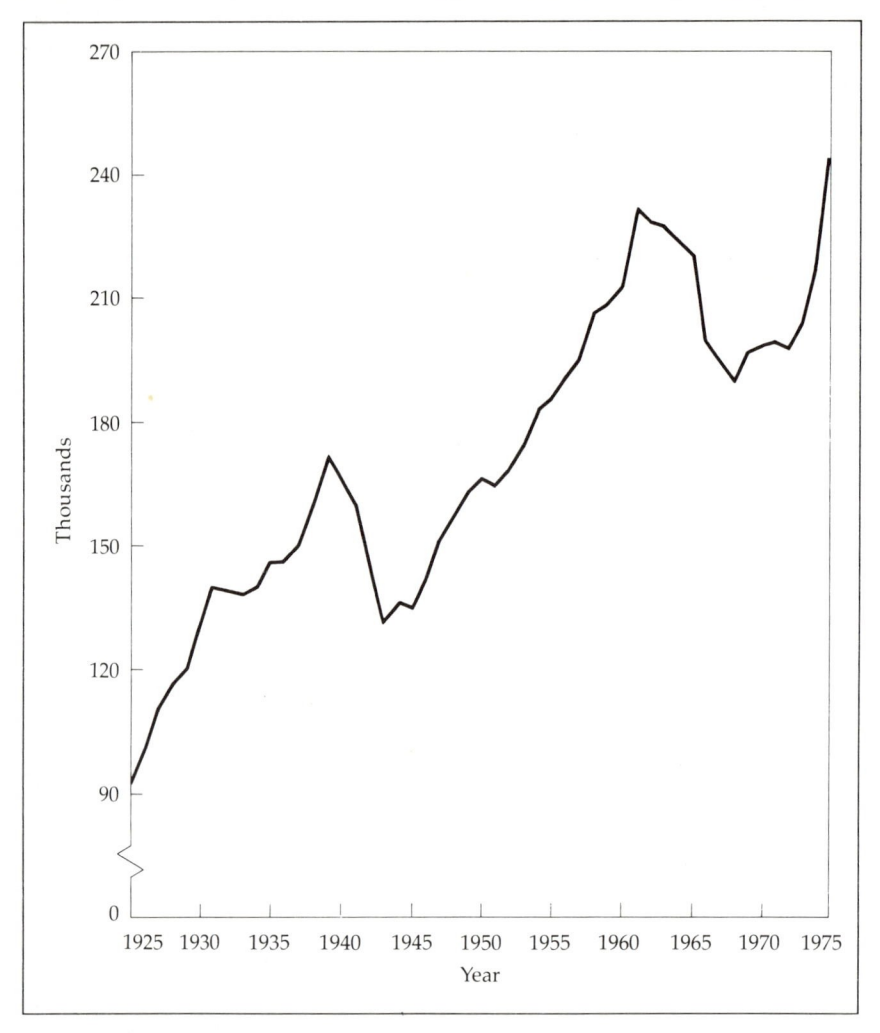

Source: U.S. Department of Justice, Law Enforcement Assistance Administration, *Prisoners in State and Federal Institutions on December 31, 1975* (Washington, D.C.: U.S. Government Printing Office, 1977), p. 14.

1961:66–70). The inmate culture arises from the fact that inmates bring into prison from the outside world a need for guidelines for everyday living. It is also a direct response to what Sykes (1958:65–78) has labeled "the pains of imprisonment." Sykes argues that prison strips inmates of most aspects of individual identity and self-worth and deprives them of conventionally valued goods and services (for example,

Table 8-2
Male and Female Prisoners in State and Federal Institutions Serving at Least One-year Sentences—1972-75

	Males	Females	Total
1972			
Federal	20,919	794	21,713
State	168,904	5,475	174,379
Total	189,823	6,269	196,092
1973			
Federal	21,883	932	22,815
State	175,644	5,752	181,396
Total	197,527	6,684	204,211
1974			
Federal	21,367	994	22,361
State	189,710	6,395	196,105
Total	211,077	7,389	218,466
1975			
Federal	23,024	1,105	24,131
State	210,874	7,745	218,619
Total	233,900	8,850	242,750

Source: M. J. Hindelang et al., *Sourcebook of Criminal Justice Statistics—1976* (Washington, D.C.: U.S. Government Printing Office, 1977), p. 686, and U.S. Department of Justice, Law Enforcement Assistance Administration, *Prisoners in State and Federal Institutions on December 31, 1975* (Washington, D.C.: U.S. Government Printing Office, 1977).

nonuniform, self-expressive apparel), heterosexual relationships, autonomy (personal control over one's life), and security (a feeling of personal safety).

Responding to an environment that is characterized by such deprivations and that seeks to reduce individuality among prisoners (through such devices as shaved heads, uniforms, and identification by number), inmates develop their own social system and culture. As Cressey (1973:118) notes, the complexity of this system never can be fully appreciated by the outsider. However, Sykes and Messinger (1960:5-19) report that it contains an elaborate value system, with explicit behavioral codes and social roles and statuses.

Inmates become part of this social system through the process of *prisonization* (see Clemmer, 1958:298-301; Wheeler, 1961:697-712; Garabedian, 1963:139-52). This is the socialization process by which an inmate is assimilated into the inmate culture—that is, comes to think and act in terms of the prison social environment. The process is characterized by "acceptance of the inferior role, accumulation of facts concerning the organization of the prison, the development of somewhat new habits of eating, dressing, working, sleeping, the adoption of local language, the recognition that nothing is owed to the environment for the supplying of needs, and the eventual desire for a good job

(Clemmer, 1958:299)." In sum, Clemmer (1958:299) notes, "prisonization is the taking on, in greater or lesser degree, of the folkways, mores, customs, and general culture of the penitentiary." Although prisonization occurs in varying degrees and proceeds at different rates among prisoners, no prisoner is totally untouched by the process.

Sykes and Messinger (1960) divide the inmate social rules, or the "inmate code," into five general categories. The first cautions against interfering with the interests of other inmates; in short, it demands loyalty and the minding of one's own business. The second involves "keeping cool"; that is, staying out of trouble with other inmates and doing nothing to bring on the attention of the prison staff. Third, prisoners are not to exploit each other, either by force or trickery; in short, they are not to lie to, steal from, or cheat each other. Fourth, prisoners are made to "stand tough"; they must not weaken or give in to staff pressures. Finally, prisoners must maintain a social distance from the staff; although they must obey direct orders, they must not overtly cooperate or socialize with guards or administrators. In sum, inmate rules—*don't squeal, be cool, be loyal, be tough, don't break your word, be right, don't be a sucker*—serve both to set the inmate world apart from the administration and to govern relations among inmates.

As in any social system, the inmate system is characterized by a number of social roles and statuses stemming from the needs of the prisoners and the degree to which various inmates adhere to "the code." Cressey (1973:135–38; see also, Irwin and Cressey, 1962) describes three inmate subcultures that reflect role and status differences in prison.

The first subculture is that of the "thief." This subculture has ties to the outside world in that professional thieves hold high status in the criminal world. They are viewed as persons dedicated to crime and a cut above the common criminal. This status is carried over into the prison world, where such criminals are called "right guys" or "real men"—inmates who adhere to the "inmate code" and neither seek out trouble nor run from it. As Sykes and Messinger (1960:8) put it, "A *right guy* sticks up for his rights, but he doesn't ask for pity: he can take all the lousy screws can hand out and more. . . ." In brief, the "right guys" are not prison oriented but simply do their time while awaiting reentry into the outside criminal world.

Cressey speaks as well of the "convict" subculture, which, unlike the "thief" subculture, is oriented toward prison life. Within this subculture are a number of roles, each accorded varying degrees of social status and each reflecting a degree of deviation from "the code." "Politicians," "peddlers," "shots," and "merchants" are all persons who successfully manipulate the system so that they gain a greater share of prison-valued goods and services. For example, a "merchant" may be assigned to a food-preparation unit and may sell or trade portions of food or coffee in return for some other valued item or favor.

In addition to economically manipulative prisoners, the inmate culture is composed of physically manipulative or coercive prisoners known as "gorillas" (or "toughs," "hoods," "ballbusters"). "Gorillas" exploit other inmates through threats and violence. They are likely to attack both weaker prisoners and staff. They sell "protection" in return for goods and services. They are considered more dangerous than other prisoners by both inmates and staff. More than any other inmates, "gorillas" depart from "the code."

Finally, Cressey points to a third subculture, that of the "square John," "straight," or "do-right." These persons are basically noncriminal, fitting in with neither the "thieves" nor the "convicts." Although they undergo some degree of prisonization, "square Johns" remain relatively isolated from other inmates. They serve their time quietly, waiting to return to the conventional world, and are little bother to the prison staff.

Most prisoners probably overlap somewhat in their membership in the above subcultures. All offer at least some allegiance to the "inmate code," though members of the "convict" subculture tend to selectively base their allegiance on the extent to which "the code" allows them to better their positions in prison. For example, merchants violate "the code" in exploiting other inmates but expect to be left alone in their endeavors because "the code" commands prisoners to mind their own business. Most prisoners are definitely influenced by the values of the high-status "thief" subculture. Yet strict imitation of the "thieves"— that is, strong allegiance to "the code"—may place an inmate in a poor position if most other inmates violate it. There are scarce goods and services to be had and, if one is to obtain them, one must play the "convict" subculture game to some degree.

Viewed from an organizational perspective, the inmate social system clearly provides inmates with what prison is designed to take from them: social solidarity (a "we" feeling) and social identity (the sense that one is not "different" yet is still seen as an individual within the boundaries of the prison). "The code" and the status system of the prison give inmates a guide for determining self-worth (whether high or low) and thereby provide each with a "social place" in what would otherwise be a social vacuum. Finally, the social system—even when marked by some inmate exploitation of other inmates—serves to place limitations on administrative control (or exploitation) of inmates. The inmate social system and culture represent a formula for survival for the inmate.

Politicization of Prisoners

As stable as the prison social system appears to have been through the years, some recent changes are observable. These involve the politicization of some prisoners; that is, the interpretation of their imprisonment and their treatment in prison in terms of political conflict in society. Rather than viewing themselves as criminals and orienting themselves toward the traditional inmate culture, some prisoners have come to view themselves as being politically oppressed and to orient their prison life toward political activism. This is especially true of black prisoners. The late George Jackson (1970:35) wrote from prison:

> Growing numbers of blacks . . . have become aware that their only hope lies in resistance. They have learned that resistance is actually possible. The holds are beginning to slip away. Very few men imprisoned for economic crimes or even crimes of passion against the oppressor feel they are really guilty. Most of today's black convicts have come to understand that they are the most abused victims of an unrighteous order . . . [and] have been transformed into an implacable army of liberation.

The militant posture of black and, in some prisons, Mexican-American prisoners has produced two important changes in prisons. First, it has increased racial tensions, as minority inmates have come to define white prisoners as oppressors, just like whites on the outside. These tensions have resulted in fighting among prison groups, especially among blacks and militant whites such as members of prison Nazi factions. Second, the increased militant or "resistant" posture of the black prisoners has resulted in a greater "gorilla" orientation among inmates. That is, more defiance and force are being aimed at guards and other prisoners. Slowly, the high status of the "right guy" is diminishing, and the detachment stressed in the "inmate code" is being granted less allegiance. Whether or not these changes will have long-term influences on the general inmate social system has yet to be seen.

Sex in Prison

Part of the inmate social system and culture involves sexual customs in prison (see Gagnon and Simon, 1968; Johnson, 1971). Some observers estimate that about one-third of most prison populations engage in homosexuality at least occasionally (Johnson, 1971:83). Most sex in prison is adaptive—that is, a response to heterosexual deprivation. Among male prisoners, most of those who engage in sexual acts with other prisoners do not view themselves as homosexuals. This self-definition stems from the fact that they always take what they see as the "male" role in sex. They sodomize other inmates but are not themselves sodomized; other inmates perform oral sexual acts on them but they never reciprocate. In short, they have sex with "female substitutes." Within the prison, persons who participate in these pseudo-heterosexual acts are not labeled "queer."

A small number of male prisoners *are* considered homosexual by the rest of the inmates. These persons are viewed as femalelike sex objects; that is, persons who perform fellatio and are sodomized. Some homosexual prisoners take on the role as a preference; they come to be known as "broads." Others, particularly young, slightly-built inmates, are coerced into the role. Coercion generally takes the form of the rape of a new, unattached prisoner. Once raped, the prisoner is defined as a "punk" and will be treated as a homosexual for the remainder of his time in prison.

The unattached "broad" or "punk" is fair game for gang rapes by "wolves"—sexually aggressive male attackers. To avoid these attacks, homosexual prisoners will often "set up house" with basically heterosexual prisoners. In these relationships, the "male" prisoner will support and protect the "female" prisoner. The homosexual partner will in turn play the role of "wife." This role is based on a very traditional view of the woman in American society: very submissive, highly feminine (especially as a sex partner), and preoccupied with keeping house. In other words, male inmates form marital or steady relationships that correspond closely to nonprison heterosexual relationships. These attachments are considered somewhat sacred by other inmates, as they are in the outside world. According to the "inmate code," rape of attached homosexuals is forbidden. Such rapes will be avenged by the "husband" or partner of the homosexual, and the penalty is usually death.

In sum, homosexuality in the all-male prison serves a number of functions. The most obvious of these is the response to the heterosexual deprivation accompanying imprisonment. The "female" role played by the homosexual "broad" or "punk" allows heterosexual prisoners to engage in sexual acts without absolute loss of normal sexual identity. Homosexuality also brings a certain amount of stability to the prison in the sense that it defines status and role hierarchies and, in the case of "marriages," defines property rights.

Control of Prisoners

No matter what their orientation (punishment, revenge, rehabilitation), prisons are first and foremost organized to gain control over inmates so that they (1) will not escape, (2) will not harm the typically outnumbered staff, and (3) will not cause disturbances (such as riots) that occasion public wrath and political interference in prison administration. Order—or, more precisely, a tolerable level of disorder—is the chief concern of prison administrators.

The primary mechanism of order maintenance is clearly the threat of force. Although the staff of a prison is generally outnumbered by the inmates, staff weaponry and resources (for example, the state militia) serve as the dominant threat against a prisoner takeover of an institution. Yet not all disorder is of the magnitude that requires "calling in the troops." In everyday attempts to secure order, prison staff rely on three control mechanisms: punishment, strategic concessions, and prisoner control of prisoners (Cressey, 1973:138–41).

Until recently, punishment was a very effective control mechanism. Prisoners were beaten to obtain discipline. Some were placed in "the hole," a dark, solitary-confinement cell. These cells were generally very small, devoid of furnishings, and poorly lit and ventilated. Prisoners were often stripped and forced to sleep in these cold cells without blankets. They were fed subsistence diets. The psychological effects of such confinement were as harmful as the physical effects. Although beatings and confinement in "the hole" are no longer routinely permitted, psychological punishment in the form of social isolation of prisoners (confinement to a cell in an isolated cell block) remains common.

Restrictions on the use of corporal punishment and solitary confinement have somewhat limited the prison staff's means of controlling prisoners. Thus, the staff has come to rely more directly on strategic concessions to prisoners. Minor infractions of institutional rules are overlooked in return for compliance with major rules and a refrain from general defiance. In essence, prison guards need cooperation from prisoners, and prisoners are aware of this. The guard whose cell block is a source of constant disruption will not do well in terms of job promotions and salary increases. Thus, guards curry the favor of inmates, especially those who are influential within the inmate social system. These inmates will "keep the lid on" in return for staff compromises. Prisoners may be placed in cell blocks with their friends. Guards may overlook contraband or even bring it into the prison. Guards may ignore homosexual marriages and rapes. Occasional retaliatory violent attacks by prisoners on other prisoners may also be allowed (McCorkle, 1956). Prisoners are also kept compliant through rewards. These usually take the form of special assignments to prison jobs (such as mail carrier or canteen worker) that place the inmate in a favorable position in the inmate bartering system.

For the most part, however, control over inmates is accomplished by other, more powerful inmates. Within any total institution, some inmates come to hold a greater share of valued goods and services: certain jobs or duties, favors from guards, high social status, a corner on a given market (such as cigarettes, coffee, new uniforms) that permits trading for other valuables. Prisoners in this position wish to preserve the status quo. To do so, they champion the "inmate code," stressing the commandments regarding not causing trouble and not interfering with other prisoners. Thus, though the inmate culture promotes inmate solidarity, it also preserves the inmate power structure, including existing patterns of inmate exploitation of other inmates.

In silent collaboration with the prison staff, the more powerful inmates—whether "right guys" trying to maintain a system that basically leaves them alone or "convicts" trying to preserve favorable social and economic positions—attempt to keep other inmates in line. Thus, a good deal of informal social pressure (such as ostracism or attribution of low status) is brought to bear against "gorillas" who, if left to their own devices, would disrupt the inmate social system and cause the kind of chaos that brings on outside interference in the administration of the prison.

Finally, internal factional struggles within the prison, if somewhat controlled, keep the inmates from plotting any organized disruption or move against the administration. Racial infighting and territorial disputes among inmates thus actually promote an acceptable level of disorder within prisons by keeping inmates preoccupied with petty squabbles.

In sum, control of prisoners takes both formal and informal shapes. On the formal side, prisoners are kept in line through threats of force and disciplinary action and through offers of incentives for good behavior. More important is the informal side of control, which is brought about by the prisoners themselves. In essence, prisoners accomplish the administration's task by emphasizing an "inmate code" that supports a power elite among prisoners and by infighting that keeps prisoners too occupied to accomplish concerted disruptions.

Women's Prisons

As Table 8–2 above indicated, far fewer women than men inhabit this country's prisons. Only 4 percent of the nation's prisoners are women. Although women's prisons still emphasize control and security, they differ considerably from men's.[3] Structurally, they have fewer perimeter-security devices and guards. They more closely resemble men's minimum-security prisons in design, with dormitories or, often, cottages and many separate buildings for educational and counseling programs. Rehabilitation is ostensibly more heavily emphasized in the women's prison, though, as some observers report, rehabilitation is primarily a matter of attempting to instill in inmates a dedication to the traditional homemaker role (Giallombardo, 1966:7–8). Smart (1977:97) argues that the penal system for women

> ... creates a situation in which realistic and potentially self-determining educational and vocational courses are intention-

---

[3]Fewer studies of women's prisons than of men's prisons are available. Among the better works are Chandler (1973), Giallombardo (1966), Heffernan (1972), and Ward and Kassebaum (1965).

ally excluded or reduced in importance ... [Women's] typically dependent status will be confirmed and their ability to control or possibly change their life-styles further damaged [in prisons]. Penal policy for female offenders is geared to preserving the typical female role, its intention is to make women and girls adapt to their pre-given passive social role which by definition is thought to preclude deviant behavior.

The women's prison differs most from the men's, however, in its social structure. Missing from women's prisons are the "thief" subculture with its "right guy" orientation and the "convict" subculture with its exploitive roles. "Merchants" are rare; "politicians" and "gorillas" are practically nonexistent. There is no equivalent to the "inmate code" of the men's prisons. Cooperation with staff is prevalent. Female inmates tend to resemble the "square John" type of prisoner, undoubtedly because so few were hardened criminals before imprisonment.

Although the inmate subculture and "the code" promote solidarity and social identity among male prisoners, the female inmates' response to the deprivations of imprisonment involves the development of small groups, which protect and sustain their members. These groups are characterized by family and kinship roles: "parents," "husband," "wife," and male and female "children." Inmates tend to form homosexual "marriage" or "steady" bonds, which, though violated as in the outside world, serve "who's who" and "hands off" functions in the prison.

Homosexuality is more pervasive in female prisons than in male prisons. As in the male prison, however, most homosexuality is adaptive—that is, carried on in prison to fulfill both sexual and emotional needs, and then abandoned upon the inmate's release from prison. Female prison homosexuality is also marked by very clear-cut sexual roles. Some women, a minority, assume a male or "butch" role, but the majority assume the more traditional female or "femme" role. For the most part, these roles survive throughout the institutional stay, and occasional wanderings are frowned upon or considered foolish.

In sum, though solidarity and identity are achieved in men's prisons through commitment to the "inmate code" and inmate culture, these entities are achieved in women's prisons through "family" commitments. Solidarity is small-group in nature—one does not exploit or bring trouble to "family" members, though non-"family" members may be exploited or troubled. Self-identity and self-worth are not obtained through one's position in prison but stem from the status accorded by one's "family."

Rehabilitation in Prison

As we noted earlier in this chapter, in the late 1950s and early 1960s there were large-scale attempts at introducing a treatment or rehabilitation orientation into prisons. Treatment referred to "making the patient better." That is, criminals were viewed as ill (emotionally or socially maladjusted) and in need of rehabilitation. Rehabilitation took two primary forms: (1) psychological counseling or therapy and (2) educational and vocational training.

Whatever their form, rehabilitation efforts within prison have come to be regarded as failures. This conclusion is based on the results of studies such as that concerned with the effects of numerous group counseling programs in a California prison (Kassebaum et al., 1971). Researchers randomly assigned incoming inmates to one of several counseling programs and evaluated their adjustment to prison and their records three years after release from prison. The researchers eventually concluded that *none* of the various types of counseling reduced hostility toward prison staff, violation of prison rules, parole violations, length of time out of prison, and seriousness of offenses while on parole. According to "the Martinson Report" (Martinson, 1974), a review of 230 pieces of prison research that were relatively methodicalogically sound, this finding is not uncommon. The report argues that education and skill-development programs and individual and group counseling techniques have been ineffective in reducing postrelease failure. It should be noted that this a general conclusion: *some* programs have been found to be effective for *some* types of offenders, but a general formula for rehabilitating prisoners has not been found (Palmer, 1975).

Before we discuss the reasons for the failure of the institutional rehabilitation model, some mention should be made of what constitutes "success" or "failure." Although all rehabilitation programs strive to make prisoners "better persons" or "more functional members of society," their ultimate goal has been the reduction of postrelease criminality or recidivism. Recidivism is sometimes measured in terms of arrests but is more often viewed as conviction for a felony or violation of parole conditions (for example, leaving the state without permission). The "failure" of institutional rehabilitation programs is a failure to reduce recidivism rates below those of prisoners not exposed to rehabilitation programs and those diverted to community-based corrections programs. In short, "failure" means that rehabilitation efforts have simply made no difference. Regardless of correctional programs to which inmates are exposed, approximately 35 percent will violate parole or be convicted of a felony within two years after release from prison. The figure climbs to 63 percent by eighteen years after release (Kitchener et al., 1977).

The failure of the institutional rehabilitation model can be attributed to a number of factors.

Lack of Political and Economic Support. Some argue that the treatment model was not given a fair chance, that insufficient funds were allocated to it. There is probably some merit to this claim. Legislators have been careful to respond to prison-reform interest groups, but they have made it clear that their priorities lie with pleasing the greater voting public. Hence, legislators resist being placed in a position that leaves them open to accusations of being "soft on criminals." The result has been a lukewarm political commitment to the funding of rehabilitation programs.

Lack of Prison Administration Support. When it was first proposed, many prison administrators resisted implementation of the rehabilitation model, fearing that it would make maintenance of order in the prison and control of prisoners difficult. However, administrators soon learned that without committing themselves to the model, they could selectively employ elements of it to better control prisoners. Chief among these elements was the indeterminate sentence, which left the decision about the length of time to be served solely to the parole board. The ability to keep a prisoner indefinitely (until "rehabilitated") could be used as a potent threat to force prisoners to conform to administration and staff wishes. Parole was thus granted not on the basis of rehabilitation success but on the basis of a prisoner's ability to stay out of trouble or provide information or services to prison authorities.

Staff Resistance. Although prison staff members were able to make use of certain aspects of the treatment model, for the most part they resisted its implementation. The model placed them in a precarious position. On the one hand, they were told that their major responsibility was maintaining order within the prison. On the other hand, they were told to rehabilitate inmates without receiving instructions as to how to accomplish the task. Given the fact that the staff members had developed means of keeping order through relationships with influential inmates and various forms of rewards and punishments, they would not jeopardize their positions by pursuing a vaguely defined rehabilitation orientation.

Inmate Resistance. In the same manner that the prison staff felt threatened by the rehabilitation model, influential and powerful inmates viewed it as a threat to the status quo inmate power structure. Basically, the model oriented prisoners to the outside world rather than to the "thief" and "convict" subcultures. Thus, stronger inmates actively resisted rehabilitation by stressing adherence to the "inmate code," which forbade cooperation and communication with prison administrators and staff. The treatment model could not survive without these elements.

Lack of Knowledge. The greatest hindrance faced by the rehabilitation model was the fact that it assumed knowledge we do not possess. Generally, we cannot cure ills without knowledge about what causes them. Yet the rehabilitation model tried to treat inmates with inadequate knowledge about the causes of their criminal behavior. The odds against the success of a model that operates only on guesses and good intentions are enormous.

These problems greatly decreased the life of the institutional rehabilitation experiment. Today the custody orientation prevails in prison. Some rehabilitative services (for example, classes for inmates) still exist, but hopes for a totally restructured correction system are gone. Some argue that the failure represents a blessing in disguise, for it allows the corrections system to begin from scratch and reconstruct a more realistic approach to the custody and treatment of offenders (Conrad, 1973). Some believe that the answer lies in the concept of community-based corrections.

Community-Based Corrections

Some convicted offenders are kept in the community rather than in the prison. In the 1970s, community-based corrections have been viewed by many as the form corrections must take if rehabilitation of offenders is ever to be accomplished.

Community-based corrections refers to all correctional activities that occur in the community. They are viewed as alternatives to incarceration and include such programs and activities as pretrial diversion and probation, halfway houses, release and furlough programs, and parole. All of these forms are described below. Before reviewing them, however, we should mention the theory and rationale behind community-based corrections.

Those advocating correction of offenders within the community argue first that this form of correction is more humanitarian than imprisonment is. Prisons are commonly viewed as being places of human deprivation, exploitation, and danger. They are labeled nonrehabilitative and, some argue, actually further corrupt the criminal. Alternatively, community-based corrections programs are viewed as mechanisms that provide incentive and motivate the offender to avoid criminal behavior. This is accomplished by integrating the offender into conventional activities and values and, especially, by raising his or her stake in the conventional economic system. Thus, one area of community corrections is employment placement. Beyond this, the programs seek to provide the offender with a full range of social services. Finally, community-based corrections work on the assumption that offenders must develop ties to and receive greater pressure from conventional persons. Thus, community-based corrections attempt to involve the offender's family (assuming it is noncriminal) and other members of the community in correcting the offender. In sum, community-based corrections programs represent more than simply moving the offender from prison to the outside world; ideally, they involve the outside world in rehabilitation of the offender.

Pretrial Diversion and Probation

On the assumption that first offenders committing nonviolent crimes may be harmed or stigmatized by exposure to the criminal justice system, some communities have developed pretrial-diversion programs (see Galvin et al., 1977). In this process, defendants meeting specified eligibility criteria have prosecutorial action on their charges suspended for a given period of time (usually 30 days to a year) in return for their participation in a community-based program of rehabilitative services. If the conditions of the diversion program are satisfied, criminal charges against them are dismissed.

Although the selection criteria for pretrial diversions vary somewhat by program, most programs are directed toward persons with no previous convictions. Offenses for which these offenders are charged must be "nonmajor"—for example, vandalism, disorderly conduct, intrafamily violence, theft and shoplifting offenses, and some sex offenses.

Probation differs somewhat from pretrial diversion. The major goal of the latter is reduction of the possible negative effects of criminal justice processing (that is, negative self-esteem, troublesome family relations, and lost employment opportunities). In contrast, probation is designed to supervise and rehabilitate offenders who have been processed and convicted by the court. Probation occurs when a judge suspends an offender's sentence and places him or her under the supervision of a court appointee—usually a state- or county-employed probation officer (see Klockars, 1972).

Depending on the seriousness of the offense and the offender's record, probation may involve simple supervision of the offender, to determine that he or she does not again commit crimes, or it may involve some form of counseling or vocational training. In some instances, the length of probation is quite short; in other cases, it is much longer. Generally, the length approximates the length of the prison sentence the offender would have received. If the conditions of probation are violated, the offender may be sent to prison to serve that sentence.

Probation, especially when combined with treatment programs, is considered the ideal form of community-based corrections. It leaves the offender in the community, takes advantage of family and employment ties, discourages affiliation with undesirable persons (usually as a condition of probation), supervises the offender, and provides assistance in adjustment to conventional life. In short, probation controls and treats offenders without exposing them to the negative aspects of imprisonment.

Halfway Houses

The halfway house concept offers yet another alternative to traditional imprisonment. Halfway houses are correctional facilities that are partly institutional, in that offenders must reside in them under supervision, and partly noninstitutional, in that residents generally come and go freely to work, shop, attend classes, and find recreation in the community. Basically, the facility resembles a home rather than a prison. Offenders may be sent directly to halfway houses upon conviction or may be transferred to them after serving time in prison. Programs within the houses vary considerably. Some are highly regimented; others are more loosely operated. Some are primarily supervisory—a form of structured probation or parole. Others are devoted mainly to counseling and therapy on either an individual or a group basis.

Halfway houses offer a number of advantages. The freedom they provide allows offenders to maintain and develop outside relationships and to offset the many deprivations of imprisonment. The facilities and programs also serve as gradual stepping-stones to successful parole. Yet the freedom provided by halfway houses also makes supervision of residents difficult, and offenders occasionally commit crimes during the course of their stay in a house. The staff attempts to counter this problem by building close ties with residents and developing in residents a sense of pride in the reputation and success of the facility. In some houses, residents work toward keeping other residents "straight."

It is doubtful that halfway houses will replace prisons to any great extent, though their potential to aid in the correction of lesser offenders has yet to be fully realized. The greatest obstacle in the path of the halfway house is community resistance. Residents of neighborhoods have often obtained court injunctions to block the opening of halfway houses. Conversely, corrections officials have been known to secretly establish halfway houses in neighborhoods that might resist them. As long as the public remains crime conscious, the future of the halfway-house concept is limited.

Releases and Furloughs

Some prison inmates are allowed to leave the prison during the day to work or attend classes in the community, returning to the prison after these activities. Programs that permit these absences are known as release programs. Occasionally, prisoners may be given leaves from prison for longer periods of time in order to take care of family problems or business or to prepare for parole or final release from prison. These leaves are called furloughs.

Releases and furloughs are seen as important methods of keeping an offender tied to the community even while imprisoned. Work and educational releases provide inmates with job skills or educational attainments that may benefit them after they have been paroled or served their sentences. Furloughs aid in the transition between incarceration and parole or release at the end of sentence, often a traumatic adjustment if not done gradually. Both releases and furloughs aid the corrections system in reducing prison overcrowding and in allowing an evaluation of a prisoner's parole potential.

On the negative side (especially in the eyes of the public), release and furlough programs carry the danger of escape or criminal behavior by the program participant. Occasionally, this does occur and causes a public furor. Yet prisoners given releases and furloughs are generally a select few and the number returning late, absconding, and committing crimes amounts to no more than 7 percent of the total (Holt, 1971).

Despite "high marks," it is doubtful that release and furlough programs will replace total confinement on a large-scale basis. The risk involved with maximum-security offenders is too great. Yet there is no reason for not fully developing these programs for medium- and minimum-security prisoners, especially in attempting to raise the likelihood of parole success.

Parole

Parole is a form of community-based corrections in which prison inmates are released into the community after they have served only part of their sentences. Their activities in the community are monitored by a state parole agent, and they are returned to prison if they violate the conditions of their parole. In theory, parole meets the needs of both the state and the offenders. The state is permitted to reimprison offenders who "are not ready for life on the outside" or who are again "headed for trouble." This option is not available if the offenders have served their full sentence in prison before release. Ideally, parole aids the offender by providing assistance in the transition from prison to life on the outside. In reality, it is the state's needs that are most satisfied by parole.

The conditions of parole vary somewhat by state. In most states, parolees may reside only in homes approved by parole agents and may not change residences or leave the county without an agent's permission. They must maintain approved employment. Every month they are required to report directly or submit reports to their parole agents detailing their activities during the past month. Excessive use of alcohol and all use of narcotics are forbidden. Parolees cannot own or possess dangerous weapons. They must avoid former convicts and persons with bad reputations. They are required to obtain written permission to drive an automobile. Most importantly, they must not violate any laws.

Unofficially, the conditions of parole are matters of the parole agent's definition. In the end the parole agent is responsible for the parolee's behavior and, therefore, he or she sets the real conditions of parole (Irwin, 1970:149–73). Some agents are extremely rule conscious. They supervise the parolee intensely and do not tolerate violations of parole conditions. Others are somewhat more tolerant and less intense in supervising the parolee. Some are primarily assistance oriented rather than concerned with supervision. Finally, some agents basically leave the parolee alone, making the only major condition of parole avoiding arrest. In the final analysis, it is the arrest record of the parolee that determines the security of the agent's job and ultimately saves the parole board embarrassment. The threat of impending arrest will make the agent consider revoking parole. Arrest itself will frequently guarantee revocation.

Whether or not parolees succeed in remaining free depends in large part on their ability to survive the immediate reentry into the outside world. As Irwin (1970:107–30) notes, parolees are liable to undergo a form of culture shock as they reenter society. Activities that were once taken for granted—making change or crossing streets—are now difficult. Meeting members of the opposite sex and getting along with family and friends become problems.

Parolees who do not do well in readjusting during the early stages of parole are not likely to succeed. Parolees who do succeed in remaining out of prison are those who manage to make it through the reentry crisis and begin "doing good." "Doing good" represents more than simply getting by. It involves holding a job that pays well, developing satisfactory relationships with those of the opposite sex, and avoiding problems with the parole agent. "Doing good," therefore, does not exclude committing further crimes. In this sense society's definition of parole success (becoming "rehabilitated") differs greatly from that of the parolee (Irwin, 1970:131–48; 176–204).

Success of Community-based Corrections

Like prison rehabilitation programs, community-based corrections programs have many goals. They seek to raise the self-esteem of offenders, to reorient them toward conventional values, to provide them with educational and job skills, and to ease the social stigma of conviction. Yet whether or not these goals are accomplished, success or failure for community-based corrections is ultimately determined by the answer to one question: Do these programs produce lower recidivism rates than imprisonment of offenders? This factor is the most crucial in deciding legislative support for community-based corrections.

According to the earlier-cited Martinson (1974) report, community-based correction programs do no better or worse than imprisonment. They simply make little difference in recidivism rates. Like Martinson's negative conclusion concerning in-prison treatment programs, this conclusion is a general one. We have not discovered a general formula for community-based rehabilitation. Yet *some* programs do work with *some* types of offenders (Palmer, 1975). These relationships must be specified.

Three major factors account for the failure of community-based corrections programs to improve upon imprisonment. First, such programs have generally been poorly designed, implemented, and evaluated. Few programs are similar enough to allow comparisons. Few are designed with evaluation in mind. For political reasons, many resist evaluations. Second, community-based corrections have proven to be correction *in* the community rather than correction *by* the community. Despite the label, community-based corrections have done little to involve the community in their programs, and the community has shown little interest in becoming involved. Finally, community-based corrections programs suffer from the same problem that ultimately caused the downfall of the institutional treatment model. Both have attempted to rehabilitate offenders without adequate knowledge of the causes of the offenders' criminal behavior. In so doing, their chances of success rest fully on guesses.

It is important to note that community-based corrections have not fared worse than imprisonment in reducing recidivism. Thus, the final choice between the two must be determined on criteria other than recidivism. Undoubtedly, the decision will involve two immeasurable factors: the potential humanitarian gains of the treatment model versus the potential general deterrent effects of incarceration of law violators. As noble as the sentiments behind community-based corrections are, it is doubtful that they will be used to treat any but low-risk, lesser offenders. These are persons least in need of rehabilitation. Thus, the value of the community-based corrections model will not lie in the correction of lesser offenders but in the protection of lesser offenders from the corrupting influence of the prison setting.

The Future of Corrections

Aside from community-based corrections programs focusing on the lesser offender, we can expect little change from the trend toward nonrehabilitative custody of more serious offenders. A "lock 'em up" philosophy is preferred to innovative rehabilitation efforts by the public for two important reasons. First, the public is basically not interested in treatment of the offender. Beyond a humanitarian concern that prisoners not be abused, the public sees little reason to spend any more tax dollars on "crooks" than is necessary. Further, the institutionalization of offenders serves the purpose of keeping them out of sight and out of mind; thus, we are spared any reminder that we may be implicated in either or both the cause and the cure of criminal behavior.

The second, and more crucial, reason for a lack of innovative correctional policies lies in the American public's conservative approach to risk taking. Above all else, this society cannot long abide disorder. Short-term disorder will accompany nearly all innovations. Within prisons, for example, increased freedom or self-government for prisoners will surely be met with abuses of privileges and of prison staff. If we could guarantee the public that these forms of disorder will only be temporary, public support for correctional innovations might be found. However, such guarantees cannot be made, and the public is not willing to risk the possibility of long-term disorder. Custody seems preferable.

The result of the return to the custody model is, in a very real sense, the self-perpetuation of the criminal justice system. The criminal justice system produces a product—officially labeled criminals. In failing to rehabilitate offenders and in likely further corrupting them through exposure to the prison setting, the criminal justice system assures itself of a steady flow of easily selected candidates for reprocessing and relabeling.

Summary

In this chapter we described the corrections system, the component of the criminal justice system that controls and, in some instances, attempts to rehabilitate officially labeled criminals. The chapter examined the constantly changing orientations of the corrections system and its current dual orientation toward protection of society from offenders and community rehabilitation of lesser offenders. The description of jails and prisons offered a bleak picture of correctional institutions. They are clearly places where little correction can occur. Yet in terms of reducing recidivism, correction in the community has fared little better than imprisonment, even with the assignment of prisoners with greater rehabilitation potential to community-based corrections programs. It seems, then, that this chapter can offer the public little hope that criminals can be made noncriminal. Indeed, the chapter has undoubtedly *encouraged* the average citizen's preference for longer incarceration of offenders. This thought represents a major theme of the following, final chapter of this book.

References

American Friends Service Committee
    1971   Struggle for Justice. New York: Hill and Wang.
Chandler, E. W.
    1973   Women in Prison. Indianapolis, Indiana: Bobbs-Merrill.
Clemmer, D.
    1958   The Prison Community. New York: Holt, Rinehart & Winston.

Conrad, J.
    1973   "Corrections and simple justice." Journal of Criminal Law and Criminology 64:208–17.

Cressey, D. R.
    1968   Offenders as a Correctional Manpower Resource. Washington, D.C.: Joint Commission on Correctional Manpower and Training.
    1973   "Adult felons in prison." Pp. 117–50 in L. Ohlin (ed.), Prisoners in America. Englewood Cliffs, N.J.: Prentice-Hall.

Gagnon, J. H., and W. Simon
    1968   "The social meaning of prison homosexuality." Federal Probation 32:23–29.

Galvin, J. J.
    1977   Instead of Jail: Volume 3, Alternatives to Prosecution. Washington, D.C.: U.S. Government Printing Office.

Garabedian, P.
    1963   "Social roles and processes of socialization in the prison community." Social Problems 11:139–52.

Giallombardo, R.
    1966   Society of Women: A Study of a Women's Prison. New York: Wiley.

Goffman, E.
    1961   Asylums. Garden City, N.Y.: Anchor Books.

Goldfarb, R.
    1975   Jails. Garden City, N.Y.: Anchor Books.

Heffernan, E.
    1972   Making It in Prison. New York: Wiley.

Holt, N.
    1971   "Temporary prison release." Crime and Delinquency 17:414–30.

Irwin, J.
    1970   The Felon. Englewood Cliffs, N.J.: Prentice-Hall.

Irwin, J., and D. Cressey
    1962   "Thieves, convicts, and the inmate culture." Social Problems 10:142–55.

Jackson, G.
    1970   Soledad Brother. New York: Bantam Books.

Johnson, E.
    1971   "The homosexual in prison." Social Theory and Social Practice 1:83–95.

Kassebaum, G. G., D. A. Ward, D. M. Wilner
    1971   Prison Treatment and Parole Survival. New York: Wiley.

Kitchener, H.
    1977   "How persistent is post-prison success?" Federal Probation 41:9–15.

Klockars, C. B.
    1972   "A theory of probation supervision." Journal of Criminal Law, Criminology, and Police Science 63:550–56.

Martinson, R.
    1974   "What works? Questions and answers about prison reform." The Public Interest 35:22–54.

McCorkle, L. W.
    1956   "Social structure in a prison." Welfare Reporter 8:5–15.

Palmer, T.
    1975   "Martinson revisited." Journal of Research in Crime and Delinquency 12:133–52.

Rothman, D.
    1971   The Discovery of the Asylum. Boston: Little, Brown.
Smart, C.
    1977   "Criminological theory: its ideology and implications concerning women." British Journal of Sociology 28:89–100.
Sykes, G.
    1958   The Society of Captives. Princeton, N.J.: Princeton University Press.
Sykes, G. M., and S. L. Messinger
    1960   "The inmate social system." Pp. 5–11 in R. A. Cloward, D. R. Cressey, G. H. Grosser, R. McCleary, S. L. Messinger, L. E. Ohlin, and G. M. Sykes (eds.), Theoretical Studies in Social Organization of the Prison. New York: Social Science Research Council.
U.S. Department of Justice, Law Enforcement Assistance Administration
    1975   The Nation's Jails. Washington, D.C.: U.S. Government Printing Office.
    1976a   Survey of Inmates of Local Jails, 1972. Washington, D.C.: U.S. Government Printing Office.
    1976b   Survey of Inmates of State Correctional Facilities 1974—Advance Report. Washington, D.C.: U.S. Government Printing Office.
    1977   Prisoners in State and Federal Institutions on December 31, 1975. Washington, D.C.: U.S. Government Printing Office.
Ward, D. A.
    1973   "Evaluative research for corrections." Pp. 184–206 in L. Ohlin (ed.), Prisons in America. Englewood Cliffs, N.J.: Prentice-Hall.
Ward, D. A., and G. G. Kassebaum
    1965   Women's Prison. Chicago: Aldine.
Wheeler, S.
    1961   "Socialization in correctional communities." American Sociological Review 26:697–712.

Suggested Readings

Two collections of readings in the area of corrections will provide the interested student with a satisfactory introduction to the topic: R. M. Carter, D. Glaser, and L. T. Wilkins, *Correctional Institutions*, 2d ed. (Philadelphia: Lippincott, 1977) and R. G. Leger and J. R. Stratton, *The Sociology of Corrections* (New York: Wiley, 1977).

    Beyond this introduction, Lloyd E. Ohlin has edited an excellent collection of papers by leaders in the field of sociology of corrections. See his *Prisoners in America* (Englewood Cliffs, N.J.: Prentice-Hall, 1973). Tom Murton's *The Dilemma of Prison Reform* (New York: Holt, Rinehart & Winston, 1976) offers an insider's look at innovations in the corrections system. John Irwin similarly points up dilemmas in the area of parole in his book *The Felon* (Englewood Cliffs, N.J.: Prentice-Hall, 1970).

    Finally, for more radical critiques of corrections in America, the reader is referred to Leonard Orland's *Prisons: Houses of Darkness* (New York: The Free Press, 1975) and Jessica Mitford's *Kind and Usual Punishment* (New York: Vintage, 1974).

Conclusion

So far, this book has attempted to provide a framework by which readers can ask common-sense questions about the potential effects of crime and anticrime strategies on their lives. ☐ Chapter 9 summarizes this framework and applies it to some recent crime control issues.

9

Summary and Observations on Crime Control

This book opened with three questions that must be asked in formulating any anticrime policy, whether at the personal or governmental level:

1. What is the nature and scope of the problem at hand? (That is, how accurate are the assumptions and figures relating to the problem?)
2. Will the proposed remedy actually aid in solving the problem?
3. What incidental side effects may accompany the implementation of the proposed remedy?

The major portion of this book has been devoted to question 1; questions 2 and 3 cannot confidently be addressed unless the first question is laid to rest. The key to answering question 1 lies in bringing together what we know about crime—its forms, its causes, its consequences. In exposing our taken-for-granted assumptions and stereotypes about crime to critical challenges, we gain a better sense of what we know and, perhaps more importantly, what we do *not* know about crime. The history of crime policy in America is a history of repeated attempts to fight crime in the absence of knowledge about it. In assessing the limitations of our present knowledge, we must wonder how we can even begin to consider responding to questions 2 and 3.

Summary

What have the chapters in this book told us about crime? Let us review our earlier discussions.

Crime in America

The increase in crime fears in the United States during the past ten years is not entirely groundless. Crime has actually increased; we cannot simply attribute the increase to changes in crime-reporting practices. Yet it is difficult to get a handle on the dimensions of the "crime problem." Our statistics are terribly flawed. Most citizens are rarely given a sense of their actual chances of being crime victims. Their picture of crime is generally distorted and highlights violent crime and downplays property and white-collar offenses. In fact, they have little chance of being violently victimized, and their chances of falling victim to a thief are really only somewhat greater. That they lose money to various white-collar offenses is a certainty. Their stereotype of crime cannot possibly allow them to make informed decisions about personal and governmental crime policy.

Criminals

Our knowledge about who commits crimes is rudimentary. Some basic crime correlates are apparent. FBI index offenses seem more likely to be committed by young, lower-class males. "Lesser" offenses are more evenly distributed among other socioeconomic classes, though not necessarily among other age and sex categories. Indeed, age and sex seem the most unambiguous correlates of criminal behavior. Youth is consistently associated with most offenses. Males commit more crimes than females do, though the gap appears to be narrowing. The relationship between criminal behavior and race and income is more complicated. Blacks and members of the lower classes seem more crime prone. However, these relationships may in part reflect differences in types of crimes committed and discriminatory criminal justice processing. In and of themselves, these correlational data do not offer a sound platform for anticrime policy.

Causes of Crime

The most pressing of criminological questions will always be: What causes criminal behavior? Our inability to provide an answer also makes it the most frustrating of criminological questions. Beyond the fact that we have discounted some biological and psychological factors (for example, the XYY chromosome pattern) as causes of any more than a few isolated crimes, we know very little about the causes of crime. This is not surprising, given the sketchy knowledge of crime correlates upon which we build our causal theories. We *suspect* that certain structural and cultural elements of society (for example, poverty) cause or encourage crime, but we cannot say precisely how these factors operate. In the final analysis, anticrime policy formulation becomes a guessing game at best.

Crime Victims

Recent research suggests that the picture of crime is incomplete without inclusion of the victim factor. That is, we are finding that victimization is not randomly distributed—some categories of people are more likely to be victims of crime than others are. Beyond this, victim involvement in some types of offenses seems to extend beyond random victimization of the passive individual. At present, we know little else about victims. We must learn more if we are to combat crime effectively.

The Criminal Justice System

In many ways, the very agencies we employ to fight crime actually create crime or at least the official picture of crime that shapes our fears. Official crime rates and official criminals are products of criminal justice organizational activity and discretion. Although we know that crime has indeed increased, we cannot always know which dimensions of the "crime problem" are real and which are purely organizational products.

Responses to Crime

Assuming that we can answer the first of our three questions to the extent that we agree that crime is problematic enough to warrant some type of response, we may ask: Can we solve the "crime problem"? Given the above summary, it appears we must respond negatively. We know little about crime and, as Wilson (1975) notes, the types of causal theories we are developing may not lend themselves to policy. If, for example, we attribute crime to poverty, how are we to remedy the situation? Past attempts have failed (see Chapter 4).

In light of this negative commentary, can we blame the public for seriously fearing crime? Though we cannot, neither should we encourage exaggerated fears. Two important factors govern the need for calm. First, although our knowledge about crime is limited, the state of the art of criminology is sophisticated enough to allow more systematic testing of hypotheses underlying anticrime policy than is presently the case. We can give question 2 ("Will the remedy be effective?") far more scrutiny than we currently do. Thus, there is no excuse for panic policy.

Second, most of the remedies now proposed to deal with crime carry potentially costly liabilities that may not be acceptable even if the remedies work and are definitely unacceptable if they do not. Thus, we argue that any attempt to curb crime is *not* better than no attempt. More attention to question 3 ("Will negative side effects accompany the proposed remedy?") will undoubtedly lead to the abandonment of many policy ideas.

With questions 2 and 3 in mind, we may take a critical look at four anticrime strategies currently in effect or suggested: (1) limited procedural rights, (2) harsher penalties for crimes, (3) lengthy incarceration of habitual offenders, and (4) gun control. Each of these responses to crime represents a "containment" approach. That is, each suggests that, if we cannot eliminate the causes of crime, we can make it more difficult for people to commit crimes.

Limited Procedural Rights

As we indicated in Chapter 1, a common response to the problem of crime is the attempted elimination of legal "technicalities" that stand in the way of arrest and prosecution of suspected offenders. The "technicalities" are, in fact, constitutional rights that protect citizens from such governmental excesses as unreasonable search and seizure and denial of counsel at the time of arrest. In the 1960s, the Warren Court wrote many decisions that liberally affirmed such procedural rights. Presently, as the current Supreme Court responds to the public and governmental definition of crime as a severe social problem, we note a trend toward conservative redefinition of some of these rights. Many of these changes have involved search and seizure laws (see West Publishing Company, 1978). The U.S. Supreme Court has recently ruled that:

1. Criminal defendants have no constitutional right to appeal state court convictions to federal courts, even if evidence used against the defendants in their trials was illegally seized.
2. Border-patrol officers at highway checkpoints can stop cars at random without suspicion and question passengers to discover illegal aliens or smuggling.
3. The Internal Revenue Service can use gambling money and records illegally seized in criminal cases as evidence in civil tax cases.
4. Police can routinely search impounded cars without a warrant and use as evidence in criminal cases whatever may be found in a glove compartment.

Effectiveness

Although the above rulings may provide easier prosecution in certain isolated cases, they will have little overall effect on the crime situation. Most deal with vice crimes rather than with the more serious offenses that concern the public. Rarely are robbers or burglars convicted on the basis of physical evidence seized in a search of their home or car; convictions generally stem from apprehension of offenders in the act of committing a crime (though other evidence may be used to buttress the prosecution's case). Indeed, few of the procedural "technicalities" affirmed by the Warren Court and modified by the current Supreme Court will influence the crime situation to any major degree. Even the famous *Miranda* decision, which placed limits on the police's ability to elicit a confession from a suspect, has had little to do with an increase or decrease in crime since so few suspects are prosecuted on the basis of confessions.

Negative Effects

Although the procedural-rights rulings may have little impact on the overall crime picture, they are nonetheless important. The Fourth Amendment ban on unreasonable search and seizure and other constitutionally defined rights were intended, as former Justice William O. Douglas so often argued, "to keep the government off our backs." Historically, the state has shown itself willing to go to great lengths to catch criminals, including abusing the average citizen. Rulings like those described above erode Fourth Amendment protections and make the right to privacy less secure. In return for establishing these conservative precedents, we have gained little or nothing in the combating of crime.

Increased Penalties for Crimes

Perhaps more than any other society, ours turns to the law to settle its problems. As crime has increasingly become defined as problematic, the legislature has responded by passing new laws or by making existing penalties harsher. This practice rests on the assumption that the greater the potential penalty for an act, the less likely an individual will be to commit the act.

Effectiveness

The deterrence issue is a complex one. The death penalty does not seem to deter homicide (see Sellin, 1967). But most murders are crimes of passion in which little thought is given to the consequences of the act. Generally, when murder accompanies some other felony such as robbery, the murder is not really planned and the consequences not really contemplated.

Can increased criminal penalties deter noncapital offenses? Several studies (see Tittle and Logan, 1973) suggest that they can when we consider three important elements of punishment: its severity, its certainty, and the public's perception of severity and certainty. It does little good to increase the penalty for a crime if the certainty of apprehension and punishment for the offense is very low. And certainty is of little consequence if a punishment is meaningless. Neither element is important unless the public is aware of it. Once public awareness is assured, certainty seems more important than severity.

Although criminologists appear increasingly willing to accept the deterrence doctrine, most are reserving final judgment until a number of theoretical and methodological problems are addressed (see Tittle and Logan, 1973; Gibbs, 1975). First, no one has yet provided an explicit theory of crime deterrence that specifies *how* penalties affect behavior and under what conditions. Second, we must find a way to measure an essentially immeasurable concept. Since we cannot really know how or when persons choose *not* to commit crimes, we must infer deterrence from changes and differences in official crime rates. Third, to really test the deterrence theory, we must eventually systematically graduate the penalties for a crime and include a "no penalty" situation. Fourth, in comparing communities with different penalty structures, we must be able to control for such extralegal factors as differences in informal community condemnation of the crime in question and differences in crime-conducive situations such as unemployment.

Negative Effects

If criminologists are somewhat inclined to believe that punishment deters crime, should we not legislate stronger penalties for crimes? Again, this policy is not without its costs. It encourages an overreliance on legislation to cure all social ills. It fosters a repressive atmosphere. It threatens the boundaries of what we now consider "just punishment" for a crime and forces us to contemplate trading justice for crime control. Finally, increasing mandatory minimum sentences for offenses undercuts the possibility of individualized justice, mercy, and rehabilitation. Judges are robbed of the discretion to make the punishment fit the crime and the ability to deal with the unusual case that really does not merit prison.

Locking Up Career Offenders

Many people feel that even if harsher punishments do not deter crime they should be enacted nonetheless to remove dangerous felons from society for longer periods. The "lock 'em up" philosophy is based on evidence that a large portion of our crimes are committed by a small number of habitual or career offenders. A study of 10,000 juveniles whose criminal records were followed until they were eighteen years old revealed that 6 percent of the sample was responsible for 53 percent of its violent attacks, 71 percent of its robberies, and 62 percent of its property crimes (Wolfgang et al., 1972). The FBI has reported that 68 percent of the persons arrested in 1971 were repeat offenders; 47 percent had committed at least three serious offenses (Federal Bureau of Investigation, 1972:36-37).

Believing that most serious crimes are the products of career offenders, critics of the criminal justice system are calling for harsher criminal penalties, greater concentration on repeat offenders by prosecutors (National Institute of Law Enforcement, 1977), and a reduction in probations and paroles given to offenders (Wilson, 1975). One study concludes that if most crimes are committed by career criminals, our crime rate could be cut by two-thirds if every person convicted of a serious crime were given a three-year prison sentence (Shinner and Shinner, 1975). A recent Rand Corporation study (Greenwood et al., 1977) of habitual armed robbers concludes that these felons are beyond rehabilitation and that their incapacitation through imprisonment may be the most effective means of reducing crime. These same sentiments are apparent in "multiple billing" laws enacted in some states. Here, a convicted offender's sentence is doubled, tripled, or quadrupled on the basis of the number of prior felony convictions on his or her record (see Sleffel, 1977).

Effectiveness

It is difficult to argue with the logic of preventing persons from committing crimes by incarcerating them. Yet we should not readily assume that this practice will greatly reduce crime when applied to repeat offenders. As Cloward and Ohlin (1960) have suggested, there may be limits on criminal opportunities in a community or neighborhood; not all would-be criminals may be able to operate at a given time. The criminal opportunity structure is determined in large part by such factors as the number of readily available victims and situations without witnesses, the offender's familiarity with the area in which he or she contemplates committing a crime, and the effectiveness of police anticrime strategies. If, indeed, there are more potential criminals than criminal opportunities, the imprisonment of repeat offenders will not alter the amount of crime in the community. Others will fill the void left by the habitual offenders.

Some readers will argue that the "limited opportunity" hypothesis is too simplistic, that opportunities to commit robberies abound ("All one has to do is get a gun and stick someone up!"). Yet if crimes are so easily committed, we wonder why career offenders do not commit more. Surely it is because there are some limits on their opportunities. Capture is not a total impossibility. Professional burglars and robbers, for example, take great pains to plan their crimes and caution against becoming too greedy ("going to the well once too often") (see Letkemann, 1973). If we assume that criminal opportunities are limited and if we accept our theories that social conditions such as poverty produce great numbers of potential offenders, we may expect some competition for exploitation of the opportunities. Career criminals may be the current exploiters; they can also be replaced.

Although we have no solid evidence to support the above contention, we can point to the territorial wars of organized crime mobs, youth gangs, drug dealers, and pimps, which continually indicate that criminal opportunities are not unlimited. However, we suggest that the "limited opportunities" hypothesis is no less plausible than the "lock 'em up" hypothesis. Neither has been adequately tested.

Negative Effects

The costs of the "lock 'em up" approach are roughly the same as those for the deterrence approach. Both eliminate the possibility for individualized justice and treatment. Both suggest that we trade just punishment for crime control. The "multiple billing" concept carries the additional liability of negating the legal ideal that individuals can pay for their crimes. "Multiple billing" of repeat offenders constitutes making them pay for the same offense twice.

Gun Control

Gun control is one of the more controversial of proposed responses to the crime problem (see Newton and Zimring, 1969; Sherrill, 1973). Those who favor gun control argue that outlawing private ownership of guns will reduce serious violent crime. Opponents claim that gun control penalizes the noncriminal gun owner for the abuses of guns by criminals. To simplify the present discussion, we will equate gun control with making private ownership of handguns illegal.

Effectiveness

Advocates of gun-control legislation attribute a great deal of our crime problem to the fact that Americans own between 24 and 30 million handguns. Nationwide, firearms are used in approximately 50 percent of the homicides, 45 percent of the robberies, and 25 percent of the assaults (Federal Bureau of Investigation, 1976:17, 20, 26). Gun-control proponents argue that in order to curb these crimes (or at least to reduce the deaths and injuries associated with robbery and assault) handguns must be made less available. To accomplish this, they seek to outlaw ownership of handguns, thereby eliminating any legitimate reason for the manufacture or importation of handguns.

Critics of gun control counter with a number of arguments. They point to the general ineffectiveness of previous local and state attempts at gun control. They argue that citizens need guns to defend themselves and their property, that gun-control laws will not stop criminals from obtaining guns, and that persons who wish to kill will do so with other weapons if guns are unavailable. Some argue that if we must have gun control, it should be directed at the "Saturday-night special," the small, cheap, imported handgun thought by many to be used in most serious crimes.

Most of the criticisms of gun-control legislation are easily rebutted. It is unfair to use past gun-control laws to evaluate the potential effectiveness of currently proposed laws. Previous laws were not uniformly written and enforced. They were also not universally enacted; it accomplishes little to outlaw guns in one city or state when they are readily available in neighboring cities and states.

Undoubtedly, many of the guns used in crimes have been stolen from citizens who bought them for protection. This frontier approach to self-defense is misguided. Statistics indicate that the presence of guns in the home is more likely to lead to the death or injury of a family member or friend than to the wounding of an intruder. Since home intrusions are generally sudden and surprising, gun owners rarely have the chance to use their weapons. In only about 2 percent of home robbery cases is a robber shot by an intended victim. Indeed, the use of a weapon to resist a crime seems to increase the victim's risk of injury (Yeager et al., 1976).

It is true that some criminals will always find guns to commit crimes. Yet gun-control laws may decrease the availability of guns enough to prevent the marginally committed, unprofessional criminals from obtaining a gun. It is those criminals who are most likely to "lose their cool" and use a gun in panic during a crime. Further, when other types of weapons are used in crimes, the risk of death to the victim decreases. The knife wound is more easily healed than the gunshot wound. Were guns less available during household disputes, fewer family members would die.

Finally, according to Sherrill (1973), the "Saturday-night special" issue is manufactured. The campaign against this form of weapon, he argues, is sponsored by American gun manufacturers who wish to be rid of the competition from importers. Classification of guns used in crimes by police also has been erratic. Some departments have classified any small gun, even if American made and expensive, as a "Saturday-night special." Sherrill's statistics indicate that the "Saturday-night special" is not so related to crime as we sometimes believe. Its disappearance will do little to alter the crime situation.

In sum, until a standardized, universally employed gun-control law is implemented, we will not be able to assess the effectiveness of gun control. Current evidence suggests that gun-control legislation *might* influence crime rates *in the long run*. There are simply too many guns presently in circulation to expect any short-term decrease in crime. Is gun-control legislation worth attempting without a guarantee of success? The answer lies in our assessment of potential negative side effects of gun control.

Negative Effects

Were gun control to have no effects other than to possibly curb crime, the risk of legislation would be minimal. Yet, as gun owners argue, there is a side effect: gun owners are being penalized for the crimes of a few. Although there is some question about the constitutionality of gun-control laws, we need not concern ourselves with it at present. Suffice it to state that gun-control laws represent one more intrusion of the government into the private lives of citizens. In this instance, they are being told what they may own. Each such intrusion sets the precedent for further intrusions. If a reduction in crime is the result of gun-control laws, some will term the laws worthwhile government interference. If crime is not reduced, we will not be allowed to go back and begin again, reinstituting private gun ownership. Thus, we had best be certain of our picture of the crime problem and the relationship of handguns to it before we enact gun-control legislation. Perhaps we should also consider the recommendation of a recent Harvard study (New Orleans Times Picayune, 1976) of gun control: rather than outlawing private ownership of firearms, we must pass stiffer penalties for crimes committed with guns. Of course, this proposal is not without its difficulties, as our previous discussion of the deterrent effect of punishment suggested.

Conclusion

No aspect of the crime problem is simple. Crime's dimensions are complicated. Its correlates are difficult to identify. Its causes are frustratingly puzzling. Why, then, do we find ourselves so often approaching the crime problem simplistically? We insist on seeing ourselves as under siege by a horde of barbarians, and we search for one-step policies to lop off their heads. If this book has accomplished anything, it has, we hope, given its readers reason to pause before they panic. As this chapter has demonstrated, all of our anticrime policies carry potential liabilities. We owe ourselves the time and effort to weigh these losses against the gains in fighting crime.

References

Cloward, R. A., and L. E. Oblin
    1960   Delinquency and Opportunity. New York: The Free Press.

Federal Bureau of Investigation, U.S. Department of Justice
- 1972 Crime in the United States: Uniform Crime Reports, 1971. Washington, D.C.: U.S. Government Printing Office.
- 1976 Crime in the United States: Uniform Crime Reports, 1975. Washington, D.C.: U.S. Government Printing Office.

Gibbs, J.
- 1975 Crime, Punishment, and Deterrence. New York: Elsevier.

Greenwood, P., M. Lavin, and J. Petersilia
- 1977 Criminal Careers of Habitual Felons. Santa Monica, California: Rand.

Letkemann, P.
- 1973 Crime as Work. Englewood Cliffs, N.J.: Prentice-Hall.

National Institute of Law Enforcement and Criminal Justice, Law Enforcement Assistance Administration, U.S. Department of Justice
- 1977 Curbing the Repeat Offender: A Strategy for Prosecutors. Washington, D.C.: U.S. Government Printing Office.

New Orleans Times-Picayune
- 1976 "Survey finds bay state gun control law a flop." August 14, sec. 1:21.

Newton, G. D., and F. E. Zimring
- 1969 Firearms and Violence in American Life. Washington, D.C.: U.S. Government Printing Office.

Sellin, Thorsten
- 1967 Capital Punishment. New York: Harper.

Sherrill, Robert
- 1973 The Saturday Night Special. New York: Penguin.

Shinner, Sholmo, and Reuel Shinner
- 1975 "The effects of the criminal justice system on the control of crime." Law and Society Review 9:581–611.

Sleffel, L.
- 1977 The Law and the Dangerous Criminal. Lexington, Mass.: Lexington.

Tittle, C. R., and C. H. Logan
- 1973 "Sanctions and deviance: evidence and remaining questions." Law and Society Review 7:371–92.

West Publishing Company
- 1978 "Searches and seizures." Pp. 16–23 in United States Supreme Court Digest: 1978. St. Paul: West.

Wilson, James Q.
- 1975 Thinking About Crime. New York: Basic.

Wolfgang, M. E., R. M. Figlio, and T. Sellin
- 1972 Delinquency in a Birth Cohort. Chicago: University of Chicago Press.

Yeager, M. G., J. D. Alviani, and N. Loving
- 1976 How Well Does the Handgun Protect You and Your Family?—Technical Report 2. Washington, D.C.: U.S. Conference of Mayors.

Suggested Readings

Chapter 9 has been concerned primarily with "reasonable" responses to crime control issues. Thus, the suggested readings for Chapter 1 are again appropriate. Beyond this, however, one book in particular and a collection of criticisms of it seem exceedingly valuable in a discussion of potential solutions to the "crime problem." James Q. Wilson's rather conservative attack on traditional criminological research and criminal justice agencies (especially the courts) in *Thinking About Crime* (New York: Basic, 1975) has apparently done much to promote a "lock 'em up" anticrime approach. A number of critical reviews of Wilson's book serve to counterbalance it nicely. See *Contemporary Sociology*, July 1976, pp. 410–18.

Author Index

Adler, F., 63, 77
Albini, J. L., 42, 48
Alviani, J. D., 231
Amir, M., 117, 125, 126, 133
Angel, A. R., 23, 24
Ares, C. E., 185, 187
Arons, S., 14, 24

Ball, H. V., 39, 48
Becker, H., 142, 143, 146, 153, 157, 161, 187
Bell, R., 154, 157
Biderman, A. D., 32, 48
Bittner, E., 30, 48
Black, D. J., 30, 48, 171, 187
Blumberg, A. S., 178, 180, 187
Bordua, D., 105, 107, 113
Borges, S. S., 126, 134
Box, S., 68, 77
Briar, S., 30, 50, 56, 79, 174, 188
Brown, C. E., 5, 78
Brown, J. W., 66, 77
Bullock, H. A., 184, 187
Burkart, J. M., 61, 79

Cameron, M. O., 60, 62, 76, 78, 155, 157
Carter, R. M., 183, 187
Chambliss, W. J., 70, 78, 143, 144, 157
Chandler, E. W., 205, 215
Chevigny, P., 174, 187
Chilton, R. J., 67, 78, 89, 113
Chiricos, T. G., 184, 187
Christianson, C. V., 133
Clark, J. P., 31, 48, 61, 78
Clemmer, D., 199, 200, 215
Clinard, M. B., 38, 48
Cloward, R. A., 106, 107, 113, 227
Cohen, A., 105, 106, 107, 113
Cohen, S., 25
Cole, G., 179, 187
Conklin, J. E., 12, 16, 24, 48, 73, 78
Conrad, J., 209, 216
Coser, L., 139, 157
Cowan, P., 20, 24

Couzens, M., 28, 50, 172, 189
Cressey, D. R., 13, 24, 59, 75, 78, 102, 104, 113, 115, 199, 200, 201, 202, 216
Cumming, E., 170, 187
Cumming, I., 187
Curtis, L., 71, 78

Davis, F., 14, 24
De Fleur, L. B., 175, 187
Dentler, R. A., 31, 49
Dieckman, D., 5, 78
Dinitz, S., 98, 116
Dominick, J. R., 14, 24, 85, 113
Douglas, J. D., 31, 49
Dunn, C. S., 5, 24
Durkheim, E., 139, 140, 157

Edell, L., 187
Empey, L. T., 3, 5, 109, 113
Ennis, P. H., 33, 49, 90, 113, 165, 187
Erickson, M. L., 3, 5
Erickson, K., 140, 157
Erlanger, H. S., 182, 187
Eron, L. D., 86, 113

Farrell, R. A., 88, 113
Figlio, R. M., 79, 231
Foote, C., 185, 188
Ford, J., 68, 78
Fox, R. G., 95, 113
Franklin, A., 126, 133
Franklin, C., 126, 133
Frank, J., 182, 188
Friday, P. L., 60, 78

Gagnon, J. H., 133, 202, 216
Galtung, J., 84, 114
Galvin, J. J., 210, 216
Garabedian, P., 199, 216
Gardiner, J. A., 40, 49, 175, 188
Garfinkel, H., 150, 157
Gastril, R. D., 59, 79
Gebhard, P. H., 126, 133
Geis, G., 38, 39, 49, 77, 130, 132, 133

233

Giallombardo, R., 205, 216
Gibbons, D. C., 71, 75, 78, 98, 114
Gibbs, J., 226, 231
Glaser, D., 77, 115
Glueck, E., 83, 94, 114
Glueck, S., 83, 94, 114
Goffman, E., 197, 216
Gold, M., 31, 49
Goldfarb, R., 194, 216
Goldstein, J., 173, 188
Gottfredson, M. R., 5, 24
Green, E. D., 24, 184, 188
Greenwood, P. 227, 229
Gusfield, J., 145, 157

Hagan, J., 184, 188
Hage, J., 60, 78
Hanlon, J., 176, 189
Harris, A. R., 61, 63, 78
Harry, J., 68, 78
Harth, E. M., 115
Hartung, F. E., 39, 49, 149, 157
Haurek, E. W., 61, 78
Heffernan, E., 205, 216
Heidenheimer, A. J., 40, 49
Helfgot, J., 111, 112, 114
Henry, A. F., 99, 114
Hindelang, M. J., 3, 5, 10, 24, 61, 70, 78, 96, 114, 167, 199
Hirschi, T., 31, 49, 58, 70, 78, 83, 84, 96, 114
Hoffman-Bustamante, D., 63, 78
Hogarth, J., 183, 188
Holt, N., 212, 216
Hooton, E. A., 93, 94, 114
Hughes, E. C., 138, 150, 157

Ianni, F. A. J., 42, 49
Irwin, J., 157, 200, 213, 216

Jackson, G., 152, 157, 202, 216
Jensen, G. F., 83, 114
Johnson, E., 202, 216
Johnson, L. A., 48
Johnson, W. T., 168, 188
Johnston, N., 115

Kadish, S., 39, 49
Kalsh, E., 14, 24
Kalven, H., 182, 188
Kassenbaum, G. G., 91, 114, 205, 207, 216, 217
Kaufman, H. R., 14
Kelling, G. L., 3, 5, 76, 78
Kitchener, H., 207, 216
Kitsuse, J. I., 150, 158
Klein, D., 61, 78

Landau, S. F., 126, 133
Lavin, M., 231

Lefkowitz, M., 113
Lemert, E., 146, 152, 158
Leonard, W. N., 39, 49
Lesieur, H. R., 75, 78
Letkemann, P., 152, 158, 227, 231
Light, I., 58, 79, 99, 114
Logan, C. H., 225, 226, 231
Lombrozo, C., 61, 79, 93, 114
Loving, N., 231
Lyman, S. M., 149, 158

Mann, L. R. H., 113
Mann, R. D., 182, 189
Manning, P., 173, 188
Martinson, R., 207, 213, 216
Mather, L. M., 180, 181, 188
Matza, D., 60, 79, 103, 104, 115, 149, 158
McCorkle, L. W., 204, 216
McDermott, E., 115
McIntyre, J., 48
Mead, G. H., 139, 158
Merton, R. K., 41, 49, 99, 100, 114, 140, 158
Messinger, S. L., 199, 200, 217
Miller, W. B., 103, 106, 114
Mills, C., 149, 158
Minyard, F. F., 41, 49
Mohr, J. W., 47, 60
Monroe, L. J., 31, 49

Nagasawa, R. H., 70, 78
Nagel, S., 183, 188
Nelson, J. F., 88, 113
Nettler, G. S., 24, 86, 114
Newton, G. D., 228, 231
Niklaus, K. C., 48, 49
Noblit, G. W., 61, 79
Nye, F. I., 83, 114

Ohlin, L. E., 106, 107, 114, 227
Orcutt, J. D., 108, 114

Packer, H. L., 178, 188
Palermo, J. S., 185, 188
Palmer, T., 207, 214, 216
Parisi, N., 5, 24
Pate, T., 5, 78
Petersilia, J., 231
Piliavin, I., 30, 50, 56, 79, 174, 188
Pollak, O., 61, 79
Pomeroy, W. B., 133

Quinney, R., 38, 39, 48, 50, 100, 102, 114, 142, 158, 183, 188

Rachal, P., 40, 50
Rankin, A., 187
Ray, M. B., 155, 156, 158
Reckless, W. C., 66, 79, 107, 108, 115
Reuss-Ianni, E., 42, 49

Author Index

Roberts, J. W., 185, 188
Robinson, W. S., 90, 115
Rosen, L., 83, 115
Roshier, B., 13, 25
Roth, L., 95, 115
Rothman, D., 192, 217
Rowe, A. R., 65, 79
Rubinstein, J., 30, 50, 170, 174, 175, 189

Savitz, L., 115
Schur, E., 80, 115, 152, 158
Schwartz, M., 108, 115
Scott, M. B., 149, 158
Seidman, D., 28, 50, 172, 189
Sellin, T., 79, 225, 231
Shah, S., 95, 115
Sheldon, W. H., 93, 94, 115
Sheley, J. F., 32, 50, 58, 61, 79, 176, 189
Sherman, L. W., 30, 50
Sherrill, R., 228, 229, 231
Shinner, R., 227, 231
Shinner, S., 227, 231
Short, J. F., 99, 114, 158
Simon, R. J., 61, 62, 79, 202
Silberman, M., 32, 50
Simons, R. L., 96, 115
Skogan, W. G., 30, 50, 118, 134
Skolnick, J. H., 18, 25, 173, 175, 176, 179, 180
Sleffel, L., 227, 231
Smart, C., 61, 79, 205, 207
Smigel, E. O., 75, 79
Smith, R. A., 38, 50
Speilberger, A., 67, 78
Steffenmeier, D. J., 148, 158
Stevens, S. S., 115
Strodbeck, F. L., 182, 189
Sturz, H., 187
Sudnow, D., 180, 189
Suffet, F., 185, 189
Sutherland, E. H., 13, 25, 39, 50, 112, 113, 115
Sykes, G. M., 113, 114, 115, 198, 199, 200, 217

Tangri, S. S., 108, 115
Tarde, G., 113, 115
Taylor, I., 94, 115
Terry, R. M., 148, 158
Tifft, L. L., 31, 48, 225
Tittle, C. R., 65, 79, 225, 226, 231
Tivnan, E., 182, 189
Toby, J., 83, 115
Tucker, W. B., 115
Turner, R. H., 9, 25

Van Loon, E. E., 25
Vaughn, T. R., 92, 115
Vold, G., 97, 116
Von Hentig, H., 117, 124, 134

Walder, L. O., 113
Waldo, G. P., 98, 115, 184, 187
Wallerstein, J. S., 32, 50
Walton, P., 115
Ward, D. A., 91, 114, 205, 214, 216, 217
Waxer, E., 77
Weber, M. G., 38, 49
Weis, A., 48
Weis, K., 125, 134
Wheeler, S., 127, 199
Wilkins, L. T., 183, 187
Wilner, D. M., 91, 114, 216
Wilson, J. Q., 40, 50, 172, 189, 223, 227, 231
Wolfgang, M. E., 48, 50, 70, 79, 115, 117, 125, 227, 231
Won, G., 68, 79
Wong, C., 58, 79
Wyle, C., 32, 50

Yamamoto, G., 68, 79
Yeager, M. G., 229, 231
Young, J., 25, 115

Zeisel, H., 182, 188
Zimring, F. E., 228, 231

Subject Index

Accounts, 149
Adversary court system, 178
Age, 64–67, 118
Aggregate data, 88–89
Arraignment, 162
Arrest rates, 172–75

Bad companions, 83–84
Bail, 184–86
Blocked opportunity, 99, 106–7
Body-type theories, 93–94
Bureau of Narcotics, 142–43

Career offenders, 226–28
Causal theories:
    biological, 95–98
    psychological, 98–109
    sociological, 108–9
Civil liberties, 17
Clearance rates, 175–76
Community-based corrections, 193, 209–14
Conflict perspective, 138–45
Corporate crime, 38–39, 132–33
Corrections:
    defined, 191–92
    orientations, 192–94
Courts, 177–86
Crime:
    amounts, 34
    fears, 15–16
    functions of, 139–40
    hidden, 57
    and media coverage, 13–14
    as a national problem, 13
    organized, 20–22, 41–44
    political, 40–41
    and political campaigns, 12
    public views of, 10–11
    self-reported, 31–32
    as a social problem, 10
    trends, 35–37
    unreported, 29–30, 165
Crime rates, 170–71

Crime statistics, 27–30, 43–44
Criminal characteristics:
    age, 64–67
    gender, 59–64
    race, 69–71
    socioeconomic status, 67–69
Criminal justice system:
    described, 161
    discretion, 166
    production, 167–70
Criminology, 1–5
Cultural transmission, 102–4

Defense attorneys, 180
Delinquency, gang, 105–7
Deterrence, 225–26
Deviant subcultures, 153–54
Deviation, primary, 147
Deviation, secondary, 152
Differential association, 102–3
Drugs:
    addicts, 155
    arrests, 178
    subculture, 154

Embezzlement, 74–76
Epidemiology, 2, 49, 55

Family influence, 85–86
Furloughs, 211–12

Gang delinquency, 105–7
Gender, 59–64
Guns:
    control of, 228–30
    Saturday-night special, 229

Halfway houses, 211
Heroin, 177
Hidden crime, 57
Homicide, 45
Homosexuals:
    in prison, 202–3, 206
    subculture, 154

Income, 120
Indictment, 162
Information, 162
Inmate social system, 197–201
Interest groups, 138–45
IQ, 96

Jails, 194–95
Juries, 182

Labeling perspective, 146–56
Law:
   criminal, 18
   procedural, 18–20, 224
   substantive, 18–19
Law and order, 18
Law enforcement, 142–43

Marijuana, 142–43, 177
Marital status, 121
Marxist theories, 100–102
Media, 13–15, 85–86
Mobilization for Youth, 111–12

Neutralization, techniques of, 103–4

Opportunity, blocked, 99, 106–7
Organized crime, 20–22, 41–43

Parole, 212–13
Personality, 97–98
Police, 170–77
Political crime, 40–41
Poverty, 81–82
Pretrial diversion, 210
Preventive pretrial detention, 22–23
Primary deviation, 147
Prisonization, 199
Prisons, 195–210
Probation, 210
Procedural rights, 18–19, 224
Prohibition, 145
Prosecution, 179
Puritan crime waves, 140

Race, 69–71, 119
Reaction formation, 105–6
Recidivism, 207

Rehabilitation of offenders, 2, 193, 206–9
Residency, 122
Rights, procedural, 18–19, 224
Robbery, 72–74

Saturday-night special, 229
Search and seizure, 224
Secondary deviation, 152
Self-concept, 107–8
Self-reported crime, 31–32
Sentencing, 182–84
Sex, 59–64, 118
Sexual assault, 46–48
Shoplifting, 148, 155
Social policy, 3, 76, 109–12, 129–31, 217, 224
Social problems, 19
Socioeconomic status, 67–69
Structuralism, 98
Symbolic law, 145

Techniques of neutralization, 103–4
Trial, 181
True bill, 162

Uniform Crime Reports, FBI, 10, 27–30
Unreported crime, 29–30, 165
Urbanization, 81–82

Vagrancy, 143
Victim characteristics:
   age, 118
   income, 120
   marital status, 121
   race, 119
   residency, 122
   sex, 118
Victim compensation, 130–31
Victimization surveys, 32–33
Victim-offender relationships, 124–31
Victimology, 117
Victim precipitation, 125–27

White-collar crime, 37–41
Witnesses, 165–66
Women's prisons, 205–6

XYY chromosome, 95